W9-AMB-525

PRIME
YO F UR
LIFE

A GUIDE FOR FIFTY AND BEYOND

WOODROW KROLL
AND DON HAWKINS

Fleming H. Revell
A Division of Baker Book House Co
Grand Rapids, Michigan 49516

Published by Fleming H. Revell
a division of Baker Book House Company
P.O. Box 6287, Grand Rapids, MI 49516-6287

Printed in the United States of America

Library of Congress Cataloging-in-Publication Data

Kroll, Woodrow Michael, 1944–
    Prime of your life : a guide for fifty and beyond / Woodrow Kroll and Don Hawkins.
        p.   cm.
    Includes bibliographical references (p.).
    ISBN 0-8007-5704-1 (paper)
    1. Middle aged persons—United States Life skills guides. 2. Middle age—United States. 3. Aging—United States. 4. Aging—Religious aspects—Christianity. I. Hawkins, Don. II. Title.
HQ1059.5.U5K76 1999
646.7'0084'4—dc21   99-20767

For current information about all releases from Baker Book House, visit our web site:
http://www.bakerbooks.com

erean Community Church
157 Kenosha Drive NW
Rochester, MN 55901
28 4179 www.bereancc.org

PRIME
Y(OF)UR
LIFE

Also by Woodrow Kroll
    Empowered to Pray
    When God Doesn't Answer
    Early in the Morning
    Tested by Fire
    The Vanishing Ministry
    Bible Country
    Prodigal People, coauthor
    Is There a Man in the House?
    The Twelve Voices of Christmas
    The Twelve Voices of Easter
    Parent Care, coauthor

Also by Don Hawkins
    Never Give Up
    How to Beat Burnout
    Worry-Free Living
    Before Burnout
    The Stress Factor
    When Cancer Comes
    Happy Holidays
    Prodigal People, coauthor
    Friends in Deed
    Master Discipleship
    Overworked
    The Roots of Inner Peace
    Parent Care, coauthor

CONTENTS

ACKNOWLEDGMENTS

Every book written is the product of more than one (or two) authors. *Prime of Your Life* is no exception.

We are grateful for the encouragement and inspiration our wives, Linda and Kathy, provided us and for their patience during the hours we put into this project. Our own parents as well as our adult children provided additional encouragement and inspiration.

Several members of our Back to the Bible ministry team made invaluable contributions. Cathy Strate and Dawn Leuschen, our administrative assistants, played key roles. Beki Garrett typed the manuscript, assisted by Carrie Nyberg and Susan Hertzler. Allen Bean provided a sounding board for concepts and an editorial eye.

Of course, this project could not have been completed without the editorial oversight of Bill Petersen. We are also grateful for Melinda Van Engen, Dan Baker, Twila Bennett, and Sara Metzger at Baker Book House.

INTRODUCTION

NAVIGATING
LIFE'S SPAN

The Longest Span

The longest interstate system bridge in the United States is found in south central Louisiana. This twenty-six-mile-long span crosses the Atchafalaya River between Lafayette and Baton Rouge, the state capital. Whether you're driving east or west, the interstate runs straight as an arrow, and as you cross the swamps, then the Atchafalaya River, and finally more swamps, it seems as if you're on the bridge forever.

It also seems at first that the scenery flashing by doesn't change much. But if you observe closely enough, you will notice changes at every hand: clumps of moss-draped trees interspersed with marsh grass, bayous of various sizes, an occasional lake, then eventually, at the top of a gradual slope, the channel of the Atchafalaya River itself, the deepest channel on the North American continent. You may even spot wildlife—ducks, geese, an occasional deer, a muskrat or alligator sunning on the bank of a meandering bayou. The landscape is constantly changing.

That's how it is as we cross the span of life. Often it seems as if one day runs into the next—sameness, monotony, routine. Yet changes (sometimes subtle, sometimes dramatic) are constantly taking place as we cross our life span—changes that sooner or later each of us must address.

Differing Spans

Stop ten people in an average shopping mall and ask them how many years make up a normal human life span. Probably more than half will say seventy. Some people are surprised to learn that the Old Testament patriarch Moses, near the end of his 120 years, wrote:

> We finish our years like a sigh. The days of our lives are seventy years; and if by reason of strength they are eighty years, yet their boast is only labor and sorrow; for it is soon cut off, and we fly away. . . . So teach us to number our days, that we may gain a heart of wisdom.
>
> PSALM 90:9–10, 12

Many people in modern life have adopted Moses' viewpoint that the normal human life span is seventy years; yet up until the present time, many humans experienced a much shorter span.

Recently, at a seniors' conference, the vice president of a company that owns retirement facilities asked, "Did you know that one out of every seven people who have lived to eighty is still alive?" A remarkable thought, isn't it? We're living in a day of longer life spans. Yet humans are like other things: Life spans vary.

Some time ago our friend Allen Bean came across a list of how long things last, compiled by Frank Kendig and Richard Hutton. The list included the following:

1. The average running shoe worn by the average runner on an average surface will last 350 to 500 miles.

2. A hard pencil can write up to 30,000 words or draw a line more than 30 miles long. Most ballpoint pens will draw a line 4,000 to 7,500 feet long.

3. A 100-watt incandescent bulb will last about 750 hours; a 25-watt bulb, 2,500 hours. The number of times a light-bulb is turned on or off has little to do with its life span.

4. A one-dollar bill lasts approximately 18 months in circulation.

5. A lightning bolt lasts 45 to 55 microseconds.

6. A normal cassette tape, played about 100 times a year, will deteriorate somewhat in sound quality after about ten years, but the tape itself will play on.

7. The projected life span of a baby born in the United States today is about 71 years, nearly double what it was at the end of the eighteenth century.

8. The longest authenticated life span of a human being is 122 years.

As we read these figures, the question that occurs to us is, What's normal, and who winds up at the average? Even though Moses, Kendig, and Hutton agree that the average is "threescore and ten," think of those who've missed the average. My friend Ernie came to faith in Christ at ninety-one, still robust and hearty. On the other hand, Jessica, the daughter of another friend, died of cancer at age thirteen. Both of my parents are still living as this book goes to press, as are Wood's. Both of us realize we could lose our parents—or for that matter, one or more of our children—at any time. After all, Job and his sorrowing wife buried seven sons and three daughters, all killed in a tornado.

The bottom line is we may not always be able to accurately project the span of life. However, based on Psalm 90:12, we believe it is imperative that we consider our life spans in the same manner Moses did: "Teach us to number our days, that we may gain a heart of wisdom." After all, as with David in Psalm 37:25, many of us can now say, "I have been young, and now am old." Hopefully, as we go through the aging process, we can agree with David about God's faithfulness in providing for our needs and that of every other generation (Ps. 37:25–26).

Stretched and Sandwiched

The first blatant evidence I (Don) encountered that I was changing—and significantly so—occurred when I ordered a cup of coffee at the counter of a McDonald's restaurant. When the young counter attendant charged me only a quarter, I asked why.

Her reply: "It's the seniors' rate."

Whom could she possibly be talking about? I wondered. *She must be nearsighted.*

Less than a week later, after I had spoken at the morning service in our church here in Lincoln, Nebraska, someone told my wife, Kathy, "You must have married an older man."

To be candid, Wood and I both feel young and energetic. We are physically active, blessed with good health, and pretty much in possession of all our mental faculties (although some of our colleagues might disagree at times). We travel a lot, maintain an extensive ministry, enjoy our children and grandchildren, and try to help care for our parents.

But the fact is, we're growing older.

You are too.

Statistics indicate that the number of Americans over fifty will increase 11 percent by the year 2001. Specifically, those in the fifty to sixty-four-year-old subgroup, which both of us fit into, will increase by 19 percent during that same time.[1] Remarkably, shockingly, an individual turns fifty every seven seconds in America.

Meanwhile, as modern technology stretches our lives to even greater lengths, many of us find ourselves—and our parents—growing older while still enjoying relatively good health. According to The Oxford Book of Aging, "For the first time in human history, most people can expect to live into their seventies in reasonably good health."[2]

As our children grow up and our parents grow older, it seems the problems we face become more complex each year. Many of those problems involve the fact that we find ourselves "sandwiched" between caring for children who are practically grown and caring for our parents as they age.

Today thirty million Americans are age eighty-five and older. By the year 2000, experts estimate there will be seven million of these "oldest old." While medical breakthroughs such as knee and hip replacements will allow millions to lead healthy, vigorous lives into their nineties, others will require longer and more intense care than has been true in previous decades. About 30 percent of this group has been diagnosed with Alzheimer's. Twenty-four percent already live in nursing homes. Most of those who are not living in nursing homes will still require significant care from children who themselves are elderly, or from other caregivers.[3]

As we began research at Back to the Bible in preparation for launching Confident Living, our new ministry specifically targeted to those fifty and older, we discovered that nearly one out of every four American households, or over twenty-two million families, currently provides informal care to a relative or friend age fifty or older. This number will increase dramatically as the elderly population doubles during the next several decades. (Couple this with the fact that disability rates among those sixty-five and over are falling—a 15 percent decline between 1982 and 1994.[4]) Currently there are seventy million Americans age fifty and older, with another seventy million right behind them. The extra fifteen to twenty years we have gained in our life spans have been added to the middle of our lives rather than the end.

Addressing Life's Challenges

As midlife becomes more crowded than Chicago's O'Hare Airport the day before Thanksgiving, there are a variety of issues we need to face. Our purpose is to address these issues from a biblical perspective, since we're both committed to the premise that Scripture contains the ultimate answer for all of life's challenges.

In the process, we'll examine our attitude toward our own aging, consider a biblical perspective on change, explore options for caring for aging parents, as well as take a closer look at our adult children and the empty-nest factor. We'll revisit a number of interrelated topics in order to gain a full perspective. For example, issues such as making a will, deciding on a nursing home, and caring for a loved one with Alzheimer's require more than a single, brief treatment. That's why you'll find us coming back to these and other crucial concerns more than once in the course of this book.

Since Scripture speaks of our spirit, soul, and body (1 Thess. 5:23), we'll examine physical health, our emotional well-being, and the all-important spiritual dimension. We'll also consider social issues, financial options, legal and ethical questions, and living environment.

Our Ultimate Destination

Our ultimate desire in writing this book is to focus our attention beyond the challenges of midlife. It's so easy for us to lose sight of the destination when the route seems monotonous, the road unbending. At some point ahead, God promises those of us who know him through faith in Jesus Christ a home that far transcends anything we can imagine. When the apostle Paul faced circumstances and trials that left him at the point of giving up—when he felt "hard pressed on every side . . . perplexed . . . persecuted . . . struck down" (2 Cor. 4:8–9)—he was able to cope by shifting his focus. As he explained it,

> Therefore we do not lose heart. Even though our outward man is perishing, yet the inward man is being renewed day by day. For our light affliction, which is but for a moment, is working for us a far more exceeding and eternal weight of glory, while we do not look at the things which are seen, but at the things which are not seen. For the things which are seen are temporary, but the things which are not seen are eternal.
>
> 2 CORINTHIANS 4:16–18

Perhaps like Paul you find midlife overwhelming. Our final chapter is designed to shift our attention to that which is of lasting and immeasurable value: our ultimate home with the Lord.

PART ONE

LOOKING
BOTH WAYS
from the TOP *of the*
MOUNTAIN

CHAPTER**One**

HELP, I'M GROWING OLDER!

OUR SOCIETY TODAY VIEWS AGING PEOPLE as less productive, less beautiful, less energetic, more forgetful, perhaps even of less value than those still in their prime. Bob Buford, founder of Leadership Network, points out in his book *Game Plan*, "Conventional wisdom holds that the first four decades of your life—the first half—are the most exciting and productive years, and that the remaining years represent first the plateau and then a gradual downhill slide into retirement."[1]

Our view, like that of Buford and a growing minority, is that midlife—ranging from somewhere in the fourth or early fifth decade of life to age sixty-five and even beyond—can actually be the best part of life. As the psalmist pointed out, "Those who are planted in the house of the LORD shall flourish in the courts of our God. They shall still bear fruit in old age; they shall be fresh and flourishing, to declare that the LORD is upright" (Ps. 92:13–15).

The "Why" Question

Why are we growing older anyway? "I'm not sure," you respond. "Nobody's getting any younger." The fact is we all age each day. Cells die throughout our bodies by the millions. Weight mass shifts, hair thins and falls out, skin acquires wrinkles. Yet even as the physical changes of age affect us, we gain wisdom through the experiences of each passing day. As our knowledge increases, our experience grows. Hopefully we develop in character and insight as well.

For most of us, the early span of life is marked by doing. During those years you worked as hard as possible just to scrape by. Perhaps you put in long hours, climbed the ladder of success, and fought off the competition. After a decade or so you began to harvest the rewards of all that hard work—higher pay, promotions, recognition. You found yourself purchasing a wide range of toys, many of which you couldn't afford, but you seldom had time to play with them.

Then you began to realize you were on a treadmill—a treadmill to nowhere. Perhaps you even experienced a midlife crisis. You may have felt like Martha as she prepared to feed the Lord and his disciples, rushing around trying to accomplish many things, feeling generally irritated with the lack of help and resources (Luke 10:40). Perhaps you even felt exasperated with the Lord. You were what Kathy Hawkins refers to as a "human doing."

Yet God created us as human beings. He's far more concerned with who we are than what we do.

Midlife Assessment

That's why the middle span of life is so important. It gives us an opportunity to make a transition from the frantic rush of what we do and focus on who we are. We can realize that we are beings created in God's image, designed to reflect his glory, meaning, and purpose beyond the routine, mundane chores and the drive to succeed, to prove significance, to win a claim.

While some of you may have experienced a full-blown midlife crisis, others simply laugh at the notion. Whether it comes as a crisis or not, however, midlife provides a golden opportunity to step back and take a good look at ourselves—particularly with a view to finding our personal significance in Christ and leaving a lasting heritage, something financial planner and author Russ Crosson recently described on our *Confident Living* radio program as "focusing on posterity rather than prosperity."

18

Looking
Both
Ways from
the Top
of the
Mountain

So where are you at midlife? Have you become worn down and fatigued by the constant pressure and stress of deadlines? Are you generally irritated and angry over the way people have treated you? Are you anxious about the future, fearful of what may happen to you, struggling to somehow find security?

For most of us the expanded span of life provides a "whole second adulthood our grandparents never had."[2] It's a great time to examine your prospects, consider new possibilities, and face the fact that God has endowed you with unique gifts, creativity, energy, and an ability to use them for his glory.

Since God has instructed us to love him with all our heart and our neighbors as ourselves (Mark 12:29–31), it seems this should be a time when each of us asks ourselves, *How can I cover the remaining span of my life and most effectively fulfill these mandates of wholehearted love for God and unconditional love for people?*

Later in this chapter we'll put together those two words most of us in midlife would rather not consider—old age. Right now, though, pause, take a deep breath, and savor the here and now. Don't focus on the past; it's already happened. Don't even look ahead to the future and ask yourself about—all right we'll say it again—old age. Just celebrate the present. After all, you're still in the span of *life*, and you're still moving ahead. Seize the moment. Enjoy!

Humankind's Decline and Fall

It's safe to say that aging wasn't part of God's original creation. In the beginning there was no aging process. Before sin entered the picture, Adam and Eve maintained their health and well-being on an ongoing basis.

Then, according to Genesis 3, our original parents sinned. Responding to Satan's temptation, they chose to partake of the forbidden fruit of the tree of the knowledge of good and evil. The consequences were both immediate and permanent.

From that point, evil permeated the environment. For the first time, a negative emotion—fear—entered Adam's mind (v. 10). Rather than taking responsibility, man looked for someone else to blame (vv. 12–13). And not only man but all of God's creation experienced the result of the curse (v. 14). Conflict, grief, pain, and toil became humankind's lot (vv. 15–18). Ultimately humankind was sentenced to death (v. 19).

But wait, you respond. That was Adam and Eve. They lived millennia ago. We're standing at the dawn of the twenty-first century A.D. How could they affect us?

The answer to that question can be found in Paul's letter to the Romans. In Romans 5:12 the apostle writes, "Therefore, just as through one man sin entered the world, and death through sin, and thus death spread to all men, because all sinned."

20

LOOKING
BOTH
WAYS FROM
THE TOP
OF THE
MOUNTAIN
❦

Human Headwaters

As it passes under the I-10 bridge near Baton Rouge, Louisiana, the Mississippi River is a muddy current, carrying pollutants of all kinds. By contrast, the first few miles of the "Father of Waters" in Minnesota appear comparatively pure. In a sense, the Mississippi River provides a graphic picture of the cumulative toxic effects of sin on a race. Pollution starts very early; in the case of humanity, it began with our original parents, Adam and Eve. Their oldest son, Cain, became the world's first murderer—and his brother Abel was the victim! Yet for generations, humans seemed to enjoy long and healthy lives.

For example, Adam was 930 years old when he died. Noah lived to be 950, and Methuselah, the granddaddy of them all, lived until he was 969—which happened to be the same year in which the flood occurred. Yet life spans decreased dramatically as sin began to take its toll. Abraham lasted only 175 years (Gen. 25:7). By the time of Moses, the average span had declined to 120 years (Deut. 34:7). And King David lived to be only seventy (2 Sam. 5:4). During the Dark Ages, life expectancies dropped even more sharply.

In recent decades, however, medical advances have restored some longevity. In addition, certain families seem to be less affected. Wood's paternal grandfather and grandmother, Andrew and Mary Kroll, lived to celebrate their seventy-third wedding anniversary. Later that year, Andrew died just short of his ninety-eighth birthday. Mary lived a bit longer, finally dying at age ninety-one. In the same way, Harry and Clara Hawkins, Don's paternal grandparents, both lived well into their eighties, enjoying nearly sixty years of married life.

Both sets of grandparents, however, saw their quality of life decrease as they aged. The Krolls spent their last years in a tiny mobile home in Florida, with a cabana attached to the side. Their grandson's last memory of Andrew Kroll was of an old man hobbling with a cane outside his little trailer, his eyesight nearly gone and his hearing severely impaired. He threw his arms around Wood, kissed each cheek, squinted his eyes, and said, "Who are you anyway?"

Harry Hawkins's last visit with the grandson he called Donald Wayne occurred in a nursing home. Harry had become an old man, propped up by pillows in a bed, eyesight gone, voice impaired, just a shell of his former self.

We've both seen firsthand the drastic effects of aging. We've also learned to link it with sin and the results of the fall.

God's Perspective on Aging

In a world in which euthanasia is openly discussed, youth seems to be favored at every turn. But how does God view aging?

Scripture contains fourteen passages in which the words "old age" appear together.[3] Earlier we mentioned Psalm 92:13–15, which seems to describe those who grow old in fellowship with the Lord. The psalmist writes, "Those who are planted in the house of the LORD shall flourish in the courts of our God. They shall still bear fruit in old age; they shall be fresh and flourishing, to declare that the LORD is upright; He is my rock, and there is no unrighteousness in Him."

For the psalmist, a godly life can still be fruitful even near its end. In this song of Sabbath celebration, the psalmist described the righteous as "planted in the house of the LORD." In language similar to Psalm 1, this psalm promises that we shall be filled with God's freshness, vitality, and vigor. "Full of scent and green shall they remain" is the way one translation renders verse 14.[4] In contrast to a world that considers increasing age a liability, God views the "silver-haired head [as] a crown of glory, if it is found in the way of righteousness" (Prov. 16:31). And while the glory of young men may be their strength, "the splendor of old men is their gray head" (Prov. 20:29). The Bible contains numerous instances in which God commends people of age: Caleb,

Naomi, and Abraham, for example, in the Old Testament, and Simeon in the New Testament.

Yet God does not provide a blanket character endorsement to all those in Scripture who grow older. King Solomon is a case in point. He married many foreign women as the splendor of his kingdom increased, yet "when Solomon was old, . . . his wives turned his heart after other gods; and his heart was not loyal to the LORD his God, as was the heart of his father David" (1 Kings 11:4).

In Psalm 71, the psalmist prayed, "Do not cast me off in the time of old age; do not forsake me when my strength fails" (v. 9). After calling for help against his enemies, he affirms, "I will go in the strength of the Lord GOD; I will make mention of Your righteousness, of Yours only" (v. 16).

Finally, reflecting over the years of his life span, he noted,

22

LOOKING
BOTH
WAYS FROM
THE TOP
OF THE
MOUNTAIN
❦

> O God, You have taught me from my youth; and to this day I declare Your wondrous works. Now also when I am old and gray-headed, O God, do not forsake me, until I declare Your strength to this generation, Your power to everyone who is to come.
>
> PSALM 71:17–18

These words reflect the promise God gave through the prophet Isaiah, "Even to your old age, I am He, and even to gray hairs I will carry you! I have made, and I will bear; even I will carry, and will deliver you" (Isa. 46:4).

Our Attitude toward Aging

So what should our attitude be toward growing older? Hopefully not that of a bitter grandfather who blurted out, "You told me to cheer up, things could be worse. So I cheered up and sure enough they're worse."

The first step toward getting a handle on growing older is to recognize that it's part of living in a fallen world. Furthermore, it includes more than just turning another page on the calendar. Growth includes developing physical stamina, emotional stability, mental alertness, and spiritual strength. Just as Jesus in Luke 2:52, we should be continually increasing in wisdom, physical stamina, favor with God, and our relationships with people.

Another thing to keep in mind is that aging is a normal process everyone experiences. If we begin to feel sorry for ourselves when we spot "silver threads among the gold," crow's feet, skin blemishes, wrinkles, or a slight weight increase, we might begin looking and feeling even worse. Part of the answer may simply be an increase in personal discipline. Exercise and proper eating habits won't change gray hair or wrinkles, but they may help with the weight gain. A more positive attitude toward life can counter the negativism that sometimes creeps into our lives at this stage. In Philippians 4:8–9, Paul reminds us to focus our thoughts on what is pure, just, lovely, of good report, virtuous, and worthy of praise.

Remember, this is not the time to throw up your hands in despair, grow cynical, or feel put on the shelf. After all, the Lord doesn't have a mandatory retirement age. Frequently, individuals achieve their greatest works at midlife or beyond. Consider the following examples:

- Michelangelo was appointed architect of St. Peter's at age sixty-six, an office he held until his death at eighty-nine. It was also at age sixty-six that he completed his famous painting *The Last Judgment*.
- Titian painted his greatest masterpiece at eighty-five.
- Thomas Edison gave us some of his best inventions between the ages of seventy and eighty.
- William Gladstone took up a new language when he was seventy; then at eighty-three he became the Prime Minister of Great Britain for the fourth time.
- Commodore Vanderbilt added about one hundred million dollars to his fortune between the ages of seventy and eighty-three.
- Immanuel Kant wrote his *Anthropology*, *Metaphysics of Ethics*, and *Strife of the Faculties* when he was seventy-four.
- Tintoretto at seventy-four painted the vast *Paradise*, a canvas seventy-four by thirty feet.
- Composer Giuseppe Verdi at seventy-four produced his masterpiece *Otello*; at eighty, *Falstaff*; at eighty-five, the famous *Ave Maria*, *Stabat Mater*, and *Te Deum*.

- Johann Wolfgang von Goethe completed *Faust* at eighty.
- Alfred Lord Tennyson wrote *Crossing the Bar* at eighty-three.[5]
- And John Wesley preached until he was called home to heaven at ninety.[6]

Moses' most significant work occurred after eighty years of preparation (Acts 7:30–36). Abraham bore a son and raised him after reaching age one hundred. Isaac, Jacob, and Joseph lived long and useful lives as well.

24

LOOKING
BOTH
WAYS FROM
THE TOP
OF THE
MOUNTAIN
❦

A Mandate to Honor

As he recorded God's law, Moses included the divine perspective we're to have toward those who are older. "You shall rise before the gray headed and honor the presence of an old man, and fear your God: I am the LORD" (Lev. 19:32). From the Lord's perspective, it's impossible to fear God while at the same time disrespect or fail to honor those who are older.

In the New Testament, Paul spelled out for a young pastor how this was to work. Older men were not to be treated harshly but exhorted as one would his own father. Older women were to be treated as mothers, and authentic widows treated with honor and supported (1 Tim. 5:1–3). In part 3, we'll explore the important mandate to care for parents as they grow older and need our support. But the principle is clear: God expects us to honor those who are older.

Furthermore, as we grow older, he expects us to set an example and teach those who are younger, passing on God's values (Ps. 71:18; Titus 2:2–5).

So you're growing older. It's no time to push the panic button. It's just another stage of life.

CHAPTER **Two**

HEALTH ISSUES
AT MIDLIFE

PERHAPS DAVID THE PSALMIST WAS AT MIDLIFE when he observed, "I am fearfully and wonderfully made" (Ps. 139:14). Without question, medical and scientific studies have documented what a remarkable organism the human body is. Made up of billions of unique cells, miles of nerves and blood vessels, hundreds of different bones and muscles, and a wide variety of organs, our bodies have the ability to grow, heal, fight off disease, and survive a wide range of environmental experiences, including abuse. Our digestive system breaks down food into usable energy and nutrients that are carried by the blood throughout the body. Different body parts communicate with each other by means of nerves, and the brain and spinal cord coordinate this communicative process.

But our bodies can't go on forever. As most of us have discovered by the time we reach midlife, sickness, injury, and other forces take their toll.

According to *The Maturing Marketplace* newsletter, the U.S. pharmaceutical industry is developing 178 new medicines to combat the debilitating diseases facing people as they live longer. The new developmental medicines include twenty-four for arthritis, seventeen targeting Alzheimer's disease, twenty-one aimed at diabetes, and nine to combat depression. Other targets include osteoporosis, twenty-three; respiratory and lung disorders, twenty-four; and Parkinson's disease, twelve. Arthritis affects nearly half of Americans age sixty-five and older. Alzheimer's is a leading cause of nursing home admissions, affecting four million Americans, and diabetes kills forty-two thousand older Americans each year.[1]

Our major concern about aging seems to relate to the matter of our health. It's a concern that crops up frequently. For example, the most common greeting between two people is "How are you?" Generally, we mean how are you feeling, how are you doing, how is your health? When someone proposes a toast, the words they often use are, "To your health." Think of how many times you've heard someone address an individual who's lost a job, a loved one, or experienced a financial setback with the words, "At least you have your health."

As we reach midlife, we notice several things about our own health. For one thing, we're not quite as physically energetic as we once were. Now, don't misunderstand; we are both still extremely vigorous. We exercise regularly, even run through airports frequently. But we must admit, we've slowed down a step or two.

Perhaps you've had the same experience. Once you may have climbed the stairs with ease, mowed the lawn or lifted heavy boxes with hardly a change in your pulse rate or respiration. Now those kinds of activities leave you exhausted.

Midlife also frequently brings prolonged illnesses or injuries. Remember how quickly you bounced back from that strained knee or sprained ankle when you were younger? A similar injury today may cause you to have to hang up your softball glove altogether. Colds, sore throats, and the flu do not respond as quickly to treatment. Infections are often more difficult to overcome.

Furthermore, as we grow older, we notice the dramatic way in which many of our friends and peers seem to be aging. If you don't believe this, make it a point to attend your next high school reunion. You'll probably react the way a friend of ours did: "I'm never going to one of those again. All the people who attended looked so much older than I do."

26

LOOKING
BOTH
WAYS FROM
THE TOP
OF THE
MOUNTAIN

It's also true that we begin to lose friends, even peers. We both recall how our parents began expressing concern over the number of their friends and associates who had died. It's not as if we thought we'd never have to face those kinds of losses; we just sort of put it out of our mind.

Sensory Losses

Hearing impairment may begin as early as middle adulthood, even though it usually doesn't come until later in life. For some reason men are more likely than women to suffer hearing loss—maybe because more of them have traditionally worked in noisy places such as factories or driven farm equipment. Jim Hawkins, Don's father, became practically deaf at midlife after four decades at the controls of a diesel locomotive.

Studies show that one in four people over fifty experiences some type of hearing loss. The most common cause is presbycusis, which is an age-related reduction in the ability to hear high-pitched sounds, such as a woman's voice or the sound of certain musical instruments. A close second, noise-induced hearing loss, probably affects us all to a degree and can cause serious problems for those who have spent a lifetime working in noisy environments. Both of these problems lead to nerve deafness, which occurs as tiny sound-sensing cells in the ear deteriorate either from aging or abuse.[2] Fifteen percent of those over sixty-five are legally deaf, usually because of degeneration within the inner ear. By the time a person reaches seventy-five or older, three out of four experience significant hearing problems.

Vision is another area of typical midlife decline. Many of us have been visually challenged since childhood—Don wears corrective eyeglasses and Wood usually wears contact lenses. We've noticed, however, that these problems tend to become more pronounced as we age. This visual decline is usually traced to a reduction in the intensity of light reaching the retina because the lens of the eye becomes less transparent, thicker, and not as elastic with passing years. Frequently, in midlife we find it more difficult to drive at night as our tolerance for glare diminishes. Our adaptation to the dark is slower, thus we take longer to recover our vision when moving from a well-lit room to semidarkness. Studies show that the area of our visual field often becomes smaller and our peripheral vision lessens as we grow older.

Midlife often also brings about significant loss of physical dexterity. From the mid-thirties on, hand and finger movements become progressively more clumsy. Sometimes the culprit is emotional, as motivation, depression, anxiety, or other factors may lower our reaction time. Stress is often a contributing factor. However, as we age, collagen, the major connective tissue in the body, loses its elasticity. This causes our entire skeletal system to grow tighter and stiffer—including our hands and fingers.

Another thing we lose as we age is our ability to taste and smell. Studies have indicated that some atrophy of olfactory fibers in the nose occurs with age. And while it's difficult to determine the effect of aging on the sense of taste since it's so closely tied to smell—about 95 percent of taste is derived from the olfactory nerves—frequently those who grow older claim less ability to taste.

28

LOOKING
BOTH
WAYS FROM
THE TOP
OF THE
MOUNTAIN

Menopause

One of the most dramatic physical changes, and one with far-reaching effects on a woman's emotional and spiritual life, is menopause. The word itself produces many different reactions for women as well as men. Many mothers have passed along horror stories to their daughters about hot flashes, mood swings, and other drastic symptoms. Fortunately, many of those adverse symptoms of previous generations can now be countered with hormonal treatment.

Menopause is the time in a woman's life when her ovaries stop producing the amount of estrogen and progesterone needed for menstrual periods. The average age of menopause in the United States today is 51.3 years, although the age may range from the late thirties or early forties to mid to late sixties.[3]

Barb was almost forty-eight when she finally made an appointment with her gynecologist. She had not been to a doctor in years, even though she had complained of night sweats, hot flashes, severe mood changes, and irritability. Her mother, Candace, told her, "There's no use in going to the doctor. If you'll just be patient, the symptoms will go away. After all, they did for me. I never had to take those dreaded hormones."

When Barb went to see her doctor, he told her that most of her symptoms could be reduced or resolved if she took estrogen and progesterone. Then he carefully explained the benefits and the risks.

Estrogen is administered in the form of a pill, an injection, or a patch attached to the skin. Physicians have found it effective in relieving hot flashes, night sweats, sleeping difficulties, mood swings, and other symptoms. Progesterone is prescribed along with estrogen for women who have not had a hysterectomy. It can sometimes affect a woman's moodiness, although her physician can usually adjust the dosage.

If a woman has cancer or is at a high risk for cancer, a physician will probably not prescribe estrogen replacement therapy, since estrogen can accelerate cancer growth. Although studies vary in results, there is some indication that estrogen could contribute to breast cancer.

Some time ago on a radio call-in program, Christian obstetrician/gynecologist Dr. Joe McIlhaney was asked, "How long do I have to take hormones?" He replied, "As long as you are willing." Then he went on to explain that hormone replacement therapy can help prevent two major lifelong risks of postmenopausal women—heart attack and osteoporosis. He explained that estrogen acts directly on the arterial walls to decrease atherosclerosis, or the hardening of the arteries caused by buildup of plaque, an effect that often happens earlier in high-cholesterol men. In addition, estrogen also helps keep calcium in the bones, thereby preventing osteoporosis, or "soft bones," which causes an increased risk of fractures.

For a woman, dealing with menopause, or "the change" as it's often called, involves a recognition that she is living through a part of what God has designed as the plan for women. She will need her husband's support and encouragement, and both will need to exercise patience in dealing with the significant physical changes she will experience and the accompanying periodic emotional instability.

Sometimes these physical symptoms and the busyness of midlife can lead to a decline in the intimate relationship between a husband and wife. It is important, therefore, for husbands and wives to care for themselves physically and be understanding with regard to life's changes. Also, men and women both need to incorporate healthy eating habits, rest, and exercise into their lives, and above all they need to carve out time to devote to each other, relating not only on a physical and sexual level but building emotional closeness, handling minor grievances and irritations, and following Peter's advice to cultivate spiritual harmony (1 Peter 3:7).

Changes in Appearance

30

LOOKING
BOTH
WAYS FROM
THE TOP
OF THE
MOUNTAIN

Have you looked in the mirror lately? Were you shocked at the appearance of the person staring back at you? Did that person appear older, more fragile, less robust than you thought you were? Claudia, in her late forties, told her friend Susan, "I can't believe it. I looked in the mirror. My stomach sags. My hair looks dull. My love handles are out of control. I have deep wrinkles around my mouth and across my face. I even noticed a double chin. I took this careful look at myself because yesterday I ran into Martha at the mall. I hadn't seen her in over five years. I couldn't believe how much older she looked—heavy, sagging, wrinkled, and gray."

Sound familiar?

Men, too, experience the inevitable inner tube of fat around the midsection, the appearance of salt-and-pepper hair or the absence of hair. (The use of topical products such as Rogaine™ and now a tablet designed to counter male pattern baldness have increased dramatically in recent years.) Men experience more muscular aches, feel a stronger temptation to become a couch potato, and are both less active and less daring than they once were.

Men don't experience a midlife physical change that exactly parallels menopause. As we move into midlife, however, we begin to reevaluate our lives and often look for answers to questions such as, Did I choose the right career? Do I still have the abilities and potential I once had? Am I truly experiencing a meaningful life? Since the spiritual component is so vitally connected to both the physical and emotional parts of our selves (1 Thess. 5:23), we can use these emotional concerns and physical changes to motivate us to reexamine our commitment to Christ and reenergize our spiritual vitality.

Unfortunately, not all Christian men respond this way. Some simply grow fearful and withdraw from the challenges of life. Others push harder, working at a breakneck pace. Many go into crash exercise programs. Still others try to act and dress like an aging adolescent. Some men experience the typical midlife crisis, perhaps succumbing as King David did to the temptation to have an affair, or falling into the trap of pornography, which is increasingly available through the Internet, videos, and cable television.

Both men and women are affected by the standards of our society that glamorize and glorify the youthful, the svelte, and the attractive. Combine this phenomenon with the evidence we've cited, and we are forced to acknowledge that physically speaking, midlife can be a risky time.

It can also be a risky time because of specific health concerns that tend to afflict those who have reached midlife. We now turn our attention to these issues.

System Problems

Think of your body as a house. When you moved in, it had relatively new systems, like the electrical, plumbing, heating, and ventilation systems in your home. But like an aging residence, the body at midlife begins to experience problems. For one thing, the quality of circulation deteriorates. We usually think of our circulatory system as something that keeps our extremities warm when it's cold, but the circulatory system does far more than that. Blood carries oxygen, nutrients, and antibodies to tissues throughout the body. By the time we reach midlife, plaque buildup in our veins or a weakened heart muscle may lessen the effects of circulation, causing parts of our body not to receive the things they need to stay healthy.

In addition, research indicates that the production of white blood cells and other antibodies peaks during or shortly after adolescence and gradually declines for the rest of our lives.[4] This means by midlife our body's defenses have less ammunition to fight off infections.

Our kidneys function as the body's "sewer system." Studies indicate that the kidneys' ability to filter out and excrete waste material declines at a rate of half a percent to three-quarters of a percent per year. Thus, by midlife we may have 25 percent less kidney function than when we were young. As a result, the potential exists for drugs that are normally excreted by our kidneys to build to a toxic level, even though the dosage may be normal.

Ailments of Aging

32

LOOKING
BOTH
WAYS FROM
THE TOP
OF THE
MOUNTAIN
❦

A recent survey of 1,752 adult men and women by *Parade* magazine[5] indicated that the number one current health concern of North Americans is weight, according to 19 percent of those surveyed, followed by heart problems, high blood pressure, arthritis, and high cholesterol. When respondents were asked, "What is your greatest personal health concern for the future?" the majority responded with cancer followed closely by heart problems, weight, and high blood pressure.

In reality, heart disease takes the life of nearly two Americans in five, while cancer will affect one out of two men and one out of three women at some time during their lifetime. In fact, three out of four American families will have to deal with cancer at some point.[6]

According to a special report in *Prevention* magazine, "Heart disease is the number one killer of women—yet it is misdiagnosed with frightening regularity."[7] Many people think of heart attacks as a man's problem, yet heart disease kills more women every year than all forms of cancer, chronic lung disease, pneumonia, diabetes, accidents, and AIDS combined—more than half a million women.[8]

Great technology for diagnosing heart disease in men and women has been around for a long time. The key tool is the treadmill stress test, which involves performing an electrocardiogram (EKG) continuously during a period of exercise. Recently, due to inaccuracies in testing women with the EKG, two new technologies have been developed. The first of these new imaging techniques involves having the patient walk on a treadmill while a radioactive isotope is injected into the bloodstream, allowing special scanners to track the blood flow through the heart. A noninvasive, less expensive alternative is the stress echo cardiogram.

Anyone with symptoms—men or women—at midlife should be tested. In fact, we recommend that everyone at midlife have a regular physical including stress EKGs.

Heart Attacks

Chest pain is the most common symptom of a heart attack. A gripping tightness or heaviness in the chest is usually accompanied by shortness of breath or sweating. For women, the symptoms may be different. According to cardiologist Dr. Roy Ziegelstein of Johns Hopkins Medical Center in Baltimore, women often experience shortness of breath or difficulty breathing and may even have pain or weakness in the shoulder, arms, or all over the body. Women are more likely than men to experience nausea or vomiting.[9] Angina, sharp pain caused by a temporary lack of oxygen to the heart, can serve as a warning sign of a future heart attack. Sometimes a person may be tempted to wait to see if symptoms will pass. But symptoms such as pain in the chest, arm, or shoulder, extreme exhaustion, or fatigue should never be taken lightly.

Cardiac surgeon Dr. John Isch told our *Confident Living* radio audience, "If you have something you think is a problem, get it checked out, and do it fast. Time is of the essence." Dr. Isch suggests you first call your doctor. If you can't reach your physician, make sure to let the person you reach know that you believe you're having a medical emergency.

Second, take an aspirin. According to many cardiologists, a 325 mg aspirin taken in the early stages of a heart attack has been shown to improve the rate of survival in both men and women.

Third, head for the emergency room. Don't worry about potential embarrassment. Studies show regular fatalities on the part of men and women who delay before going to a hospital. If you are experiencing a heart attack, your chances of survival are much better if you're at a hospital.

The risk factors for heart attack include smoking, high cholesterol, high blood pressure, high triglycerides, and obesity. For men the risk of heart attack and stroke soars after age forty-five. In women, a comparable increase occurs at approximately age fifty-five, probably as a result of the gradual reduction in estrogen levels. Past age sixty, one out of four individuals is likely to die of heart disease.

Cancer

For many people the word *cancer* is tantamount to a death sentence. Throughout our lives, many factors influence the cells in our bodies. Some such as tobacco and tobacco smoke, industrial agents, or toxic substances are external. Others operate on us internally. For example, the high-fat, low-fiber diets that are so common today, sexual practices that increase exposure to sexually transmitted viruses, medical treatment such as X rays or hormones (such as DES), or excessive exposure to sunlight can trigger the changes in a cell that lead to a mutation in which a single abnormal cell becomes two abnormal cells, then four, and so on. Some fast-growing cancers may double in size in a matter of weeks. Others take months, even years. Medical authorities explain that it is the silent period of cancer growth, when a tumor is too small to be detected, that makes this disease so difficult to deal with.

Genetics also plays a role in whether a person will develop cancer. Cancer researchers have noted that some individuals can work for years, perhaps an entire lifetime, with repeated exposure to strong carcinogens such as asbestos and yet remain free of cancer. Other individuals have contracted lung cancer or other forms after only a brief exposure to asbestos or other carcinogens. This variation indicates a link between genetics and cancer susceptibility.

Cancer cells can spread or metastasize throughout the body, using the blood or the lymphatic system—the body's drainage system—or they can spread from one tissue mass to another. Left untreated, cancer almost always leads to death. This disease, however, is no longer considered an automatic death sentence. Incredible strides have been made in recent years through effective modalities and research. The most common treatments for cancer include surgery, chemotherapy, and radiation therapy, although new strategies are currently under research.

The most common form of cancer in women is breast cancer, which affects one out of every nine women in America. For men, prostate cancer is the most common form.

34

LOOKING
BOTH
WAYS FROM
THE TOP
OF THE
MOUNTAIN

According to the American Cancer Society, there are seven major early warning signals that those of us at midlife need to heed. These can be remembered by using the acrostic CAUTION.[10]

C—Change in bowel or bladder habits
A—A sore that does not heal
U—Unusual bleeding or discharge
T—Thickening or lump in the breast or elsewhere
I —Indigestion or difficulty in swallowing
O—Obvious change in a wart or mole
N—Nagging cough or hoarseness

While regular checkups can help alert our physician to the possibility of cancer, we need to make sure we heed any of these warning signs and schedule an appointment in a timely fashion.

The approach we advocate in regard to cancer is based on the principle of waiting on the Lord found in Isaiah 40:31. Most people misunderstand the concept of waiting; they think it simply means to sit passively and hope for something good to happen. Actually the term as used in Scripture indicates a proactive, even stretching, experience. In fact, a closely connected word, from the same root as the term translated "wait" or "hope" in Isaiah 40:31, is found in Joshua 2, where Rahab was instructed to stretch a scarlet cord through the window as a sign of her faith in Israel's God. Our definition of waiting is to "do everything the Lord has empowered and instructed you to do, and leave everything else up to him and other people."

When it comes to the possibility of cancer or serious illness, we believe this means we should exercise the best preventive care as possible, see a physician for regular checkups and whenever we suspect cancer, heart disease, or other serious medical problems, and most important of all, trust the Lord both daily and through medical crises to work things out for our good and his glory. As a friend once said, "When you're caught on a lake in a thunderstorm, it's best to pray hard and row to shore." We think the same approach applies to serious medical problems.

Chronic Illnesses

We've already identified the leading causes of death during midlife and beyond: heart disease and cancer. Others include stroke, diabetes, and lung diseases such as pneumonia and influenza. But as we grow older, many of us suffer from illnesses that are not terminal yet cause pain and restrict our ability to enjoy life.

One such illness is arthritis, an inflammation of the joints accompanied by pain, stiffness, and difficulty with movement. We might never have thought of it that way, but inflammation is actually how the Creator designed our bodies to fight infection. However, once the infection is gone, the inflammation is supposed to leave as well. With arthritis the inflammation continues, resulting in tissue damage.

About thirty-seven million Americans are affected by arthritis, one in every seven people. The most common kind is osteoarthritis, although medical experts have documented over one hundred different versions of this painful ailment.

As we reach the mid-range of midlife, osteoporosis begins to affect many of us. This disorder involves extensive deterioration of bone tissue and is the main reason many older adults walk with a stooped posture. It generally begins to make its presence known in midlife, although it can happen earlier.

Although usually regarded as a woman's disease, osteoporosis can also affect men. As male hormone levels begin to decline after age sixty, men begin to lose bone mass at about the same rate as women. By the time we reach our seventies, close to half of all men and women have some degree of osteoporosis. Inactivity, poor diet, cigarette smoking, and heavy alcohol use are often contributing factors to this as well as other health problems.

Steps to Midlife Wellness

Despite the health issues we have discussed, there are practical steps we can take to cultivate a healthy, physical "you" at midlife. In the following sections we will talk about some specific ways to improve our health. Generally speaking, however, we find in Romans 12 a series of principles that can help us maintain physical well-being during the critical midlife years.

36

LOOKING
BOTH
WAYS FROM
THE TOP
OF THE
MOUNTAIN

First, treat your body like the temple it is. In Romans 12:1, the apostle Paul urges believers to "present your bodies a living sacrifice, holy, acceptable to God, which is your reasonable service." Paul wrote the Corinthians to remind them that "your body is the temple of the Holy Spirit" (1 Cor. 6:19). The point is clear. Our bodies belong to God, not us. That should be motivation enough to care for them. This includes eating right, getting regular physical exercise (even walking up and down a flight of stairs rather than taking the elevator can help), taking enough time for rest, and getting regular medical checkups.

On a recent edition of our *Confident Living* program, nutritionist Sharon Sneed pointed out:

> You can get away with a lot of poor choices in your twenties and thirties, but right about age thirty-five the tide starts to turn. At midlife we lose lean body mass. We also lose our zeal for exercise. At that point those bodily engines that burn calories at a faster rate shut off. Then it becomes very easy to gain ten to twenty pounds every year.
>
> By the time we reach the fifties and sixties we shouldn't be as worried about things like ideal weight. What we need to do is devote about forty-five minutes a day to physical activity, including some simple stuff we used to do in grade school—like modified pushups (where you do them on your knees) and some stomach crunches, even a brisk walk. You may also need to change the way you eat; decrease your calorie intake while you increase your calorie expenditure.

We may not think of issues such as exercise and eating as spiritual, yet according to Galatians 5:23 the fruit of the Spirit is self-control. And 1 Corinthians 10:31 reminds us that "whether you eat or drink, or whatever you do, do all to the glory of God."

Second, avoid the "squeeze" of conformity to the world; instead focus on pleasing God. Romans 12:2 points out, "And do not be conformed to this world, but be transformed by the renewing of your mind, that you may prove what is that good and acceptable and perfect will of God." As we noted earlier, the world tells us that young, slim, and beautiful are in and good. We may be tempted to become obsessed with health and fitness rather than simply giving balanced attention to this matter. To do so is dangerous, both since it can place us at physical risk and it can detract from our spiritual focus.

Midlife is a time to remember that God has given us a body to care for as a stewardship; it should not be the primary source of our personal esteem. True, we need self-discipline—that's what Paul meant in 1 Corinthians 9:27 when he wrote, "But I discipline my body and bring it into subjection." The apostle also reminded his protégé Timothy of the importance of "a spirit of self-discipline" (2 Tim. 1:7 NIV).

One issue we may not normally connect with conformity to the world has to do with a stress-filled lifestyle. Dr. David Hager teaches medicine at the University of Kentucky Medical School. He and his wife, Linda, coauthored a book titled *Stress and the Woman's Body*. Recently, he told our radio audience:

> We're living in a day and age when there are many more stressors on us. If you look at the fight or flight reflex, I think the key is to find a spiritual resolution. In my practice I see how stress affects us in different ways—the workings of the brain, the hypothalamus, and the pituitary gland, for example. When a woman is highly stressed—she has an unhappy marriage, a child who's gotten into trouble with the law, or she's unhappy with her job—then she's generally going to suffer more as she goes through the menopause, both physically and emotionally. Stress also increases the risk of heart disease or a heart attack, both for women and men. That's why it is important that we minimize stress to the degree that we can, while learning to deal with those we cannot eliminate.

Third, evaluate yourself realistically. Romans 12:3 points out that each of us is "not to think of himself more highly than he ought to think, but to think soberly." Sometimes we are tempted to deny the reality of our own aging, to live in the past, even to neglect physical care, medical checkups, or the need for exercise. Yet Paul urges a sober or realistic self-appraisal, one not based on personal ability or achievement but on the measure of faith God has given to each of us individually.

Fourth, utilize other members of the body to help you physically through accountability. As Paul points out in Romans 12:4–5, "For as we have many members in one body, but all the

38

LOOKING
BOTH
WAYS FROM
THE TOP
OF THE
MOUNTAIN

members do not have the same function, so we, being many, are one body in Christ, and individually members of one another." Since we have different gifts, we need to use those gifts to build each other up, to encourage each other, and to help each other.

Our colleagues Allen Bean and Kirk Chestnut have encouraged each other significantly over the past few years through their early morning racquetball appointments. Allen is at midlife; Kirk is a bit younger, yet each benefits from the camaraderie, friendly competition, and accountability of meeting each other at the Sports Court for an early morning session. In similar fashion, at times we have observed our entire secretarial services team, led by their manager, Dawn Leuschen, walking briskly around the indoor hallways at Back to the Bible's International headquarters building.

We should always keep in mind, however, Paul's summary statement in Romans 12:21, which provides us with a measuring rod to evaluate all our physical activities: "Do not be overcome by evil, but overcome evil with good."

A Healthy Diet

Perhaps the most basic step to healthy living at midlife is healthy eating. Usually this means eating less. As a rule, adults must consume fewer calories as they age in order to maintain their weight. The reason for this is that our metabolic rate, the rate at which the body burns calories, drops about two percent every decade.[11] That's why nutrition authorities suggest that it takes only a hundred calories a day of extra food eaten and stored as fat to gain ten pounds in a year at midlife. You can see how easy it is to allow those extra pounds to accumulate, even when you continue eating the same amount of food—or even less— than you have before.

There are some commonsense rules we need to follow when it comes to diet. First, minimize or eliminate dietary fats. Total fat intake in our diet should be decreased to no more than 30 percent of the total calories we eat. At one time authorities thought polyunsaturated fatty acids such as those in corn and safflower oil were healthy in any amount; current research has indicated, however, that polyunsaturated fats such as corn, soybean, and sunflower oils should be considered along with meat and other saturated fats and monounsaturated fats (such as olive oil) when determining our total amount of fat intake.

According to the *Parade* magazine survey "How Healthy Are We?" more than half of those who responded have changed to healthier eating habits, avoiding fats and eating more fruits and vegetables. But about a quarter of those who responded still smoke, more than half drink alcohol, half do not exercise, and almost 90 percent say they don't exercise as much as they should.

Taking vitamins and minerals is another commonsense dietary tip, but you should remember you'll never make up for a poor diet by taking a pill. Eating the right kinds of food is essential. A healthy diet must include a certain amount of fiber, a term applied to a variety of nondigestible carbohydrates. Most physicians who specialize in disorders of the intestine and colon recommend that we consume twenty-five grams per day of cellulose fiber. It's been suggested that this can decrease the incidence of colon cancer by more than 50 percent.[12] The right kinds of fiber can also help lower blood cholesterol.

Getting Enough Rest

Studies indicate that approximately fifty million Americans have significant problems getting regular sleep. Some simply can't fall asleep or have trouble staying asleep; others try "burning the candle at both ends." The psalmist pointed out that "it is vain for you to rise up early, to sit up late, to eat the bread of sorrows" (Ps. 127:2); yet we both know many individuals who are so obsessed with their work or other factors that they have trouble sleeping.

So how much sleep is the right amount? There's no one set amount of sleep that fits everyone. Some people require as many as nine or ten hours, while others can get by on five or six. The average person needs between six and eight hours. Medical authorities tell us the quality of our sleep is important; in other words, we need both the lighter, dream-filled Rapid Eye Movement (REM) sleep and the deeper non-Rapid Eye Movement sleep.

What are the factors that hinder our sleep? Heavy foods eaten late in the evening just before bedtime can lead to both indigestion (since it's difficult to digest food while we're horizontal) and insomnia. Vigorous exercise just before bedtime

40

LOOKING
BOTH
WAYS FROM
THE TOP
OF THE
MOUNTAIN

may keep us awake, although regular exercise for thirty to forty minutes three to four times a week can help promote better sleep as well as physical fitness. Caffeine and nicotine are proven to interfere with sleep, as is alcohol—some people think alcohol will help you fall asleep faster, but you're likely to wake up during the night and not experience restful sleep. Scientists have identified at least seventy different types of sleep disorders. Some, such as sleep apnea, can actually be life threatening.

So how can we get sufficient rest? First, we need to establish a regular sleeping schedule. Going to bed and getting up at the same time every day, even on weekends, can help. Use your bed for sleeping only and not for eating, working, or studying. If you find yourself lying awake for half an hour or more, sleep authorities suggest you get up, read, or engage in some other activity, then return to bed only when you feel tired. The continuous sleep you finally get will be better than periodically dozing off and waking up.

It's also important not to brood over work or personal problems in bed. We recommend the approach Paul advocates in Philippians 4:6: "Be anxious for nothing, but in everything by prayer and supplication, with thanksgiving, let your requests be made known to God." Commit your concerns to the Father, perhaps write them down along with ideas for dealing with them, then let the Lord "give His beloved sleep" (Ps. 127:2).

Avoiding the Sedentary Life

The older we get, the easier it is to become a couch potato. When I (Don) reached forty, I realized I had gone from an exercise program that included running up to five miles three times a week and playing a vigorous game of basketball at least once a week to practically nothing. Realizing my lack of exercise, I decided at forty it was time to resume running. I began with a mile a day three times a week. Within a year, I had increased to a mile and a half three times a week, and I've maintained that pace ever since. I'll never compete with my friend Paul Heitzman, who, in his early sixties, runs marathons, but I have no doubt that I'm in better shape as a result of my physical exercise.

Lifestyle Changes

Many of us realize as we near midlife that we haven't taken good care of ourselves. Perhaps we're overweight, experiencing health problems, not feeling too well, lacking in energy. Maybe we're a bit like Sandy who in her late forties found herself carrying an extra twenty pounds on her five-foot-six-inch frame. When Ruthie, a friend and personal trainer, asked Sandy about her plans for working out, Sandy rushed into her bedroom, returned with a dress that was two sizes too small, and said, "My goal is to get into this dress in time for my Christmas party." Shaking her head, Ruthie realized there was no way Sandy could lose that amount of weight, maintain her health, and keep the weight off, all in three short weeks.

We've found that unrealistic goals and inappropriate motivation are two of the biggest midlife obstacles to good midlife health. We have many friends who have lost a great deal of weight using crash diets—a quick ten or fifteen pounds at a time—then usually gained it all back, and then some. We've even had fellow workers who lost into the triple digits—that's right, over one hundred pounds—only to gain it all back in a matter of months.

The trouble with a good deal of our motivation is that it just isn't appropriate. We've gorged over Thanksgiving, and we have to lose the extra pounds in time for Christmas; we can no longer get into that stunning new outfit; a spouse has been dropping hints about our need to reduce; a good friend has taken off ten pounds with a successful crash diet and looks great—never mind the fact that he or she will gain it all back, with interest, before long.

What is the right kind of motivation for the arduous, lifelong struggle to maintain the discipline that leads to good health?

First and foremost, things done in the body will be evaluated at the judgment seat of Christ (2 Cor. 5:10). The apostle Paul has our walk and witness uppermost in mind in his comments to the Corinthians. The fact that he uses the phrase "the things done in the body" indicates God is concerned with how we handle the physical temple he's given us.

Second, although the body is not to be the primary focus of our concern (Matt. 6:25), it is the dwelling place or temple of the Spirit of God (1 Cor. 6:19) and, therefore, is deserv-

42

LOOKING
BOTH
WAYS FROM
THE TOP
OF THE
MOUNTAIN

ing of our care. Along that line, Paul urges the Romans, "Do not let sin reign in your mortal body, that you should obey it in its lusts" (Rom. 6:12).

Third, even though our bodies have been affected by the fall, one of the significant hopes we have as Christians is what Paul refers to as "the adoption, the redemption of our body" (Rom. 8:23). None of us at midlife needs look any further than the mirror to find evidence of the effects of sin on our physical lives. On the other hand, our present physical condition is not permanent, and for this we can rejoice. The fact that we won't always face this struggle can motivate us to diligent discipline during our present life.

Fourth, there are legitimate appetites built into our created bodies, such as hunger and the sex drive (1 Cor. 6:13). Yet these are to be submitted to the Lord and fulfilled only in ways that glorify him. Many Christians who consistently shun sexual immorality may never consider the fact that gluttony displeases the Lord and does our bodies a disservice. Furthermore, sexual sins are a violation of and harmful to our own bodies (1 Cor. 6:18).

Fifth, Paul indicated that self-discipline of our bodies is of primary importance if we are to finish well in life. As he told the Corinthians, "I discipline my body and bring it into subjection, lest, when I have preached to others, I myself should become disqualified" (1 Cor. 9:27). Since God has empowered us to exercise the discipline of self-control (Gal. 5:23), it is imperative that we make appropriate choices, especially with regard to eating, exercise, and personal purity.

Room for Improvement

It is important for all of us to accept the fact that there will always be room for improvement in most areas of our lives, including diet and exercise. We'd both love to have time for thirty minutes of cardiovascular exercise every day and to always sit down to a healthy, balanced diet. There are times, however, when it just isn't possible to do so. We both travel a great deal, and we both find ourselves extremely busy from time to time at home. But the important thing is that we don't give up when schedule gets in the way of fitness or health. When possible, we come back to our regimen and start over, determined to resume the discipline of healthy living.

For many individuals, a vital step toward cultivating good health is to avoid the trap of television. This one device has probably contributed more to our sedentary lifestyles and furnished more junk food for the mind and spirit than any other product of the technological era. A major reduction or elimination of television time can increase our time for physical exercise and other worthwhile pursuits.

Another idea is to consult a fitness or health expert. Linda and Wood began seeing a registered dietitian at our family physician's office. Because of Don's diabetes, Kathy and Don consult with her as well. The four of us are probably significantly healthier in terms of what we eat because of her input and counsel. As Proverbs 12:15 points out, only the wise seek (and heed) counsel.

It's always appropriate and important to set limits when you are exercising. Pay attention to how your body feels. Have you experienced a great deal of pain in your ankles and knees after running? Perhaps you should run a shorter distance or switch to a nonimpact activity such as bicycling or swimming. Some time ago, cardiovascular authority Dr. Kenneth Cooper pointed out during a radio interview that individuals who run more than fifteen miles a week are running for something other than cardiovascular fitness.

Another important factor is balance. Take, for example, the spiritual realm. We both believe in spending significant chunks of time studying God's Word on a regular basis. Yet, if you spend all your time studying the Word, when do you pray? If all your time is taken up with prayer and Bible study, when do you witness or fellowship or worship? All of life involves balance, including the physical. If your physical stamina improves because of exercise, that's a good sign, but if you find yourself drained and exhausted because of that six-day-a-week aerobic regimen or your marriage is suffering because of your workout routine, then you may need to make some adjustments.

Finally, the ultimate goal for our body is to reflect the glory of Jesus. Paul expressed this in 2 Corinthians 4:10 when he said, "Always carrying about in the body the dying of the Lord Jesus, that the life of Jesus also may be manifested in our body."

44

LOOKING
BOTH
WAYS FROM
THE TOP
OF THE
MOUNTAIN

No matter how difficult life becomes, whether our bodies are affected by the illness or decay brought about by the fall, or whether we need to achieve the discipline to maintain the good health with which we've been blessed, our ultimate goal is not to build a beautiful, healthy body for the sake of appearance, stamina, or anything else. The ultimate goal is exactly as Paul expressed it: that our mortal bodies may reflect the life of Jesus Christ.

CHAPTER THREE

CAREER CHANGES AT MIDLIFE

ARE YOU FAMILIAR WITH THE PHRASE "the winds of change"? Perhaps Prime Minister Neville Chamberlain of England should have received a royalty payment each time this phrase was used. He was the one who coined it to describe the rise of communism during World War II.

But neither Neville Chamberlain nor his successor, Sir Winston Churchill, or even H. G. Wells, who wrote *War of the Worlds*, or George Orwell, author of *1984*, could have imagined all the changes that have affected life at the end of the twentieth century.

Just one year before the end of the nineteenth century, Charles Duell, head of the U.S. patent office, observed, "Everything that can be invented has been invented."

To prove how wrong Mr. Duell was, look at your wristwatch and see how many inventions you can recall within the span of a minute. By the way, you receive extra credit if you move beyond such obvious developments as the aircraft, the space shuttle, the diesel locomotive, the computer, and the incandescent light bulb.

Speaking of changes, take another look at your watch—chances are it's digital. Fifty years ago, the world's best watches were Swiss. Eighty percent of all watches were made in Switzerland. A little over thirty years ago, the concept of the digital watch was offered to Swiss watchmakers. They turned it down because they believed they already had the best watches and the best watchmakers. At that time Swiss watchmakers employed eighty thousand people. Today that number has dropped to eighteen thousand.[1]

48

LOOKING
BOTH
WAYS FROM
THE TOP
OF THE
MOUNTAIN

Resistant to Change

Change never seems to come easy, does it? There's something about our human nature that resists change, even fears change. In fact, change can rattle our emotional cages like little else.

Changes affect every dimension of our lives, including our homes, our work, and our churches. Change could be described as transition, a shift from one era to another, from using an old skill to developing a new one, from employing an old method to acquiring a new one, or leaving an old relationship to establishing a new one. Change is the transition from the past to the future.

According to Dr. Cynthia Scott and Dennis Jaffe, we respond to change through a sequential process consisting of four observable steps: denial, resistance, exploration, and commitment.[2]

In the denial phase our focus is typically on the past, or "business as usual." We often remain stuck at this stage, denying the need to change to preserve our comfort level.

During the second phase, resistance, we maintain our focus on the past, but our response shifts to emotions such as anger, anxiety, or even depression. At this stage individuals are worried about their own particular role and responsibilities in change.

In the third or exploration stage of change, the focus moves from the past to the future. For many of us this is an awkward phase, a time of feeling inadequate or struggling with what is new. There may be confusion, a lack of focus and direction, even chaos. The older we are, the more conscious we are of the changes in this phase and the less likely we are to be comfortable. This is a time, however, to ask questions, explore new opportunities, even allow ourselves to fail.

The final stage of change, commitment, is marked by a clarified focus, a new sense of cooperation, and a commitment to new opportunities made possible by the change.

Whatever the process, it seems change always involves resistance.

Changes and Responses

In 1884 when the first baby carriage was invented, people protested violently that such carriages posed a danger to pedestrians. As trains began to come into widespread use, farmers in Suffolk County, New York, tore up a track and burned down a depot in an effort to stop what they considered "an evil contraption." In 1842 when the first bathtub was invented, a group of physicians went on record warning that these newfangled contraptions could pose a menace to public health. Philadelphia even issued an ordinance prohibiting bathing between November 1 and March 15. Another state levied a thirty-dollar-per-year tax on every family that owned a bathtub!

Christians are not exempt from emotional resistance to change. Some time ago two ladies who were a step or two beyond midlife were talking. One said to the other, "That young pastor and those elders are going to kill off my church." When asked why, she responded, "They've changed the Sunday school time from 9:45 to 9:30."

We may not like change, but we are changing. A pastor told of asking a woman, "So you've been married for fifty years to the same man?" The wife sweetly replied, "Well, no, honey, he's not nearly the same man he was when I married him."

Over the years, we've experienced vast changes in lifestyle, employment, living conditions, even morals and values. For example, most of us today live in cities in contrast to just a few generations ago when the majority of people lived on farms. At the beginning of the twentieth century there were only eleven cities worldwide with populations of more than a million people. Today there are nearly three hundred, and according to the United Nations, there will likely be more than five hundred within twenty years.

Even the cycle of life has changed drastically over the last generation. Today many nine-year-old girls are showing signs of puberty, while ten-year-old boys carry guns to school—and some shoot fellow students and teachers. Some sixteen-year-olds are filing for divorce against their parents, while forty-year-old women are just beginning to have children. Fifty-year-old men are forced into early retirement, while some men of sixty run marathons.

Change as Opportunity

50

LOOKING
BOTH
WAYS FROM
THE TOP
OF THE
MOUNTAIN
🍃

For those of us at midlife, responding to change generally takes one of two forms. Most commonly we struggle with it, or resist it. Our initial response involves emotions such as anger, fear, or anxiety. Sometimes, however, we respond positively, looking at change as an opportunity for growth. This chapter will consider one major aspect of change at midlife—that of career—and the positive ways we can respond to such a change.

First, however, let's consider the concept of change from the point of view of Scripture. The term itself is used twenty-three times, ranging from Jacob's reminder to his household to "change your garments" in preparation for meeting Esau to the reminder of the necessity for the change of the priesthood and the law in Hebrews 7:12. Certain changes are viewed as impossible: "Can the Ethiopian change his skin or the leopard its spots?" (Jer. 13:23). God himself is viewed as unchangeable (Mal. 3:6). But some change is both inevitable ("I will wait, till my change comes" [Job 14:14]) and desirable ("We have heard him say that this Jesus of Nazareth will . . . change the customs which Moses delivered to us" [Acts 6:14]).

Scripture shows that while God is unchangeable, he oversees a creation permeated with change. Many of these changes result because of the fall. In fact some are a direct consequence of divine judgment because of sin: "The LORD will change the rain of your land to powder and dust; from the heaven it shall come down on you until you are destroyed" (Deut. 28:24). Frequently God initiates and desires change on the part of his people: "You will change them, and they will be changed" (Ps. 102:26). At other times God warns his people against change: "My son, fear the LORD and the king; do not associate with those given to change" (Prov. 24:21).

From this we can draw several observations about change. First, although God himself is unchangeable, he frequently changes his response to people based on how they respond to him. One good example of this is in Jonah 3 in which God relented in his stated intention to destroy the Ninevites when they repented and turned in faith to him.

Second, change itself is neither morally good nor evil; instead, change must be evaluated based on God's unchanging Word (Matt. 24:35).

Third, some changes are a natural result of living in a fallen world. "They will perish, but You remain; and they will all grow old like a garment" (Heb. 1:11).

Changes at Midlife

Let's fast forward in our consideration of change from the biblical perspective to midlife implications.

Brad didn't mind when he hit forty. After all, that's when life begins he'd heard often enough. But during the decade between that birthday and the "big 5-O," his marriage to Janice began to lose its spark. Where once they shared feelings, hopes, and dreams, now he doled out criticisms and sarcastic barbs. She in turn withdrew.

Things were just as bad at work as at home. Brad spent the past two decades moving up the management ladder at a firm that developed computer software. At forty he seemed on a career track that was likely to take him to a senior VP post. He even had an outside chance of one day becoming CEO.

However, a couple of years after his fortieth birthday, Brad was passed over for the key promotion he had worked so hard for. As a result, he became discouraged and depressed, began condemning himself for his career failures. Then two years later, when another company bought out his firm, Brad was downsized. "Imagine the shame of managing a Wal-Mart while your former buddies are headed for the corporate top management team," he moaned.

In addition, Brad found himself and Janice more and more isolated from former friends—partially because of the hostility that had crept into their marriage after his job loss. To top it off, their eldest son, Tommy, had begun getting into trouble with the law, smoking pot, and occasionally coming home drunk. Several times Brad became enraged and threatened to "throw the kid out."

In addition, Brad's parents were struggling healthwise. His father had suffered a second heart attack, and his mother had been diagnosed with Alzheimer's. Before long, Brad and his sister and brother would have to face some difficult decisions about caring for their parents—decisions that sent a bolt of fear into Brad's heart every time he thought of their mortality and his own.

To some, midlife is the prime of life, a time to "feel fabulous."[3] For others it's the "beginning of the end" or a time of significant crisis—check your bookstore or library to see how many books have been written with titles that contain the words *midlife* and *crisis*.

52

LOOKING
BOTH
WAYS FROM
THE TOP
OF THE
MOUNTAIN

Count on Change

However, the common denominator for everyone in midlife is change. It's a time of transition, physically, emotionally, vocationally, relationally, and even spiritually. In fact, part of the problem in Brad's life was that his relationship with the Lord, once passionate, had been allowed to deteriorate and grow cold.

Midlife is usually the time when individuals begin to evaluate where they are, where they've been, and ask the question voiced by pop singer Peggy Lee, "Is that all there is?" According to counseling authority Dr. Gary Collins, "Some define the middle years as a time when there is a growing realization that all goals will not be reached, that time is running out, and that one must decide whether to keep moving in the same direction or to make changes before it is too late."[4]

Some view the prospects of change as overwhelming; others decide to make the best of changes and grow through them. Psychiatrist Victor Frankl, who experienced incredible changes and stresses while in Nazi prison camps, wrote that

> the transitoriness of our existence in no way makes it meaningless, but it does constitute our responsibleness; for everything hinges upon our realizing the essentially transitory possibilities. . . . The pessimist resembles a man who observes with fear and sadness that his wall calendar, from which he daily tears a sheet,

grows thinner with each passing day. On the other hand, the person who attacks the problems of life actively is like a man who removes each successive leaf from his calendar and files it neatly and carefully away with its predecessors, after first having jotted down a few diary notes on the back. He can reflect with pride and joy on . . . all the life he has already lived to the fullest.[5]

Clearly our own perspective becomes a major factor in how we deal with change.

Career Changes

"Why didn't you ask for directions, Brad? Mr. Ellis told you it would be hard to find Right Path." Janice grimaced as her husband cut across two lanes of traffic, steered into a parking lot, slammed on the brakes, and shoved the car into park.

"It's right there, Janice, right where I knew it was. See the sign? Right Path! I was on the right path all along."

A few minutes later the couple found themselves seated on a couch in a corner of Lee Ellis's office. "I appreciate your taking the time to talk with us," Janice began as Brad sipped a diet soda. Lee Ellis ran his hand through his close-cropped salt-and-pepper hair, nodded at Janice, then turned to Brad. "Why don't you tell me what happened, Brad? I take it you were downsized? I know it's hard for us as men to talk about losing a position, a job, but I want you to know that I've been there and I've talked to a lot of other men who have and who've survived."

"I should have seen it coming when I was passed over for the senior VP post. I'd put in a lot of extra time, and the position should have been mine."

Lee noted Brad pressed his hands together so tightly they had become white. "There I was, headed for top management. Now I'm running a Wal-Mart. I just can't begin to tell you how embarrassed I am."

"No question about it," Lee replied gently. "I think for us men it's especially hard. Our work becomes who we are. When the work goes away, there's a lot of shame."

"Plus, there's the economic factor," Janice chimed in. Brad glanced at her and frowned, but she continued. "I think we're both concerned about what's going to happen to us long term."

When Janice paused Brad continued. "She's right, Mr. Ellis. A big part of the shame is because I want to be able to provide for my family. I've always worked hard to do that—and been proud of being able to care for their needs. I think that's one of the main ways a man demonstrates love. Now we're barely making ends meet.

"But the main thing is, I feel totally confused. I'm not sure what I want to do, what I can do. I've already been through one part of the change—the downsizing part. I can't believe they kept people who were under me and let me go."

54

LOOKING
BOTH
WAYS FROM
THE TOP
OF THE
MOUNTAIN
❦

Nodding, Lee responded, "That often happens, Brad. By the way, feel free to call me Lee. My experience has been that companies frequently choose to keep younger, less experienced men and let key middle or upper management people go. It's part of what they call 'trimming the fat.'"

"So what do you plan to tell me to help with this career change?" Brad asked, his hands gripping his knees. "I don't see any easy way out of this thing. We're praying about it—in fact, the people at our church are praying with us, especially our small group Bible study. I don't mind telling you, I really feel shaken."

"Brad, we're going to take a look at several things," Lee replied. "First, I want you to know I don't have any pat answers or quick solutions. But I've walked through this process with a number of men and women who've been right where you are. The good news is there's hope. One of the things we'll do is put you through some tests I've developed. They'll help us look at your personality, your interests, your skills, and your values. Then we'll talk about putting a strategy together that works."

Walking to an acrylic board, Lee picked up a marker and wrote two words. The first was *process*, the second *results*.

"Process is your responsibility, Brad." Lee continued, drawing a circle around the first word. "There are certain things God expects us to do. He gives us choices, and we have responsibilities. Those include things such as doing a résumé, networking, carrying on a job search, taking an assessment that helps you know what your God-given talents are. It also includes getting good counsel. You've talked to your pastor; you're talking to me. So you're on the road to doing those things you can and should be doing.

"On the other side, though, God takes care of the results."

Lee paused, underlined the second word, then continued. "So you have to do your part and allow him to open doors and close doors and provide the godly counsel you need. You also have to be willing to listen, because sometimes the counsel you receive isn't what you wanted to hear."

Lee capped the marker, set it down, then returned to his chair. He looked at Brad intently. "Here's the great and exciting thing, Brad. If you do your part—you and Janice—and you allow God to do his part, you don't get what you want, you get ten times better. In fact, a hundred times better, because God is faithful. It goes back to what Paul told Timothy. Even if we don't believe, God is faithful. You can trust him. And he's going to support you with his Holy Spirit to give you the confidence to keep going, even when you can't see how things are going to turn out."

Few forms of change carry as much impact as a job transition, yet more and more of us at midlife are encountering the reality that the only constant, when it comes to a career, is change. In an earlier era, our parents went to work at the same factory, office, store, or shop where their fathers worked, put in forty years or more, then retired with a pension. Don's father, James Hawkins, invested forty-two years working for Southern Railway. The company itself changed when it merged with the Norfolk and Western to become the Norfolk Southern. Yet his dad, who had begun as a fireman shoveling coal from the tinder into the hot belly of a steam engine, continued running diesels until he finally decided to retire just before he turned seventy. Wood's father, although he was a pastor, followed the same basic career track, shepherding the same flock for more than thirty years.

Today things generally happen differently for those of us at midlife. Both of us have been through several career changes en route to our current roles at Back to the Bible. For both of us they included pastoring, Christian education, and previous experiences in Christian radio. And while we're both happy at Back to the Bible and willing to serve here until the Lord returns, he may move either or both of us on to something else. None of us knows the future. Changes can come.

Reasons for Career Changes

During a recent broadcast of our live call-in program *Confident Living*, Lee Ellis talked about the kind of changes Brad was experiencing, and about the reasons why career changes are so common at midlife. As Lee explained, "When you're in that situation you just have to keep doing your part, and trusting God to do his. It requires patience. We live in a society in which we want instant results, and we want it to be just what we dreamed of.

"I've seen it in my own career transition. When I retired from the air force, there was a job I thought was perfect for me. Unfortunately, I came out number two in that race. I trusted God with that decision and look what's happened since. I've written several books and gotten to work with a wonderful boss, Larry Burkett. God has just blessed my direction, and I'm so thankful that I waited and trusted him."

During the course of the program Lee identified the four major types of changes people experience in midlife in regard to career. They are:

56

LOOKING
BOTH
WAYS FROM
THE TOP
OF THE
MOUNTAIN

1. changes that are forced on us by job loss, downsizing, plant closings, etc.

2. changes that come about because our passion is gone or our values no longer match our work

3. changes that come about because of need, perhaps due to overcommitment, health problems, etc.

4. changes that grow out of conflicts at work, personality mismatches, etc.

Forced to Change

According to Lee, "Some of the people who've been the most happy about their career changes were those who lost their jobs and were forced to make a change. They actually may have made some bad career decisions to start with."

When asked to elaborate on bad early career decisions, Lee answered, "A lot of people just take the first or easiest job they can get, and that usually doesn't work out. Some people take jobs because of the money. They think the more money the better the job. Well, that's not true. All you have to do is talk to some people who've made good money but aren't happy in their job, and you find out that doesn't work. Other people think a good title means a good job, and you're therefore successful. That's not true either. Just because your friends are working a certain place, your parents are doing a certain job, or you're trying to fulfill your parents' unfulfilled expectations, or even because you have the basic ability to do a job doesn't mean that's what you should do."

Like Brad, Clem found himself forced into a midlife career change. As he explained to our radio audience, "I'm going through a plant closing. I'll be laid off next Friday, but it's been a wonderful faith-building experience, once we finally came to the point of giving thanks and acceptance and trusting God for what he could provide."

When I asked Clem how difficult it was to come to that perspective, he replied, "It was very hard. I'd worked at the plant for thirty-four years. To see a place close like that is like going through grief. But our grief and despair finally turned into acceptance and joy when we started to give thanks that we had employment for thirty-four years, and we now have a new opportunity to try something different, even though we're uncertain what that might be."

In response to Clem's call, Lee reminded all of us that in North America we've typically been spoiled because we have it so good in contrast to many who live in Africa, Latin America, parts of Asia, even in Europe. Sometimes when we face a transition, life becomes difficult. We may even have to suffer a bit. Lee continued, "I'm convinced that God is faithful. He will use that. He redeems everything, including our suffering, and actually will use it in our lives down the road to help others."

As I thought about Lee's words, my mind went back to something the apostle Paul wrote to the Corinthians nineteen centuries ago.

Blessed be the God and Father of our Lord Jesus Christ, the Father of mercies and God of all comfort, who comforts us in all our tribulation, that we may be able to comfort those who are in any trouble, with the comfort with which we ourselves are comforted by God.

2 CORINTHIANS 1:3–4

As I think about some of the transitions I've encountered, I remember that not all of them were easy. I recall how, years later, God used those experiences—especially the difficult ones—to provide me with the resources to encourage others who were going through hard times. Paul experienced God's incredible encouragement in his trouble, and he shared the truth that we can comfort others, even those who are in different kinds of trouble, when we have received and responded to God's encouragement. I'm convinced that even though both Clem and Brad were forced into a change they didn't ask for and endured hardship in the process, they will be uniquely prepared and qualified, because of their experience, to comfort others who are going through hard times.

58

LOOKING
BOTH
WAYS FROM
THE TOP
OF THE
MOUNTAIN
❦

"My Passion Is Gone"

The second key reason for midlife career change is a loss of passion. The issue isn't a company-mandated change, the problem isn't money or job security. Perhaps our values have changed, or the company's values have shifted, or maybe we've finally decided to wake up one day and smell the coffee—and we discover it's not a brand we feel passionate about.

That's what happened to Ellen, another of our radio callers who was honest enough to admit that "my passion is pretty much gone." We listened as Ellen explained her situation.

"I'm forty-five, single, and completely and financially independent. My father is dead, and my mother is on social security. I have a good job as a licensed professional. I generally work for nonprofit organizations, and the changing political climate with different priorities on healthcare and money being funded through different sources has brought about a lot of pressure to produce. I've been doing this for over twenty years. Most of the people who entered the field when I did weren't in it for the money. But now, many of the younger people switching into the field are doing so for the money. So there are different kinds of people in my field.

"Anyway, I'm kind of a one-to-one person. I don't do well with a lot of people, but the organization I've worked for, and felt comfortable with for fifteen years, has really shifted its priorities and management styles. I really feel like I don't fit in anymore. I've been praying to the Lord about it, and this may have been his opportunity to show me, 'Okay, Ellen, now you can leave. There's nothing there to make you comfortable anymore.'"

As Lee Ellis explained to Ellen and the rest of our radio listening family, "The primary issue that's driving this is a values issue. It relates to the organization and the change in the environment. My first counsel, Ellen, is to look for other settings or other organizations in which you could exercise your profession and your talents, but in an area that would be more compatible with your values and the way in which the work is done.

"I think you need to develop a plan, get some wise counsel. If you want to explore the possibility of becoming self-employed, talk to some people about what this means. If you get enough information and process through this, God's going to show you the way and bring about the results you're looking for."

Many people like Ellen feel stuck in a work rut at midlife, no longer passionate, just putting in their time. When the thrill is gone, the passion diminished, and it's just "a job is a job is a job," you may be ready for a midlife change.

A Needed Change

For some of us, a midlife job change may come about in response to pressure rather than passion. That was the case with another well-known Nebraska resident who participated in our radio program. Dr. Tom Osborne had completed a successful twenty-five-year career as the head coach of the Nebraska Cornhuskers, leading his team to a third national championship in a five-year span. Then he stunned the state of Nebraska by announcing his decision to walk away from it all. He explained in an interview we recorded via telephone that as he drove to a speaking engagement in western Nebraska, "I realized there were other things that were important, more important than working seven days a week, wearing two hats, being my own offensive coordinator. I wanted to have more time for my wife and family. I wanted to take care of myself physically—I've had some health problems in recent years—and I wanted to have more time for my spiritual life."

Frequently, a midlife career change will be precipitated by job stress. Some time ago *Newsweek* carried a list of the top ten stress-producing jobs, as determined by the National Institute on Workers' Compensation. They included inner-city high school teacher, police officer, air traffic controller, medical intern, stockbroker, journalist, secretary, waitress, and—not surprisingly—customer service complaint department worker.[6]

The apostle Paul never changed his career after he became an apostle, yet he experienced incredible stress at times. In 2 Corinthians 6:4–7 he listed ten different forms of stress, then detailed eight specific inner qualities that helped him cope with the pressure he faced. He faced troubles, pressures, hardships, and what we might describe as "tight spots." He was beaten, imprisoned, shipwrecked, and found himself sleepless after working night and day; yet he coped with his stresses by relying on the power of the Holy Spirit and God's protection and by cultivating such qualities as purity, godly knowledge, steadfastness, kindness toward people, sincere love, and the armor of righteous living.

60

LOOKING
BOTH
WAYS FROM
THE TOP
OF THE
MOUNTAIN
❦

Thinking about the current stresses of work, it's not surprising that a man with the wisdom and insight of a Tom Osborne can see the need to cut back. We have to allow time for the priority of cultivating the spiritual resources that can protect us in stressful times.

Another important principle to help us counter the tyranny of the urgent is to follow the advice of management guru Stephen Covey in his book *First Things First*. Covey titled section 2 "The Main Thing Is to Keep the Main Thing the Main Thing."

Centuries earlier Jesus put it even more straightforwardly when he told those who listened to what we call the Sermon on the Mount, "But seek first the kingdom of God and His righteousness, and all these things shall be added to you" (Matt. 6:33). When you examine Jesus' public career, it is clear that his life demonstrated a perfect balance between dealing with urgent demands and maintaining the priority of the important. After what most Bible scholars label "the single busiest day in his entire ministry" (Mark 1:16–34)—a day in which he called disciples, taught in a synagogue, cast out a demon, healed a seriously ill woman, and ministered to an entire city—Jesus awakened well before daylight the next morning, went out to a solitary place, and prayed (v. 35). Throughout his life Jesus maintained a critical balance between the urgent and the important. He never carried a pager, wore a watch, or used modern technologies, yet he was always on time and always found the time to do what mattered most. And those things he focused on always seemed to reflect the two ultimate priorities he detailed: loving God wholeheartedly and loving people unconditionally (see Mark 12:29–31).

Sometimes the only way to make the main thing the main thing is to change careers. Throughout life, in big decisions or in small, we make choices based on what we value most. Perhaps like Coach Tom Osborne, you need to step back, take a look at all the things that are crowding into your schedule, and consider a career change. This can open a door to freedom from some of life's pressures and allow you to invest significant time in things such as grandchildren, your marriage, a new Bible study course, caring for a struggling teenager in your household or those parents who need your help.

During a follow-up appointment with Lee Ellis, Brad and Janice detailed some of the struggles in their relationship with their son Tommy and his troubled lifestyle. They also explained how they needed to invest more time with their parents, especially since Brad's father's heart attack and his mother's Alzheimer's diagnosis. "My previous job just didn't allow the time for any of those relationships," Brad admitted candidly. "Maybe God actually did me a favor by allowing me to go through a job loss."

Conflicts on the Job

A fourth reason some people need to consider a midlife career change has to do with our personalities and those we work with. Lee explained it this way: "Some people are good talkers and they like to network. They know a lot of people everywhere; they're very good at verbal communications. They like meeting new people all the time.

"But everybody is not that way. Don and I were just talking at breakfast about how we spent the first few years of our marriage trying to change our wives to make them more like us. Then we finally learned better. You see, there are other people who are more one-on-one. They prefer to communicate with just a few people, perhaps people they know very well. They'd rather work in a more solitary setting. God wired them that way, and many of them can focus in a way Don and I would have a hard time focusing, and staying focused on one thing."

In two of the books he coauthored with Larry Burkett, *Finding the Career That Fits You* and *Your Career in Changing Times*, Lee has provided a wealth of material to help individuals understand their personality strengths. According to Lee and Larry, "Personality is the most intriguing and probably the most useful guide in helping you choose your basic line of work."[7] As they explained, personality includes all the behavioral traits of an individual, including things such as assertiveness, sociability, patience, confidence, accuracy, compassion, enthusiasm, independence, and flexibility. As Lee explained to our radio audience, some people are more dominant, more naturally inclined to try to control their environments; they're usually assertive, direct, and strong willed. Other individuals are more influencing; they are driven naturally to relate to others. They are verbal, friendly, persuasive, optimistic, and enthusiastic. A third group are more steady; they're usually patient, considerate, dependable—and they're excellent team players. They seem to work best in a supportive environment. Finally, there are those who are very conscientious; they tend to be more cautious, they focus on doing things right, usually they're detail oriented and find it easy to follow prescribed guidelines.[8]

Family authority Dr. John Trent has studied some thirty different instruments used to analyze the human personality. In the process, John developed some unique labels for the four basic personality types. His user-friendly titles include the dominant "lion," the fun-loving "otter," the structure-loving "beaver," and the easygoing, helpful "golden retriever." From John's perspective, the combination of these different personality types can produce what he calls a "wild kingdom" at work or at home.[9]

Sometimes personality differences, or finding ourselves feeling "like a square peg in a round hole" at work, may bring us to the point at which we conclude it's time to make that midlife career change. If we are to do so we need to deal with three specific steps.

First, we must learn to accept ourselves. Sadly, some of us have difficulty accepting the personality God gave us; we'd

62

LOOKING
BOTH
WAYS FROM
THE TOP
OF THE
MOUNTAIN
❦

rather be somebody else! However, radical personality shifts at midlife are about as rare as brain transplants. God wants us to recognize and build on the strengths he's given us, while working on our weaknesses.

Second, we need to recognize the value of others who differ from us. As Solomon pointed out in Proverbs 27:17, "As iron sharpens iron, so a man sharpens the countenance of his friend." There is always something we can gain from every other individual, something that can sharpen us so we will develop in character and become more effective in our performance. It may seem as though my overbearing boss, my passive employee, or my fellow worker whose personality is on the opposite end of the spectrum holds no positive benefit for me. Even among Jesus' disciples, however, we can see how the popular and powerful Peter could benefit from the more perfectionistic and peaceful John—and vice versa.

Finally, before we leap into a midlife career change based on personalities, we need to be sure we've learned all the lessons God wants us to learn where we are. Change for the sake of change is seldom effective—and usually not the right thing to do.

Career Change and God's Will

As Brad and Janice wound up their initial session with Lee Ellis, Brad raised a question about the will of God. "A few weeks ago our pastor preached a message from Romans 12 on the 'good and acceptable and perfect will of God.' How do I know when something is God's perfect will? Could his perfect will mean some kind of ministry? I mean, I don't feel like I'm called to be a pastor or a missionary, but I wonder if God could bless me in another management job."

"I'm glad you asked, Brad," Lee responded. "Personally, I don't think we need to get too hung up on God's perfect will. One reason is Christians often tend to be perfectionists. They look for God's perfect will to be written on the sidewalk, or written in the sky with lightning in letters that say, 'Show up at Joe's Factory on Monday.' Or, 'Take the top management position.'

"I don't really think it works that way. I believe there are a number of career fields I could probably work in and be in God's will. The real key to his will is my heart and my motivation and my desire to honor him, whether I'm the manager at Slacks Incorporated or working at Joe's Auto Parts. I don't think that's as important to God as how I'm carrying it out, how I'm doing the job and using the position for his glory. Now things may run smoother for me at one place than another, but God can redeem those areas where we may be in less than his 'perfect will.'

"But one of the important issues, Brad, is control. When I went through one of my career changes I had to stand and wait on the Lord. When I was a prisoner of war I had to depend on my enemy to feed me, so I really learned to rely on the Lord. Through that, I learned what it was like to be totally out of control in my life. I couldn't control anything. That experience, however, developed in me a faith that has really stood by me. God has used that trial; he taught me some things during that difficult time that have proven invaluable."

64

LOOKING
BOTH
WAYS FROM
THE TOP
OF THE
MOUNTAIN
❦

We strongly agree with Lee's assessment that not everyone is called to vocational ministry. Nor should everyone feel obligated to make a midlife career change into a vocational ministry. However, we think everyone should at least pray about and consider the possibility. As Lee explained on the radio program, "I have a number of friends who reached midlife who could afford to take a little time off and do some things. One friend runs a landscaping business about six to eight months out of the year, then he spends three or four months in Siberia on a mission trip, leading people from our church and community. They build church buildings, teach Bible school, and actually teach the Bible in Russian schools. It's a tremendous opportunity, and through my friend a number of other people have become involved.

"I guess the encouragement I would give people is, give something a try. Step in the water and get your feet wet, then you'll find out what the pros and cons are and where your talents lie."

Additional Factors to Consider

When we face a potential career change, there are additional factors to consider. Perhaps the one most of us fear is the financial factor. That's why we need to exercise good stewardship and build reserves. The best example of this is found in Proverbs 6:6–8, in which Solomon explains how the ant, with "no captain, overseer or ruler, provides her supplies in the summer, and gathers her food in the harvest."

A second factor to consider, according to Lee, has to do with success. As he explains, "We have this idea about success and position. We like to talk about our job titles. We need to set that aside, because in reality job titles don't mean that much any more. Some of our most valuable employees don't have a title at all, but they have a lot of talent they bring to the organization. They're not managers; they're researchers, writers, people who can develop seminars, people who can go out and train others."

The third factor is the workaholism issue. Some of us are literally addicted to work. Psalm 127 says, "It is vain for you to rise up early, to sit up late, to eat the bread of sorrows" (v. 2). One of the great risks of midlife is becoming addicted to work, pouring yourself into your career so much that you neglect your health, your family, and most of all the Lord. A midlife career change can either take us in the direction of more drivenness and a greater time commitment to our work, or to more time for the Lord, our family, and to "stop and smell the flowers." We need to carefully evaluate any midlife career change opportunity with this factor in mind.

Finally, there is the fear factor. We'll talk about emotions in the chapter that follows. But if you're afraid of making that midlife career change, consider the words of David: "The LORD is my light and my salvation; whom shall I fear? The LORD is the strength of my life; of whom shall I be afraid?" (Ps. 27:1). Sure, change is fearful, but God is faithful.

Chapter Four

The Emotions of Midlife

WHEN WE FIND OURSELVES CONFRONTED with the complexities of change, the necessities of transition, and the inevitability of decay, we find our emotions kicking into gear. We feel fearful, lonely, angry, depressed. Our minds are clouded with worry, cluttered with disappointment, gripped with grief.

Perhaps the place to begin is by considering the nature of emotions. Most of us use the word *feelings* without thinking about it. Family authority Dr. Dan Allender, however, defines emotions as "the cry of the soul." He goes on to say, "They expose what we are doing with the sorrow of life and in turn reveal what our heart is doing with God."[1]

Dr. Allender's definition grows out of his own candid assessment of his experience with aching joints and "the looming specter of crippling arthritis." As he describes it, "I feel loneliness, then fury. How can this happen? My fury glides into envy, then I round the corner into stark, naked terror. All in the span of minutes, my emotions race like a wind through an open window, blowing every unfastened paper into a chaotic debris."[2]

Who among us hasn't felt the chilling blast of emotions heralding the winds of change? Frequently, our initial response is to deny our emotions, numb our feelings, and pretend they don't exist. "The Bible commands us not to be angry," we piously affirm, neglecting the fact that we are misquoting Ephesians 4:26. However, denial never works, as Jesus so clearly pointed out in his confrontation of the Pharisees in John 8, when he reminded them that "the truth will set you free."

Perhaps you've wondered, why do we have to feel things anyway? Why did God create us with emotions in the first place? After all, if we had the personality makeup of Data, the character from *Star Trek: The Next Generation,* for example, we wouldn't hurt; we'd only have an intellect. Scripture makes it clear, however, that our personalities were formed in the image of God, who has both intellect and feelings. God loves; God hates; God can be angry. God wants us to experience the full range of emotion from exultant cheer when our favorite team scores a touchdown, to the incredible pride of hearing "The Star Spangled Banner," to the anger we feel toward those who burn the flag the song describes. David—a man of intense emotional peaks and valleys—recognized, "I will praise You, for I am fearfully and wonderfully made; marvelous are Your works, and that my soul knows very well" (Ps. 139:14). David knew God had formed him, and whether you are a very emotional person or one whose feelings stay buried beneath the surface, God made you as you are. So you might as well face the fact that God made you an emotional creature.

Not only can we not bury our head in the sand like the proverbial ostrich when confronted with the emotions that accompany midlife changes, we also cannot pretend that our emotions are simply "okay." Frequently, God uses anger, fear, worry, and other feelings to expose our sinful motivation, our desire to control life. They reveal our insistence that God fulfill our demands, remove our pain, and provide us with the stability, security, and comfort we think we so richly deserve.

In an earlier chapter we considered the physical changes of midlife. Perhaps no change is quite as shocking as the role reversal we experience when our parents begin to need our care and the multitude of emotions that go with this experience.

First we begin to notice a decline in their well-being. They seem more unsure of themselves. They seek our advice. We knew

68

LOOKING
BOTH
WAYS FROM
THE TOP
OF THE
MOUNTAIN
❦

they would get old, but when we first noticed Mom's unsteady gait or received word about Dad's heart attack or Mom's stroke, suddenly we were forced to face the fact that our parents are mortal. Then comes the biggest shock of all: The individuals who always looked after us now need our help.

You didn't plan for it. Even though adult children have cared for aging parents in countless generations past, it sometimes seems as if our generation thought it couldn't happen to our mothers and fathers. But as more of us move into our fifties and our parents turn seventy or eighty, an increasing number of us face this incredible challenge.

Many of us struggle, even stumble, when the roles are reversed and we find ourselves parenting those who parented us. It's difficult to face the fact that our parents can no longer be trusted to balance their checkbooks or take their medications. Of course there is a natural reluctance to intrude into another adult's personal life. In addition, old power struggles with our parents, even emotions from our own childhood, can be resurrected at this point. All these factors can make this relationship with our elderly parents one of the most challenging transitions in our lifespan.

Grief

Perhaps the core emotion with which we struggle at midlife is grief. Frequently, anger, fear, or other emotions grow out of this grief. Simply stated, grief is our emotional response to loss. The loss can be as overwhelming as that of a spouse, or as seemingly small and insignificant as that of a misplaced credit card.

Grief is incredibly common at midlife. Though we typically associate this emotion with death, there are numerous midlife situations that can bring grief, in addition to the death of a spouse. Divorce produces major grief. The loss of a job due to either retirement or downsizing, the departure of a child for college, the breakup of a friendship, the move of a pastor to another church, or the death of a pet—these and many other circumstances can generate grief.

In fact, one of the givens as we grow older is that we will suffer losses. C. S. Lewis wrote, "As we grow older, life consists more and more in either giving up things or waiting for them to be taken from us."[3]

Two classic New Testament passages deal with grief, both related to the subject of death. In John 11, Lazarus, Jesus' friend from the town of Bethany, became ill and eventually died. When Jesus arrived, the burial had occurred four days earlier, yet the family—sisters Martha and Mary—were still surrounded by many friends and neighbors who were present to "comfort them concerning their brother" (John 11:19).

Throughout the passage there is never a hint that grief is wrong or inappropriate. Jesus himself shared the agitated emotions of Mary and the Jews who wept with her (John 11:33). Then, standing at the tomb, John recorded those memorable words so frequently quoted: "Jesus wept" (John 11:35). Even though the Savior knew he was about to raise Lazarus to life, he still entered into the grief of his friends.

70

Looking
Both
Ways from
the Top
of the
Mountain

The second passage dealing with grief is found in Paul's first letter to the church in Thessalonica. Believers there were confused because many of them had experienced the death of loved ones, and they were wondering whether they would see them again. Paul wrote to counter their ignorance of the facts regarding the death of Christians and to prevent them from sorrowing "as others who have no hope" (4:13). He did not forbid them to grieve, nor did he suggest that grieving was a sign of weakness or made them less stable in their faith. He simply made it clear that there are two kinds of grief: the hopeless variety experienced by those who do not know the Savior, and the grief of the Christian whose hope in the risen Christ enables him to view deceased loved ones as "those who sleep in Jesus" (v. 14).

Coping with Grief

From this passage we can draw several applications that can help us deal with this strong midlife emotion. Perhaps the most important thing we can learn is that grief is a universal and appropriate response to loss. Since midlife often brings with it an increased number of losses, we should expect to experience more grief at this point in our journey. Genesis 37 tells of Jacob's mourning over the loss of his son Joseph. Second Samuel 12 records David's intense grief and agitated response to the death of his infant son. Later the king was "deeply moved" as he mourned for his beloved son Absalom (2 Sam. 18:33). When godly King Josiah was killed in battle, all Judah and Jerusalem mourned, including the prophet Jeremiah (2 Chron. 35:24–25).

Perhaps the greatest source of grief at midlife is the loss of a spouse. Recently, I (Don) had lunch with Dick Semann, a gifted motivational speaker and veteran of Christian broadcasting. I came away from the meal impressed with how deeply Dick loved his wife, Sandy, and how, although he traveled much of the time, he relished and enjoyed returning home to her companionship and the things they shared together, including two children and nine grandchildren.

The next morning I was shocked to receive a voice mail message informing me that Dick had been found dead in his hotel room. It was later determined that an aneurysm of the brain had ended his earthly life.

Later that day I talked with Sandy by telephone. She was experiencing all the shock and pain of the loss of someone to whom she had been married for over four decades. Yet hers was not the mind-numbing, hopeless sorrow of one who will never again see a loved one. Although she felt incredible pain, hurt, and loneliness over losing her husband, Sandy was able to acknowledge the fact that "I will see Dick again in heaven."

If we are going through a period of grief or are trying to help someone else at midlife deal with this emotion, there are several practical steps to take.

First, allow it to happen. Jesus permitted himself to feel all the emotion and pain surrounding the death of Lazarus, as well as the sorrow felt by Mary and Martha. Romans 12:15 reminds us to "rejoice with those who rejoice, and weep with those who weep."

Second, recognize that because of Christ, a Christian's grief is different. Because Jesus overcame death, we can claim the encouragement of knowing that "death is swallowed up in victory" (1 Cor. 15:54). We don't deny or minimize the reality or pain of loss due to death (or for that matter divorce, job loss, health decline, or other forms of loss), we simply acknowledge that the ultimate answer for all the loss and pain we experience is the gain that is ours in Christ.

Third, see grief as a time to focus on the Lord. Frequently, those who grieve struggle with the "why" question; even Job wrestled with this after an overwhelming series of losses including the deaths of his seven sons and three daughters. Sometimes this leads to bitter, angry feelings. Yet grief affords a great opportunity to focus on the Lord, rest in his goodness, trust him for strength to work through our emotions, and come to the place where Job was when he wrote, "He knows the way that I take; when He has tested me, I shall come forth as gold" (Job 23:10).

Fourth, realize that grief requires time. It takes time to face and accept the reality of the loss, to recognize and come to grips with the pain we've experienced, and to begin to accept life without the object of our grief. Studies of widows have shown that up to three or four years may be needed before stability is regained.[4]

72

LOOKING
BOTH
WAYS FROM
THE TOP
OF THE
MOUNTAIN
🌿

Nor is grief easy. There will be times of intense sorrow, waves of strong emotions such as anger or depression, even physical symptoms. The way we grieve is an intensely individual matter. Eventually, though, most people return to a state of emotional and physical well-being. But it doesn't come easily or quickly. As C. S. Lewis wrote following the death of his wife, Joy, "There is a sort of invisible blanket between the world and me. I find it hard to take in what anyone says or perhaps hard to want to take it in. It is so uninteresting, yet I want the others to be about me. I dread the moments when the house is empty."[5]

With time, however, our focus needs to shift from our losses to the blessings promised by the Lord. The psalmist reminds us, "Bless the LORD, O my soul, and forget not all His benefits: who forgives all your iniquities, who heals all your diseases, who redeems your life from destruction, who crowns you with lovingkindness and tender mercies, who satisfies your mouth with good things, so that your youth is renewed like the eagle's" (Ps. 103:2–5).

Fifth, recognize the valuable contribution that listening and talking make to the process of working through grief. Frequently, those who are grieving wish to withdraw, and it's important not to force ourselves on them. However, there is great value in simply sitting quietly with a grieving friend as Job's three friends did with the patriarch before they began to condemn him.

If someone close to you has suffered a loss, be available, reach out, call, visit. Don't become pushy, but take the initiative to make contact and cultivate the ability to listen. There are times when grieving people need to be able to discuss their feelings and express their emotions. Don't condemn honest expressions of guilt, anger, confusion, or even despair. Resist the temptation to preach or paste a biblical Band-Aid on the pain. When the time is right, however, share comforting words from Scripture, and of course pray for those who grieve.

Finally, if you are experiencing grief, allow hope to serve as an anchor to your soul. During a particularly difficult time in his own life, the psalmist affirmed, "My expectation is from Him. He only is my rock and my salvation; He is my defense; I shall not be moved" (Ps. 62:5–6). As you work your way through the routines of life, allow God to strengthen you so you can avoid the two extremes of denying your feelings or being overwhelmed by them. There will be times when it is appropriate to let your emotions out, but recognize that even in the worst losses of midlife, we can reflect on the reality of Jeremiah's words: "This I recall to my mind, therefore I have hope. Through the LORD'S mercies we are not consumed, because His compassions fail not. They are new every morning; great is Your faithfulness" (Lam. 3:21–23).

Anger

If grief is the foundational emotion, anger is perhaps the one most commonly expressed. Like grief, anger is a response. In fact, it would be safe to say the two are "emotional cousins." Anger typically involves our response to a threat, either real or perceived. It may be a threat to our own well-being or to someone or something close to us. Anger is commonly related to our sense of self-preservation. When I feel threatened or when I sense a threat to something that is of value to me, I am likely to become angry.

Our two most typical responses to anger are to deny it or to justify it. "Me, angry? You must be kidding. Not a chance. I may be mildly irritated or concerned, but certainly not angry." Frequently, this kind of denial is linked with the mistaken belief that anger is always a sin. But other times we may consider our anger to be righteous when perhaps it is not. Dr. Dan Allender describes unrighteous anger as "a dark energy that demands for itself a more tolerable world now, instead of waiting for God's redemption according to divine design and timing."[6]

Anger can take many forms, most of which are fairly evident at midlife. Perhaps the most common manifestation of anger is an explosive outburst of indignation. That's what Susan experienced when, on their thirtieth anniversary, Phil was late for dinner—again. Besides, he had forgotten the day—she had to remind him. And he could have chosen any other day to work late at the office. The moment he walked through the door she launched into a tirade, berating him for his lack of sensitivity, his repeated tardiness, and his failure to recognize their anniversary. The problem was she felt threatened.

Phil could have retaliated by expressing the same kind of anger. Instead, he demonstrated another kind. While Susan's anger was aggressive, Phil's was passive. Setting his lips firmly in a grim line, he listened for a few moments as the decibel level rose. Finally, he'd had enough. He turned away from his wife in mid-sentence, placed his coat in the closet, quietly retreated to his home office, and firmly closed the door, cutting himself off from his wife, her anger, and their anniversary.

Passive anger may be more difficult to handle than aggressive anger. In fact, if we had interviewed Phil later that day, he would have affirmed his wife's anger while denying his own. Procrastination frequently comes under the heading of passive anger, as do halfhearted efforts, the silent treatment, and personal withdrawal. In essence, the person who practices passive anger is sabotaging the relationship.

A third form of this emotion is what we might call cumulative anger. Frequently, it is identified as bitterness or even resentment, a graphic though often misunderstood term that explains how we are capable of bringing up and "re-feeling" the strong, intense emotions of anger over an incident that happened days, months, or years earlier.

Scripture and Anger

Scripture has a great deal to say on the subject of anger. A casual examination of a concordance reveals well over six hundred references to anger or wrath in the Bible. Anger is an attribute of God, mentioned even more frequently than his love. Since it is a part of his holy nature, anger cannot be intrinsically evil. As James I. Packer points out, "God's wrath in the Bible is never the capricious, self-indulgent, irritable, morally ignoble thing that human anger so often is."[7] Instead, God's anger is his

74

LOOKING
BOTH
WAYS FROM
THE TOP
OF THE
MOUNTAIN

righteous response to evil in the universe. Perhaps the best example of this in human terms can be seen in Jesus' cleansing of the temple when he unleashed his own perfect fury on those who had turned his Father's house of prayer into a den of thieves.

Scripture is clear to point out, however, that "the wrath of man does not produce the righteousness of God" (James 1:20). That's why James urges us to be "swift to hear, slow to speak, and slow to wrath" (James 1:19). Since God is perfect, omniscient, and sovereign, his anger is always perfect. Unlike him, we see things imperfectly and are not always able to distinguish between legitimate, just issues over which we should be angry and those things that are simply affected by our own faulty self-interest or our lack of complete information.

Dealing with Anger

Anger is not a uniquely midlife emotion. The problem is, by the time we reach midlife we've developed a series of rationalizations that we use to give ourselves permission to be angry—when in fact we shouldn't. These include:

- feeling entitled to explode on occasion—after all, you've lived long enough and you've earned the right to let off steam
- feeling inclined to carry a grudge—after all, you've been beaten and slapped around long enough
- feeling less inclined to exercise self-control—after all, you're tired of all the hassles you've been through

Like fire, anger can have significant positive uses, or it can possess incredibly destructive tendencies. If you want to see how destructive it can be, allow yourself to explode at your spouse on your anniversary or vent your anger at your boss during your next job review. Yet there can be a positive result from anger. MADD (Mothers Against Drunk Drivers) was founded by a small group of California residents in 1980 after a thirteen-year-old-girl was killed by a drunk hit-and-run driver. Choosing to use their anger and grief in a positive way, they formed an organization that has spread nationwide. MADD has had a direct effect on reducing the number of drunk drivers and improving the safety of our streets and highways.

Anger is a force that affects many of us at midlife. It is important that we cultivate an ability to understand and deal with anger both in ourselves and in those around us. Several biblical principles come to mind.

First, we must acknowledge the presence of anger. In perhaps the key New Testament passage on the subject, Paul urges the Ephesians to "be angry, and do not sin" (Eph. 4:26). The Greek word he uses, *ginomai*, suggests the idea of becoming angry or becoming aware of anger. Counselors frequently refer to this as "overcoming denial" or "getting in touch with your anger."

Second, we need to understand the true nature of the anger we're experiencing. Are we righteously indignant over the abuse of a grandchild or the unfair firing of a colleague? Or are we simply upset because a teenage son has used up the gasoline in our car or a clerk in accounting has failed to credit those overtime hours we worked two weeks ago?

Third, we should always practice the "slow to wrath" rule originally stated by James (James 1:19). There are times when it is essential that we take a stand for our convictions or rights or for the rights of others. In his book *Mind over Emotions*, Dr. Les Carter lists several appropriate ways of using anger, including publicly stating your beliefs and opinions, saying no when necessary, setting boundaries, openly seeking to clarify issues, and assertively asking for favors.[8] Even when using anger appropriately, however, we should exercise caution, not allowing ourselves to rush to an angry response in the heat of the moment when a more measured response might be best. After all, the fruit of the Spirit is self-control (Gal. 5:23). As Proverbs 15:1 explains, "A soft answer turns away wrath, but a harsh word stirs up anger."

Fourth, we must respect the biblical time limit on anger. Ephesians 4:26 warns, "Do not let the sun go down on your wrath." Later in the chapter, Paul warned, "Let all bitterness, wrath, anger, clamor [brawling], and evil speaking [or slander] be put away from you, with all malice" (v. 31). Bitterness can become an emotional cancer, eating away at us. It's an all-too-common ailment at midlife, and it must be dealt with vigorously. The key is to resolve anger issues quickly before they develop into

76

LOOKING
BOTH
WAYS FROM
THE TOP
OF THE
MOUNTAIN

❦

resentment or bitterness. Like a concrete finisher who must wash his tools quickly after finishing a sidewalk, we must allow the Spirit to wash away any residue of anger before it hardens.

One of the classic examples of how to deal with anger can be found in Psalm 73. Asaph, musician and writer of Scripture, begins by recognizing God's goodness, then quickly acknowledges his own near disaster when he became angry and envious at the prosperity of the wicked. Asaph's emotional response was remarkably similar to that of Warren, a midlife missionary. Warren became embittered while home on furlough after experiencing the hospitality of several fairly well-to-do Christians and supporting churches. He became upset because he didn't think these relatively wealthy believers were giving enough to missions. Instead of coming to grips with his resentment, Warren allowed his anger to harden. As a result, although he and his wife returned to the field, he became angry and irritable, constantly at odds with the native people as well as his missionary colleagues. Eventually, he resigned and returned to the States before his next term was up.

Instead of cultivating a smoldering bitterness, as Warren had allowed himself to do, or torching those around him with anger, Asaph brought his grieved heart and vexed mind into the presence of the Lord. Humbly he acknowledged, "Whom have I in heaven but You? And there is none upon earth that I desire besides You. My flesh and my heart fail; but God is the strength of my heart and my portion forever" (Ps. 73:25–26). Then after confessing the foolishness of his feelings (v. 22), the psalmist recognized the truth that "it is good for me to draw near to God" (v. 28) and trust him.

If you find yourself struggling with anger, perhaps you can practice the remedy David used when he said, "While I was musing, the fire burned. Then I spoke with my tongue: 'LORD, make me to know my end, and what is the measure of my days, that I may know how frail I am'" (Ps. 39:3–4).

David's instructions for dealing with anger include the reminder "be angry, and do not sin. Meditate within your heart on your bed, and be still" (Ps. 4:4). Later he wrote, "Do not fret because of him who prospers in his ways, because of the man who brings wicked schemes to pass. Cease from anger, and forsake wrath; do not fret—it only causes harm" (Ps. 37:7–8).

Typically, our initial response to anger is to leap into action and look for a battle—frequently with tragic results. Instead, we ought to think carefully and clearly, asking ourselves questions such as:

78

Looking
Both
Ways from
the Top
of the
Mountain

- Why am I feeling angry?
- What do I know about this situation or person?
- What is the threat to me or someone else in this situation?
- Is my anger righteous or unrighteous?
- Does my anger reflect the desire to control?
- Does my anger reflect the desire to get even?
- If I were to lay my anger before God, how would he evaluate it?
- How would others, including the person toward whom I feel angry, view my anger?
- What can my anger teach me about the character of God, who was willing to pour out his wrath on his own Son to pay for every sin I committed?

Finally, Scripture makes it clear that there are things we can do to prevent anger. One is to understand what Scripture teaches about this volatile emotion. Second, allow the Spirit of God to produce the fruit of self-control in our lives (Gal. 5:23). Third, cultivate a relationship of accountability with our spouse or a same-sex friend. Fourth, avoid people and even situations that tend to generate anger. Proverbs warns us to steer clear of various people, including those whose lives are marked by anger (Prov. 22:24–25). Fifth, learn to handle disagreement and conflict by having a confrontation when necessary. In other words, follow Paul's exhortation to speak the truth in love (Eph. 4:15). Finally, remember there will be times when we blow it and feel or express inappropriate anger. When we do, it's time to confess, then claim God's grace to move on.

Emotional Cousins of Anger

An entire family of emotions could be developed from anger. One is guilt, a feeling of remorse based on an understanding of

God's standard of right and wrong and our own violation of it. Scripture describes a "godly sorrow [that] produces repentance" (2 Cor. 7:10) that leaves no regret. There is an authentic sadness when we have sinned and acted contrary to God's standards. That sadness is appropriate. It leads to humility, repentance, and a change of life.

On the other hand, many people, especially at midlife, become overwhelmed by a form of false guilt that focuses on our own lack of worth rather than facing, confessing, and dealing with our failures. Sometimes we feel overwhelmed with guilt, wondering how God could possibly forgive us of a sin we committed perhaps years earlier.

Scripture makes it clear that the guilt for our sins was placed on Jesus Christ, and therefore, we can experience forgiveness. Our goal is not to avoid feeling guilt or simply to put all guilt out of mind. Instead, we need to eliminate the mental and emotional clutter of false guilt—frequently promoted by Pharisaical thinking—while allowing true guilt to cause us to respond with confession, repentance, and additional growth.

Depression

"No godly person should ever get depressed," I recall hearing a pastor say years ago. "After all, depression is a sin." Years later I realized there was an occasion when Jesus himself "took with Him Peter and the two sons of Zebedee, and He began to be sorrowful and deeply distressed. Then He said to them, 'My soul is exceedingly sorrowful, even to death'" (Matt. 26:37–38). Since Jesus was sinless and perfect, depression must not be a sin. For those of us who may struggle with depression, it is encouraging to know that even Jesus was not immune to feelings of despair and depression. Other instances of depression can be seen in Scripture as well. King Saul, Elijah, Jonah, and Moses also experienced it.

Depression is so widespread today that some authorities have referred to ours as "an age of sadness" and labeled depression "the common cold of mental health." Statistics indicate that depression affects more than 20 percent of women and 10 percent of all men at some point in their lives. Modern clinical authorities recognize that some instances of depression originate in the medical or physical realm, while others begin in the mental, emotional, or even the spiritual realm.

Depression is a feeling of profound sadness. Often underlying it is another emotion, despair, which includes a sense of hopelessness. There are four similar terms found in the dictionary, *despair, desperation, despondency,* and *depression,* which describe a range of feelings and responses of individuals who have lost strength and hope.

80

LOOKING
BOTH
WAYS FROM
THE TOP
OF THE
MOUNTAIN
❧

Depression at Midlife

Many factors make depression an extremely common midlife emotion. For one thing, we have begun to experience losses— the death of one or both parents, a job loss, perhaps a divorce or the death of a child. We may also be overextended, "running on fumes" as it were, with our physical and emotional tanks nearly depleted. Furthermore, midlife is the point at which we finally come to face the fact that many of our dreams, hopes, and aspirations simply will never become reality.

Can godly people feel depressed? Listen to these words from respected pastor and radio teacher Chuck Swindoll:

> How much like the tide we are! When our spirits are high, we are flooded with optimism, hope and pleasant expectations, but when low, with our jagged barnacles of disappointment and discouragement exposed, we entertain feelings of raw disillusionment. We usually hide the plunging inner tide line from others, protecting ourselves with a thick coat of public image shined to a high gloss . . . embellished with a religious cliché or two, but all the while, at ebb tide within, cold winds blow across the empty, empty sand.[9]

Have you ever been there? Perhaps you have never felt that way. We've known a few individuals who have never been depressed, as far as we know. We've also known other godly people and studied the lives of still others who have experienced intense depression. Martin Luther, Charles Spurgeon, William Cowper, Dr. Howard Hendricks, Dwight L. Moody, and many others have all felt the black cloud of depression.

When you are depressed, life looks bleak and hopeless. It's almost as though you're seeing things in black and white rather than in color. Your mood is one of sadness. You even look sad. You feel sorry for yourself, helpless to change things, and generally hopeless about the future.

When depression strikes, especially at midlife, frequently two elements are related. One is the sense of loss caused by grief. The other is the fact that emotions such as grief, anger, guilt, or loneliness have been turned inward. That's why depression is often linked with anger.

Dealing with Depression

Many good books have been written on the subject of depression. However, the best approach for handling it is to follow the three steps utilized by the Lord Jesus in the Garden of Gethsemane when he felt "sorrowful and deeply distressed." First he called on his friends Peter, James, and John for help and encouragement (Matt. 26:37). When we feel depressed, we need to reach out for the help we need—the encouragement of a friend or even appropriate medical care.

Second, Jesus verbalized his feelings of despair to God. In the Garden he prayed, "Father, if it is possible, let this cup pass from Me" (v. 39). Later, on the cross, he echoed David, who called out, "My God, My God, why have You forsaken Me?" (Ps. 22:1). Ultimately, both David and Jesus called on God when they felt the depths of depression.

Finally, Jesus faced the source of his despair—his appointment at the cross—without flinching. "Father," he continued, "not as I will, but as You will" (Matt. 26:39). Then he urged his disciples to join him, faced his accusers, and allowed himself to be led away to experience the cross.

Tragically, depression has often been viewed as a sign of spiritual weakness or even an evidence of the presence of sin. Like the priest and the Levite confronted by the wounded traveler, our approach to depressed Christians has often been to ignore them and "pass by on the other side of the road." It is encouraging that many Christians are now willing to get involved in the lives of others who feel depressed, those who've been left devastated along the road of life by feelings of despair. Just as it is appropriate to face our own feelings of depression honestly, we should seek to provide encouragement, help, and hope to others who are affected by depression.

Loneliness

82

Looking
Both
Ways from
the Top
of the
Mountain

When Oliver came in to see his pastor, he explained, "I feel so tense I can't sleep at night. I feel angry a lot of the time, and I worry." As Pastor Tom gently probed Oliver's emotional thunderstorm, it turned out that the problem had to do with bitterness he felt toward his brother, Hal. Both men were in their early fifties, and Hal was dying of cancer. Oliver yearned to recapture the joyful times when the two brothers played together, fought off the neighborhood bully, built a treehouse with a rope ladder, and slipped into the neighborhood fire station to ring the bell on the hook and ladder truck at five o'clock in the morning, waking all the firemen. Tears poured down Oliver's cheeks as he talked about the toxic inner bitterness that had isolated him from his brother.

"I hate him, I hate him, I hate him!" He shook his head vehemently. "I want him to die. He's rejected me, humiliated me— and I didn't deserve it."

Oliver's experience illustrates a common reason for loneliness. Frequently, lonely people have experienced significant isolation in their relationships, often at midlife.

Betty and Marge were the only two girls in a household in which there were five brothers. They looked out for each other, cared for each other, wept together, and checked up on each other. After they married, they lived nearby and talked on the phone each day.

Then when they reached their upper forties, something happened. Harsh words were expressed over a seemingly minor incident. Accusations were compounded, harsh attitudes formed. When asked about their number one emotional problem, both women identified loneliness, but each refused to give up bitterness.

Bitterness isn't the only cause of loneliness. Other factors such as having an introverted personality or a reluctance to cultivate deep relationships can factor into this. We'll explore that more in the chapter on relationships. However, it's important to acknowledge what's behind our loneliness, including bitterness.

Oliver admitted to Pastor Tom that his unresolved anger toward his brother, Hal, made it virtually impossible for him to get over his feelings of loneliness and isolation. "But I just don't think I can give it up, Pastor," he insisted.

"Let me offer a suggestion," Pastor Tom said. "Suppose your brother were able to sit here with us. What if he were seated in the chair across the room and he offered to let you tell him everything you resent about him—explain exactly how you feel? Now, he isn't here, but why don't you just speak to the chair as though he were here?"

Oliver glared at the chair, then began a rapid-fire list of several incidents in which his brother had embarrassed or angered him. His eyes blazed with anger as he kept up the barrage of complaints for almost ten minutes.

Finally, he paused, and Pastor Tom said, "Good work, Oliver. It's hard isn't it? But you're doing what Ephesians 4:15 calls for—speaking the truth. Next I want you to tell Hal something positive, anything you can think of that's good about him, and let him know you love him."

Frowning, Oliver replied, "I can't think of a thing. There's nothing good about him."

"Has he ever been good to anyone else?" Pastor Tom asked.

Finally, Oliver nodded.

"Tell him about it," said Pastor Tom, gesturing to the chair.

"Hal, I hate to admit it, but you did a good job taking care of Mom when Dad died. I remember when you were a lifeguard at summer camp too. You actually saved a couple of kids' lives."

It was obvious to Pastor Tom that the wall of isolation between the two brothers was beginning to weaken. He continued, "Oliver, now let's pray for him."

"I can't pray for him! He's rejected God; he's been mean to me."

"That doesn't matter, Oliver," Pastor Tom interrupted. "You're not discounting any of the things that hurt you. All you're doing is what God told you to do: Pray for those who've despitefully used you and hurt you. That's what Jesus said in the Sermon on the Mount."

"I don't think I can," Oliver replied.

"Your brother's in the hospital, Oliver. He's not going to last much longer. Don't you want that wall to come down?"

Finally, Oliver nodded. "I'll give it a try," he said.

The two men bowed their heads.

"Dear God," Oliver said, "please help Hal. I know he's hurt me, but he helped Mom. He's going to die and he needs you. Please bless him and help him. Amen."

When the two men raised their eyes, tears were streaming down Oliver's cheeks. Before long the two men had made the short drive to the hospital. Oliver and Hal experienced a tearful reunion. The wall between them had come down.

Many people who suffer some interpersonal conflict such as that experienced by Hal and Oliver confine themselves to a lonely dungeon of solitude. They continue to poke at the emotional wounds that fester for years, often believing the best course of action is to avoid those who caused them such deep pain. Yet the ultimate answer is to confront those who have hurt us, face our own feelings, and ask God for the help we need to deal with the isolation, pain, and hurt.

Remember, you may feel lonely at times, but you're never alone. Hebrews 13:5–6 points out, "For He Himself has said, 'I will never leave you nor forsake you.' So we may boldly say, 'The LORD is my helper.'"

Sometimes loneliness happens because of the death of a spouse at midlife or earlier, or perhaps a divorce. The very word *single* carries a component of aloneness. Yet God understands your feelings. He's willing for you to pour out your deepest emotions to him. His Holy Spirit is your encourager, the One "called alongside to help."[10] Ultimately, Peter's words of affirmation provide us with a great antidote for loneliness: "Casting all your care upon Him, for He cares for you" (1 Peter 5:7).

For many of us, midlife is a time of intense loneliness, even though we may have many friends and spend a great deal of time in the company of others. Several factors may contribute to this; for example, even though you're married, you may rarely connect emotionally with your spouse anymore. Furthermore, you've been hurt enough in the past that you now just withdraw rather than making the effort to relate at work, church, or with friends or family. Or you may have decided that connecting with

84

LOOKING
BOTH
WAYS FROM
THE TOP
OF THE
MOUNTAIN
❦

others just isn't worth the effort. After all, you've tried before and it hasn't paid off.

The ultimate answer to loneliness is found in our need for people. After all, loneliness is a form of self-preoccupation. We need to understand and apply the many "one another" statements of Scripture that stress the importance and value of fellowship and relationships. One of the most basic of these is the instruction not to abandon our assembling together, as some have done, but to give ourselves to encouraging each other (see Heb. 10:24–25). Encouragement can provide a strong, positive antidote to loneliness.

Worry and Fear

Scripture has much to say against worry and fear. Yet many of us at midlife have come to know these emotions all too well. While both have a legitimate side—the phrase "fear of the Lord" is found throughout Scripture, and the term for anxiety is also used for legitimate concern in several instances (it is translated "care" in 1 Cor. 12:25; Phil. 2:20)—in most cases both indicate a weakness in faith.

Many have reached midlife without experiencing inner peace. We may have achieved relative financial security, live in nicely decorated homes, hold a fistful of credit cards with fairly high limits, and drive comfortable automobiles. Yet many of us are affected by life's most toxic emotions—fear and anxiety.

Fear was humanity's first negative emotion. Shortly after our original parents chose to disobey God and eat the forbidden fruit, Adam admitted, "I was afraid because I was naked; and I hid myself" (Gen. 3:10). We have been covering up to compensate for fears ever since. Frequently, we allow the cares of this world, the desire for wealth, and our concerns about the future choke out our legitimate concern for the Lord and other people (Luke 8:14). Sometimes we become paralyzed by fear over some threat, real or imagined (Prov. 29:25).

The Hebrew word for fear, *yare*, appearing more than three hundred times in the Old Testament, describes a response to a threat. It was used positively for the fear of the Lord. More commonly it refers to fear of death, circumstances, or other people. Fear, an apprehension or dread usually related to a specific object, and anxiety, a less specific concern about the future, are devastating emotions. Like the dry wind of summer they can rob us of vitality and stability.

Several years ago Rodney, a midlife friend, listed several things that were producing significant fear in his life. They ranged from prospective loss of his job (rumor had it his company was merging with another), to the health of his aging mother, to misbehavior and even the possibility of pregnancy on the part of his teenage daughter, to concern over how people felt about his involvement in ministry at the church. One day he finally admitted, "I think I'm just struggling with worry and fear."

86

Looking
Both
Ways from
the Top
of the
Mountain
❦

Faith, the Antidote

We like to tell people that worry and fear are like the red lights on the dashboard of a car. When they light up, it's time to check for the cause. So what do we do about these toxic emotions?

First, the ultimate antidote to both worry and fear is faith. In the process of warning his listeners against the dangers of anxiety, Jesus slipped in a phrase that defined the essence of the root problem behind worry: "O you of little faith" (Matt. 6:30). On another occasion, after stilling a storm on the Sea of Galilee, he asked his disciples, "Why are you so fearful? How is it that you have no faith?" (Mark 4:40). Clearly the issue when both fear and worry are present is one of trust. Are we depending on the Lord or on ourselves or some other factor?

Second, to combat anxiety and fear we need to put first things first. As Jesus explained in Matthew 6:33, "Seek first the kingdom of God and His righteousness, and all these things shall be added to you." Frequently, at midlife we struggle with multiple masters, trying to live life under the control of competing demands. When the Lord has first place, our choices and our worry are much easier to deal with.

Third, the ultimate key to countering both worry and fear is to live life one day at a time. As Jesus explained in Matthew 6:34, "Therefore do not worry about tomorrow, for tomorrow will worry about its own things. Sufficient for the day is its own trouble."

Fourth, we should always respond to feelings of worry and fear with prayer. Frequently, in Scripture those who were plagued with fear cried out to God. David wrote Psalm 31 during one of the most volatile times in his life. Living among the rocks and caves, threatened daily by King Saul, he wrote, "In You, O LORD, I put my trust; let me never be ashamed; deliver me in Your righteousness. Bow down Your ear to me, deliver me speedily; be my rock of refuge, a fortress of defense to save me. For You are my rock and my fortress; therefore, for Your name's sake, lead me and guide me. Pull me out of the net which they have secretly laid for me, for You are my strength" (Ps. 31:1–4).

The apostle Paul reflected the same values and the same approach in Philippians 4:6: "Be anxious for nothing, but in everything by prayer and supplication, with thanksgiving, let your requests be made known to God."

Just as in the case of grief and depression, much has been written on the subject of worry and fear. The bottom line for each, however, is to cultivate trust in the Lord. As Jeremiah 17:7–8 points out,

> Blessed is the man who trusts in the LORD,
> and whose hope is the LORD.
> For he shall be like a tree planted by the waters,
> which spreads out its roots by the river,
> and will not fear when heat comes;
> but her leaf will be green,
> and will not be anxious in the year of drought,
> nor will cease from yielding fruit.

When our hearts are fixed on the Lord and we trust in him instead of relying on ourselves and allowing our hearts to wander from him, we can handle all the emotions of midlife—loneliness, envy, guilt, depression, anger, fear, worry, and all the rest. The reason is simple: The Lord wants our hearts—our inner emotional and rational being—to be focused on him.

CHAPTER FIVE

SPIRITUAL CHANGES AT MIDLIFE

THE APOSTLE PETER CONCLUDED HIS SECOND EPISTLE to the churches of Asia Minor with these words: "But grow in the grace and knowledge of our Lord and Savior Jesus Christ" (2 Peter 3:18). His reference to spiritual growth was without regard to any of the categories into which we divide ourselves—nationality, gender, ethnicity, age, and so on. All believers are to be constantly progressing from spiritual infancy to spiritual maturity.

But this isn't always easy. And as we age, sometimes it becomes downright difficult, a significant challenge. One reason for this difficulty is the myth that age necessarily means spiritual maturity. It doesn't.

Myths and Misconceptions

With the aging process comes a plethora of myths. Some were documented by Bert Kruger Smith in *Aging in America*. For example, it is a myth to believe that older people cannot learn. We've all been told that "you can't teach an old dog new tricks," but later in life many come to believe it. Still, people aren't dogs. Unless a person's mind is diminished by dementia or similar physical maladies, learning need never stop, both in the intellectual and the spiritual realm.

Another myth is that older people do not want to work. While many look forward to the golden years of retirement, a majority of people who have retired find they just can't handle all the time they have on their hands. Many of them now greet you at Wal-Mart or take your order at McDonald's. Most older people want to work, not only for income but also because they want to be useful and productive.

90

Looking
Both
Ways from
the Top
of the
Mountain

Perhaps one of the most serious misconceptions about older people is that they have it all together spiritually, that they have settled all their spiritual accounts and have no place to go but up—literally. The myth is that senior saints have reached a spiritual high that cannot be achieved without years of prayer and Bible reading. They can go no higher.

But the Bible paints an entirely different picture. Christians need a plan for spiritual growth that lasts a lifetime. It is not only good for the soul, it's also good for the body.

Spirituality and Life

Older people continue to be interested in spiritual things. Nine out of every ten older Americans say religion is important in their lives, and nearly three-fourths say it is very important.[1] A recent survey found that 80 percent of people age sixty-five or older are members of a church or synagogue, and over half (52 percent) worship there at least once a week.[2]

But do these "religious" adults continue to practice their religion, and does a life of faith have any effect on their health? The answer is yes on both counts. Nine out of ten seniors indicate they pray frequently when faced with worries or personal problems. And what's more, a growing number of Christian physicians feel at liberty to pray with their patients as a routine part of an examination. One study found that two-thirds of a sample of family physicians and general practitioners felt that prayer with an older patient was appropriate and that younger physicians were more likely to have positive attitudes toward addressing religious issues.[3]

Spirituality and Health

But what about the effects of spirituality on health? Is there a cause and effect relationship between spirituality and good health? Empirical evidence shows that when a person, young or old, walks closely in a vibrant relationship with the Lord, there is a beneficial effect on his or her health. Ellen L. Idler supervised a study of 2,811 New Haven, Connecticut, residents age sixty-five and over. She discovered that those who attended church and were vitally involved with the people of their church exhibited "fewer chronic conditions, lower functional disability and depression."[4] In other words, they were in better health than the nonchurchgoers in the study.

Harold G. Koenig, director of the program on religion, aging, and health at Duke University Medical Center, has become the modern guru of studies documenting the relationship between spirituality and good health. He notes fourteen spiritual needs of physically ill older people that are intimately related both to physical and psychological health, and therefore, ought to be addressed by health professionals.[5] Unfortunately, David O. Moberg seems to be right when he says, "Most gerontologists tend to ignore faith and practice or even, in some instances, try subtly to impose nontraditional faiths or atheistic agnosticism upon elders with whom they work."[6]

Despite ardent research attempting to prove otherwise, a growing body of evidence shows a positive link between maintaining a healthy spiritual dimension and a healthy physical dimension. This becomes even more necessary as we age. The older we get and the more physically challenged we become, the more we need to maintain a close walk with God.

The question is, How do you do it? How does someone in midlife and beyond continue to live under the shadow of the Almighty? And more particularly, how does someone who is aging and whose mind may not always understand continue to maintain the spiritual aspect of life? Here are some biblical solutions.

Set Life Goals and Stick to Them

It is often we men who spend our energies and lives pursuing goals that have little eternal meaning. But with more women in the workplace today, many women have discovered that the men were right after all: It's a jungle out there, and the rat race is for the rats! Christians often become caught up in life goals that do not reflect eternity and do not reflect the teaching of Jesus. When they do, these Christians find a spiritual vacuum that only grows with the aging process. That's why it's important to set life goals early and stick to them—life goals that satisfy, even in old age.

What are some life goals that do not satisfy and can even destroy us? Two come to mind immediately.

Materialism. People today seem to be on the treadmill of materialism. They work harder, longer, and put up with more because the boss expects it of them. They invest in risky and questionable investments in an attempt to get rich quick. They buy a couple of lotto tickets each night at the Seven-Eleven in hopes of hitting it big. They buy and show. They buy and store. Finally, they buy and sell. Have you noticed the dramatic rise in yard sales, garage sales, and flea markets in the waning years of the twentieth century? It's a cultural testimony to the fact that we all have too much stuff we'll never use. And yet, we take the money from the yard sale and buy more stuff we'll never use. It's a sickness. More accurately, it's an addiction to materialism.

When people are addicted to materialism, they face a severe problem as the years wear on. They have less and less money to buy the things they don't need but can't do without. So they become fearful and often bitter. If their sense of worth is found in the possessions they have, when they are faced with losing those possessions or selling their home to move into an extended-care facility, it's little wonder they become depressed, even suicidal. Materialism will not sustain us in our golden years, even if we still have lots of stuff.

Self-centeredness. When we live for ourselves, plan for ourselves, even scheme to benefit only ourselves, our self-centeredness usually comes back to haunt us in later years when we are no longer the center of our universe and must look to someone else for advice and primary care.

Self-centered people are everywhere. The papers are filled with horrific accounts of workers who were so self-centered that, when they did not get the promotion they felt they deserved,

92

LOOKING
BOTH
WAYS FROM
THE TOP
OF THE
MOUNTAIN

they came to work the next day with a .357 Magnum. Husbands and wives were so self-centered that, when they did not feel their spouse was meeting their needs, they walked away, leaving their family in shambles.

Unfortunately, as we grow older we often tend to become even more self-centered, and sometimes more materialistic. We have watched older people become more demanding of their mates, more demanding of doctors, more demanding of everyone but themselves. We've also watched them cling more tightly to their possessions, hiding money from their spouse or vocally reminding their children, "That's mine. You can't have it!"

To maintain spiritual growth in later years requires jettisoning every life goal that reflects materialism or self-centeredness. After all, the words of Jesus have no age limit: "Do not lay up for yourselves treasures on earth, where moth and rust destroy and where thieves break in and steal; but lay up for yourselves treasures in heaven. . . . For where your treasure is, there your heart will be also" (Matt. 6:19–21). Nor are the words of Paul restricted by age: "Let nothing be done through selfish ambition or conceit, but in lowliness of mind let each esteem others better than himself. Let each of you look out not only for his own interests, but also for the interests of others" (Phil. 2:3–4).

We do not stop laying up treasures in heaven when we retire from the company. Eternal treasure building should be a major life goal during our golden years when our time is becoming critically short. And we should not become increasingly self-centered when we need so desperately those who reach out to us. Maintaining the spiritual dimension requires increasingly taking on the mind of Christ, and that requires a good spiritual diet and a program of spiritual exercise.

What are some life goals that will help you maintain your spiritual dimension as you grow older?

Find What You Need in Your Bible

When we were young in our Christian faith, we often read the Bible for answers. There were so many questions, and our faith was new to us. The Bible was an encyclopedic source of information. "And truly Jesus did many other signs in the presence of His disciples, which are not written in this book; but these things are written that you may believe that Jesus is the Christ, the Son of God, and that believing you may have life in His name" (John 20:30–31).

Perhaps later in our Christian growth we read the Bible more for enlightenment. We wanted to know more so we could grow more. We read portions of the Bible that at first didn't attract our attention—books such as Ezekiel, Song of Solomon, or Hebrews. "My son, do not despise the chastening of the LORD, nor be discouraged when you are rebuked by Him; for whom the LORD loves He chastens, and scourges every son whom He receives" (Heb. 12:5–6).

As we aged further we often read the Bible for comfort. We found ourselves migrating to the psalms and other portions that brought encouragement to us. "Yea, though I walk through the valley of the shadow of death, I will fear no evil; for You are with me; Your rod and Your staff, they comfort me" (Ps. 23:4).

But when we face the final years of our life, the greatest benefit we may gain from reading the Bible is confirmation. "I will never leave you nor forsake you" (Heb. 13:5). "O God, You have taught me from my youth. . . . Now also when I am old and gray-headed, O God, do not forsake me" (Ps. 71:17–18). "Mark the blameless man, and observe the upright; for the future of that man is peace" (Ps. 37:37).

For whatever reason you read, spiritual growth, even in the latter stages of life, is inextricably bound to reading the Word of God. Now that you may have more time on your hands and are looking for something beneficial to do, plan to read through your Bible and take note of those passages you've long neglected. Set a time each day. Pick a place. Don't allow anything to interrupt you. And if your eyesight is causing you to have trouble reading your Bible, even that giant print edition you have, ask someone to read to you. Who knows? It may do them even more good than it does you. Or if no one is available secure a cassette player and tapes of the Bible. Good ones are available.

Embark on a Prayer Journey

Let's take a hypothetical situation. Suppose you have a strong enemy. He is big, ugly, and brutish. That you can handle, but he is also crafty and shrewd, which makes him dangerous. For-

94

LOOKING
BOTH
WAYS FROM
THE TOP
OF THE
MOUNTAIN

tunately, you have a weapon, a strong weapon, and with that weapon your enemy knows he doesn't stand a chance against you. What would your enemy do if he wanted to disarm you and defeat you?

First, he would try to take away your weapon. He would do everything in his power to dismantle it, disengage it, or destroy it. But what if he couldn't? What if it were not in your enemy's power to destroy your strong weapon? Would he give up? Not a chance. He'd simply go to plan B.

And what is plan B? If your enemy can't destroy your weapon, he'd try to convince you it doesn't work or it isn't really that effective. He'd attempt to get you not to use your weapon by convincing you it wouldn't be effective.

That's exactly what our enemy, Satan, does every day. He knows we have this superpower weapon. We call it prayer. With our weapon we can call in the firepower of the sovereign God. Satan cannot destroy our weapon, but he doesn't have to. Instead, he whispers in our ear, "Don't bother to pray. It doesn't work anyway." When we listen to him, we lose.

One of the best ways to cultivate the spiritual dimension of your life in midlife and beyond is to maintain a consistent prayer life. It's interesting, isn't it, that we often place prayer some-where near the bottom of service to the Lord. But we can serve God by praying for others, and we can remain close to God by communing with him on a daily basis.

Even in old age, when we are no longer capable of doing all we once did in our youth, we can still pray. Did you know you can pray even if you have arthritis? You can be on Medicare and still pray? You can retire and find that God has given you your most important life's work—the work of prayer. If we stop listening to the devil, we may find that the secret to maintaining the spiritual dimension in our life is only a prayer away.

Age has little bearing on our ability to pray. Even with Alzheimer's and an increasing inability to get words out of his mouth, my (Wood's) father can pray lucidly and meaning-fully. Fostering a more meaningful personal prayer life can be like taking spiritual vitamins. It will put the life back into your years.

Get Back in the Race

I had a friend years ago named John. He was an excellent automobile mechanic. I can still hear John say, "You know the problem with cars these days? We don't run them enough. Engines are made to be run. If you don't run them, you can't properly maintain them."

People are like car engines. We are made to run for Jesus, to serve him. That's what Ephesians 2:8–10 says. Read verse 10. God did not create us a new creature in Christ just so he could fill up heaven. God created us to serve him, and we are never truly fulfilled until we do. And once we stop, that fulfillment of our spiritual dimension wanes quickly. A great deal of our satisfaction in retirement, not to mention our sense of worth in old age, comes from how we view our continuing service to God.

Embedded in the conventional notion of retirement are some assumptions that may be hazardous to your spiritual health. For example, many people view their life's work as something they did for thirty or forty years (roughly until age sixty-five), and then suddenly it was over. They never would work again. They relied instead on a company pension, social security, and their savings. Of course there's nothing wrong in pursuing a goal of retirement, unless retirement means dropping out of life.

The same can happen in the spiritual dimension. If you have worked hard for the Lord for years, and suddenly you drop off the face of the planet, the work of the Lord may suffer, but not nearly as much as you will. If you want to maintain the spiritual dimension in your life, you've got to get back in the race. But how do you do that?

To find something you can do in your retirement to maintain your spiritual health, you have to be honest. You may face many limiting factors that you didn't before, factors such as age, ability, health, opportunity. Begin, therefore, by identifying your abilities and opportunities. You may be surprised that they are many and varied. Become an usher at church. Join a ladies' Bible study or host one at your home. Mentor a young mother. Become a regular at the men's prayer breakfast. Go on a missions trip. Use your computer to feed information and encouragement to your missionaries. Become a greeter at a Bible conference. Volunteer to help with the maintenance at a Bible camp. Use your

96

LOOKING
BOTH
WAYS FROM
THE TOP
OF THE
MOUNTAIN

knowledge of accounting by helping single mothers or widows at church complete their income tax forms. Learn a new skill and teach it to others. The list is almost endless.

If your health won't permit you to be this active, find a less physical way to stay in the game spiritually. Use your telephone to provide a listening ear to those who need it (see James 1:19). Don't gossip, but have the compassion Jesus had for the multitude (Matt. 9:36–38; 14:13–14). Give people a sympathetic ear. Pray over the telephone with those who hurt. Volunteer to be a senior companion to someone who is lonely. Sit with someone who has Alzheimer's while the caregiver runs some errands. This list is only limited by your imagination.

The bottom line is clear: Car engines run as long as they are used and properly maintained. When they are not, they rust. Christians are the same way. To maintain your spiritual life, plan to spend time with the Lord and with others, then keep on running. The apostle Paul didn't say "I have finished the race" (2 Tim. 4:7) until the last chapter of the last epistle he ever wrote. Get back in the race.

A Final Word to Caregivers

"I don't have time to take care of myself." Sound familiar? That is the outcry of many who have reached midlife and find themselves in the role of caregiver. You devote so much of yourself and your energy to giving care to others, you find no time for your own life. Giving care to a spouse or parent with cancer or AIDS or Alzheimer's is about the most stressful job in the world. This stress can be damaging to you as well as to the one you love. And if this stress is draining you spiritually, it can be damaging to your relationship with the Lord. So what do you do? Follow the example of Jesus. He was the ultimate caregiver, giving care to multitudes of people, to the Twelve, and to one or two at a time. Here's what Jesus did.

Jesus had a realistic attitude about the world. Many caregivers are in denial about the disease and its effect on the person for whom they care. They say, "It's not so bad; he'll get better. Our lives are just on a temporary hold." But that temporary hold, more often than not, is a permanent deterioration. Be realistic.

If you are giving care to a spouse, a mother, or a friend, that care will likely last the rest of his or her life, or yours.

When Jesus sent his disciples into the world, his view of what they would find was not a fantasy. Jesus didn't say, "It's not so bad out there. It's just a temporary setback. Man is basically good. Just go and do the best you can. Things will get better." In fact, Jesus warned, "Behold, I send you out as sheep in the midst of wolves" (Matt. 10:16).

Don't let your best hopes for the future blind you to the present realities of life. You cannot put your spiritual life on hold while you wrestle with another's disease or dementia. You must face the aging process and all the debilitating side effects realistically. While you give care, take care to maintain your own spiritual health and, to the highest degree possible, the spiritual health of the one you love.

Read the Bible together. Pray together. Talk about spiritual things together and recall spiritual victories and defeats. Look back at your life for those spiritual landmarks that document your spiritual journey together. Do as much in the spiritual realm as you can together, but if that becomes impossible, don't let your own spiritual life diminish while you are giving care to another. You owe it to yourself to keep on growing; you owe it to God too. Besides, if the one you are providing care for is a Christian, do you really believe he or she would want your relationship with God to suffer just so your relationship with him or her can flourish?

Jesus took a break occasionally. I am amazed at how many times the Lord left a crowd hanging. Here are just a few examples.

The multitudes followed Jesus wherever he went. When he came to Capernaum, the centurion begged Jesus to heal his servant. Jesus did. Then he sent the centurion away and entered the house of Peter to get away from the crowd (Matt. 8:14). That evening those possessed by evil spirits were brought to the Master for deliverance. He healed them, but Matthew 8:18 says, "Now when Jesus saw great multitudes about Him, He gave a command to depart to the other side." The people needed Jesus, yet he slipped away by boat.

As the Lord taught by the Sea of Galilee, a multitude gathered. They needed to know important truths, eternal truths. Only

98

LOOKING
BOTH
WAYS FROM
THE TOP
OF THE
MOUNTAIN
❦

Jesus could provide the answers for them. So he taught them the parable of the sower. There were more parables to be taught, so Jesus tutored them about placing a light under a bushel. But there were still more parables to be taught, and Jesus would teach them too—but not today. "Now when they had left the multitude, they took Him along in the boat as He was" (Mark 4:36). People needed him; he slipped away.

Again, when Jesus had finished the parable of the wheat and tares, Matthew records, "Then Jesus sent the multitude away and went into the house" (Matt. 13:36). The multitude wanted to know what the parable meant; so did the disciples. But Jesus sent the crowd away. He took refuge indoors.

After a hard afternoon of feeding four thousand men, besides women and children, Matthew 15:39 records that he sent away the multitude and took a ship to Magdala, where there were no crowds. He left them hanging again.

Time and again Jesus left the crowds begging for more. Why? Because Jesus knew there was more to his life than meeting the needs of others. He healed the sick and caused the blind to see, the deaf to hear, the demon-possessed to be free. But he also took a break occasionally, climbed in the disciple's boat, left the crowd hanging, and simply slipped away. Jesus knew when it was time to move on and when it was time to come back. And most importantly—and as a caregiver you dare not miss this—Jesus left the needy crowd without a hint of guilt. They needed him but he sailed away free from guilt, even though he did not meet their need.

The next time you need a break from giving care to someone you love, don't feel guilty. Especially if you are the only caregiver, don't allow guilt feelings even a foothold. Jesus was the only one who could meet the needs of the people, but there wasn't even the slightest twinge of guilt when he entered the boat and left the crowd crying for more. Taking a break should be a guilt-free way of being restored to continue caregiving. Here's how to do it.

Take your break with your Bible. Let the Spirit of God enrich your life, refresh your soul, and renew your mind. Get away from the stress of giving care and constantly meeting needs by letting the Word speak to you and meet your needs. Don't neglect your own spiritual dimension while you are attempting to minister to your loved one's physical needs.

Sneak away. Find a quiet corner. Kick off your shoes. Read your Bible and pray. Let the Holy Spirit fill you again. And do it all without any twinges of guilt. If Jesus, the Son of God, the only Savior this world will ever have, could walk away from a multitude when they cried out for him, don't you think you can walk away and get refreshed spiritually without guilt?

Jesus spent time alone with God. One of the great secrets to spiritual renewal is spending quiet time alone with God. How often we caregivers are so busy with the needs of the one who demands our full attention that we often neglect the One who deserves our full attention. To maintain your own spiritual dimension, find some time each day to be alone with God.

Jesus often left the crowd to get away, but what did he do when he got away? More often than not, he got alone with his heavenly Father. Mark 6:45–46 says, "Immediately He made His disciples get into the boat and go before Him to the other side, to Bethsaida, while He sent the multitude away [getting alone]. And when He had sent them away, He departed to the mountain to pray [getting alone with God]."

Matthew 14:23 informs us that when Jesus went into the mountains to pray, "he was there alone." Just God the Son and God the Father. No crowds. No needy people. No disciples. No neighbors. Just Jesus and Jehovah. That's the way it must be if we are to be renewed, refreshed, and revitalized to handle the many pressures of being a caregiver.

Who is the great example of a caregiver in the Old Testament? It has to be Moses. He was giving constantly to the grumbling Israelites. He did everything for them. They complained, yet he loved them and cared for them. They threatened to stone him, yet he prayed on their behalf and interceded for them to God. They disappointed him. Sound familiar?

But God knew what Moses needed. The caregiver needed some personal time with the great Caregiver. Moses needed to withdraw from his demanding kinsmen and to be held in the everlasting arms of God. Exodus 24:1–2 tells us that God said to Moses, "Come up to the LORD, you and Aaron, Nadab and Abihu, and seventy of the elders of Israel, and worship from afar.

100

LOOKING
BOTH
WAYS FROM
THE TOP
OF THE
MOUNTAIN

And Moses alone shall come near the LORD." "Moses alone." The two most helpful words when you're at your wit's end—you alone. And God.

When the one for whom you are giving care nods off, when that person you love dearly is peaceful and quiet, don't just pick up a good book. Pick up the Good Book. Spend a few uninterrupted, uninhibited, unhindered minutes alone with God. Talk to him. Read his Word. Sit quietly, motionless. Give your self, your stress, your loved one to him. Let him enfold you in his love. Let him create a new spirit within you. Let him do what he has promised. Let him give you rest (Matt. 11:28). Let him be your hiding place (Ps. 32:7). Let him shelter you as you escape, even if only for a moment, under the refreshing shadow of his wings (Ps. 91:1–4).

Maintaining the spiritual dimension for one who is aging is tough enough. Don't let yourself become spiritually run down so that you fail to give the best care possible. "He makes me to lie down in green pastures; He leads me beside the still waters. He restores my soul" (Ps. 23:2–3). Do you need that? Then you need him. Take care of your spiritual dimension, caregiver. After all, you're important to God too!

CHAPTER SIX

RELATIONSHIPS
AT MIDLIFE

"I'M TIRED OF PEOPLE," Cheryl exclaimed as she seemed to shrink into the chair in her pastor's office. "I'm fifty-three years old. I don't have anyone close to me. Before Jack died we had plenty of friends from right here in this church. While he was lying there in the hospital wasting away with cancer, our friends began to desert us one by one. Pastor, I'm not going to start hanging out with that old widows' club!"

With those firm statements, Cheryl dissolved into tears. Meanwhile Pastor Matt bit his lip and resisted the temptation to speak. *After all,* he thought, *almost anything I say will be wrong.*

Finally, as the silence stretched on he asked, "What about Tammy and Jerry?"

"Those grown kids are so wrapped up in their own lives they don't have time for me. Tammy's getting married this fall—to a cowboy of all things—and all Jerry cares about is that job of his and that new sports car. The only time I see either one of them is when they need money."

"What about work?" Pastor Matt asked, continuing to probe gently.

"That dog-eat-dog office? There's no room for relationships there. It used to be there was time for several of us to sit down after a project, go out for a meal together or drink coffee, but since the downsizing, it's one crazy deadline after another. Nobody seems to care about people anymore.

"Then there's Jack's mother in the nursing home. I try to visit her at least once a month, but she doesn't remember who I am. All she can talk about is 'Jack this, Jack that.' She doesn't even seem to realize he's dead. And my own parents—they need more help than I can give them. So there's no time for a relationship.

"The other day Tammy was over talking about her wedding, and she asked why I didn't start dating again. I guess she'd forgotten how upset she and Jerry both were when Bob Martin took me to dinner last summer. I know the kids miss their dad, but you'd think I had committed the unpardonable sin."

Unfortunately, Cheryl was having the same kind of relationship struggles that many people experience at midlife. The fact is our relationships can go smoothly and provide us with a great deal of support. They can also be as bumpy as a rut-filled backwoods road. Frequently, by the time we reach midlife our relationships resemble the moving parts in a car with well over one hundred thousand miles logged on the odometer. Due to friction the parts no longer work together smoothly, there are many rattles, and frequent breakdowns result.

As we think about the different types of relationships we all experience, the most basic, the one God established in the Garden of Eden, is the marriage bond between husband and wife. The next level includes the immediate family parent-child relationship, as well as relationships with other relatives. Other relationships exist at work, where we relate with associates and establish professional contacts. In the church we experience relationships with fellow members, some of whom may become close friends. We also develop relationships with our pastors. In the community we have relationships of one kind or another with neighbors, and we may be involved with clubs or other common interest groups.

Most relationships fall into one of two kinds. Primary relationships occur between individuals or within small groups and are by nature intimate. Examples of primary relationships include

104

LOOKING
BOTH
WAYS FROM
THE TOP
OF THE
MOUNTAIN
❦

the marriage relationship, close friendships, and mentoring relationships. Secondary relationships, which involve larger groups and are more impersonal, include relationships between customers and store clerks, professors and students, and supervisors and employees to name a few.

In his book *We Need Each Other,* pastor and seminary professor Dr. Guy Greenfield identifies eight levels that can be applied to these various relationships.[1] They vary from shallow to deep and include avoidance, greeting, separate interests, common interests, social interactions, caring, sharing, and the closest, intimacy. If you took the time to list all the relationships in your life, you'd discover that each one fits somewhere on Dr. Greenfield's continuum.

The Bible and Social Relationships

The Bible has a great deal to say on the subject of relationships, and if we are to navigate successfully through life without running into the relational dead end Cheryl experienced, we must get a handle on what Scripture has to say.

First, Scripture makes it clear that social and interpersonal problems and conflicts have existed throughout human history. Adam and Eve disagreed over the reason for their disobedience to God's command in the Garden of Eden. Their oldest son, Cain, murdered his brother. Before long Scripture recorded that "the earth was filled with violence" (Gen. 6:11). The Old Testament was marked by family feuds such as the conflict between the herdsmen of Abram and those of Lot, a long-running feud between Jacob and Esau, violent crimes involving members of David's family, especially his cousin Joab, and a series of tribal and regional wars.

The New Testament doesn't show much improvement. Jesus' disciples seemed to spend a great deal of their time bickering over who would be greatest in the Master's kingdom. The early church experienced conflicts over provision for the needy (Acts 6) and the relationship between law and grace (Acts 15). Even longtime colleagues Paul and Barnabas couldn't agree over the role of John Mark in their ministry (Acts 15:37–40).

But the Bible doesn't simply document the history of social and interpersonal conflict; it presents God's clear-cut answer, expressed in the word *love*. On several occasions during his ministry Jesus discussed the greatest commandment (see Matt. 22:35–40; Mark 12:28–34; Luke 10:25–38). His perspective on the primary mandates the Lord requires can be summarized in two statements: "Love God wholeheartedly" and "Love people unconditionally," or as yourself.

Jesus and his listeners understood the concept of love based on the Old Testament words *ahav* and *rahirem*, both of which are translated "to love." According to one source, "Love in the Old Testament is basically a spontaneous feeling which impels to self-giving."[2]

106

Looking
Both
Ways from
the Top
of the
Mountain
❦

Love's Characteristics

Four characteristics summarize the Old Testament concept of love. First, it is passionate. Prophets Jeremiah (31:3) and Hosea (3:1) compared the relationship between a husband and wife to God's love for Israel to demonstrate how the Lord relentlessly pursued his people. The opposite of passion for too many is indifference, a characteristic common to many relationships today, including Christian marriages and friendships.

A second element of biblical love is that it is powerful. While the word *passionate* refers to the response of love, *powerful* describes the energy of love itself. Listen to these words from Solomon to his beloved Shulamite bride:

> Set me as a seal upon your heart, as a seal upon your arm; for love is as strong as death, jealousy as cruel as the grave; its flames are flames of fire, a most vehement flame. Many waters cannot quench love, nor can the floods drown it. If a man would give for love all the wealth of his house, it would be utterly despised.

Song of Solomon 8:6–7

One of the prime examples of this is the power of the love Jonathan expressed toward David. Jonathan's love was so strong that he overlooked the threat that David would one day occupy the throne that by inheritance should have belonged to him. He refused to succumb to the hostile threats of Saul, his angry, resentful father. His love for David not only ran the risks, it stood the test of time.

Third, love is permeating and touches every area of life. When Moses came down from Mount Sinai to deliver God's detailed law to the Israelites, he spelled out clear-cut guidelines for interpersonal relationships among the people of God. After warning against cheating their neighbors, cursing the disadvantaged, exercising partiality against the poor, gossiping or doing injustice to others, Moses summarized God's principles for personal relationships:

> You shall not hate your brother in your heart. You shall surely rebuke your neighbor, and not bear sin because of him. You shall not take vengeance, nor bear any grudge against the children of your people, but you shall love your neighbor as yourself: I am the LORD.
>
> LEVITICUS 19:17–18

Tragically, by Jesus' day the religious authorities had drawn a narrow, exclusive border around the application of this broad principle. The term *neighbor* had come to be used only of those who were both nearby and of the same racial or national origin. Gentiles were certainly not considered neighbors, nor were the despised Samaritans.

The term Jesus used for love, *agape*, took the statement from Moses in Leviticus 19:15 and elevated it to "selfless, choice-motivated, sacrificial love shown by the Father in sending Him and by Himself in laying down His life."[3] This is the quality that is to become the guideline and mandate for all Christian relationships.

Love Each Other

Fifteen times the New Testament instructs God's children to love each other, including four times by Jesus in the upper room discourse (John 13:34; 15:12, 17). On the night before his crucifixion, the Lord clearly identified love as the ultimate badge of discipleship and the primary commandment, the ultimate "new commandment" summarizing and superseding the Old Testament law.

Writing to the Romans, the apostle Paul pointed out that the foundational obligation of every Christian is fulfilled in obeying the command to love each other (Rom. 13:8–9). Furthermore, authentic love never harms another; thus it fulfills both the letter and the spirit of the law. From Paul's perspective, love provides the expression of the liberty to which we as God's children have been called (Gal. 5:14).

Paul understood this quality of agape love as something that affected relationships on a practical level. As he explained to the Thessalonians, practicing love means minding your own business rather than getting involved in gossip or trying to manipulate the lives of others (1 Thess. 4:11). He warned the Galatians against using others for their own selfish ends or bitterly attacking each other in the manner of angry dogs (Gal. 5:13, 15). He also pointed out that authentic love avoids the works of the flesh such as immorality, hatred, strife, selfish ambition, and self indulgence (vv. 19–21), choosing instead to allow the Spirit to produce joy, peace, longsuffering, kindness, goodness, faithfulness, gentleness, and self-control (vv. 22–23). And as he explained to the Philippians, the one who genuinely loves will "esteem others better than himself" (Phil. 2:3).

Peter and John also underscored the importance of love as the core value in human relationships. From Peter's perspective, loving each other passionately was the natural outgrowth of obeying the gospel (1 Peter 1:22). And from John's prolific pen, true love transcended simple emotion to reach out with compassion to those in need. We should never refuse to meet the needs of those we are able to help (1 John 4:20–21).

The Marriage Relationship

Dealing with the Loss of a Spouse

As Pastor Matt listened to Cheryl pour out the intense feelings that surrounded her midlife loneliness and despair, he realized she needed more than a simple explanation of the nature of love. Like many women at midlife and beyond, Cheryl was experiencing widowhood. According to authorities on change, no loss is greater than the earth-shattering loss of losing a mate.

None of us likes to think about death, yet in almost all marriages one partner will outlive the other. Usually that spouse is a wife, but when either spouse dies the other's life changes in drastic ways. Gone are the shared joys, the jointly-met challenges, the daily interaction. Somehow, even though we know

108

LOOKING
BOTH
WAYS FROM
THE TOP
OF THE
MOUNTAIN

that Scripture makes it clear that "it is appointed for men to die once" (Heb. 9:27), we'd rather forget about the appointment.

For the widow the immediate sense of loss is crushing. Life suddenly becomes fragile and filled with grief. How long does grief last? For some the worst is over in a year or less. For others, the grief process may take two years or longer. Some may never completely come to grips with the death of a spouse.

Many factors affect the length of time grief takes. For example, was the death anticipated or was it unexpected? Was there a high degree of dependence on the spouse? Does the widow have significant coping skills? Were there unresolved resentments within the marriage, or other unfinished business? And of great importance, does the widow have a supportive network of caring family and friends?

Scripture mandates that God's people extend compassionate care to widows. Jesus frequently reached out to widows during his ministry, raising the dead son of the widow of Nain (Luke 7:12–15), referencing a poor widow in his parable about persistence in prayer (Luke 18:1–5), and commending the generous widow who donated two mites to the temple treasury (Luke 21:2–4).

In 1 Timothy 5, Paul instructed Timothy on the importance of caring for widows, spelling out the responsibility of children and grandchildren to provide the first line of care, followed by the local church for widows sixty and over (vv. 5:5–9).

In their excellent book *Coping with Life after Your Mate Dies*, Don and Rita Cushenberry list a number of important things for widows and widowers to keep in mind when dealing with the loss of a spouse. These include:

- It is sensible to grieve and shed tears.
- It is not a sign of personal weakness to seek help from others during bereavement.
- The crisis of grief may serve as a stimulus for creative activities.
- No one's grief is just like anyone else's.
- The intense pain and grief of losing a spouse is not a sign of being deserted by God.

- No words of comfort from friends or relatives will provide sudden lifting of feelings of grief.
- No one should allow another to minimize the importance of the life of a spouse or push the widow or widower to get on with life.[4]

In short, there is no relational trauma greater than the loss of a spouse. Even if one marries again, the deceased spouse cannot be replaced.

Recently I (Don) hiked around the lakeshore at Odosagih Bible Conference while talking with Phil, a small, dapper man in his early sixties. As we walked together, Phil told me of the loss of his first wife, Trudy. "I loved her dearly," he explained. "When she died it was like my life ground to a halt. Nothing or no one could replace her.

"She and I had been friends with my present wife, Janice, and her husband, Sam. But after Sam died, I lost touch with Janice. God brought us together, and we've enjoyed a wonderful marriage. She didn't replace my first wife, but I'm thankful that God allowed us to remarry. We've shared some very special times together."

Keeping the Fire Burning

Unfortunately, even those at midlife who haven't lost a mate aren't assured of close relationships. Even in good marriages, expectations and roles can change. Frequently, by midlife marriages can become as stale as a week-old loaf of bread. Husbands and wives take each other for granted. Meaningful conversation is replaced by increasing periods of silence. The vitality of romance has been banished to the dim and distant past. Physical desire has diminished, and instead of enjoying life together, a couple feels bored. Frequently, the midlife marriage is at risk for an extramarital affair.

In addition, rather than lessening at midlife, marital conflicts may become more serious. Boredom and frustration lead to irritability. Both parties are less willing to apologize, admit they're wrong, or ask for forgiveness. Frequently, a husband or wife may conclude, "My spouse will never change; why bother trying?" Personal attacks may grow, and since the couple's lengthy mar-

110

LOOKING
BOTH
WAYS FROM
THE TOP
OF THE
MOUNTAIN

riage has made each keenly aware of the other's hot buttons and vulnerable points, the pain level increases exponentially.

By midlife a husband and wife may also have different goals. Early in most marriages, financial struggles, buying a home, raising children, and establishing careers typically have both partners pulling together at least to some degree. But as the children leave home and the nest empties, many wives head in a new career direction. A husband may also choose to change careers at midlife. Material values may differ, and "yours-mine" rather than "ours" becomes the approach. Tragically, while new goals can afford an opportunity for mutual encouragement and support, they can also drive a wedge into a marriage.

Another factor that can have a negative effect in a midlife marriage is spiritual dissonance. It is the opposite of spiritual harmony, in which a couple may not be at the same level spiritually but are both in step with the Lord and in agreement with each other on spiritual values. Sadly, it is not unusual at midlife for one partner to become spiritually motivated while the other resents the spouse's spiritual passion. Midlife can lead to either spiritual closeness or spiritual isolation.

What kind of steps can a husband and wife take to rejuvenate their marriage at midlife?

First, analyze and evaluate the situation. Do you still spend time talking to each other? Are you able to share feelings without anger escalating to the point of major conflict or withdrawal? Do you and your spouse feel supported, loved, and accepted in the marriage?

Second, do you listen and make an effort to understand each other? Or do you constantly interrupt each other? Have you learned to follow James' exhortation to be "swift to hear, slow to speak, slow to wrath" (James 1:19)? Are you following the biblical mandate to speak the truth in love (Eph. 4:15)? Have you been guilty of answering before listening (Prov. 18:13)? Have you forgotten that "a soft answer turns away wrath, but a harsh word stirs up anger" (Prov. 15:1)? Are you neglecting the truth that "a word fitly spoken is like apples of gold in settings of silver" (Prov. 25:11)?

Most important, are you still praying together? Do you attend church together regularly? Are you functioning as a team spiritually, vitally concerned about each other's walk with the Lord? Do you pray regularly for each other? Are you involved in ministry together? Are there areas in which you serve the Lord and people as a team?

These areas are vital because in many respects the spiritual relationship between a husband and wife is like the cornerstone of the foundation of a building. No other social relationship at midlife, or for that matter at any other time, can function effectively if you and your life partner are out of sorts spiritually. That's why Peter warned husbands and wives to relate to each other in a way "that your prayers may not be hindered" (1 Peter 3:7).

112

LOOKING
BOTH
WAYS FROM
THE TOP
OF THE
MOUNTAIN

The Immediate Family

For individuals at midlife the immediate family typically involves either teenagers or adult children. Relationships with such individuals can be difficult indeed. Frequently, the rebellion, frustrations, and struggles of teenagers hit us with frightening force, particularly when they coincide with our own midlife struggles and transitions.

Cheryl, whose visit with Pastor Matt we chronicled earlier in this chapter, had already begun to weather the relational storm of a teenage child. Her son, Jerry, in whom she and her late husband, Jack, had delighted, was no longer a delightful child. Almost overnight he had become a defiant, angry teenager, demanding increasingly more freedom and seldom listening to the advice Cheryl was quick to give him. "He never hears a word I say," she had told Pastor Matt in an earlier visit. "If he just understood the value of the lessons I've learned, many of them the hard way, I could help him avoid a lot of disasters. The other thing I don't understand is why he always chooses to have a crisis at the worst possible time for me."

The problem is life never seems to run on a convenient schedule. Teenagers can be sources of incredible personal pressure. Their problems strike us in the middle of our own transitions. Their emotional upheavals and unpredictable behavior cause us intense anxiety and fear. Their friends often frighten us. Their schedules leave us tempted to pull out our hair. And their choices cause us great inner turmoil. King Solomon wrote, "A wise son makes a glad father, but a foolish son is the grief of his mother" (Prov. 10:1).

In our own experience with teenagers—and for that matter young adults—certain things have proven helpful. First, parents need to practice authentic Christian character and integrity. Teenagers are absolute masters at detecting hypocrisy. Pastor Matt thought back to a recent conversation with Todd, an eighteen-year-old from the church youth group. "You wouldn't believe my dad, Pastor. He teaches Sunday school. You guys all think he's a wonderful Christian. At home all he does is yell at Mom and put me down. The only time he picks up his Bible is when he's getting ready to show off his knowledge to his Sunday school class."

As parents it is imperative that we demonstrate Christlike character, develop our own convictions, and learn how to communicate them firmly yet lovingly to teenagers and young adults. Furthermore, our ability to maintain self-control during times of crisis and demonstrate wholehearted trust in the Lord can provide a powerful example for teens and young adults who may not have the spiritual experience or maturity God has given us.

The Extended Family

Midlife can be a wonderful time of fellowship and growth with extended family members—or it can be a time of unbearable tension.

For years Robert and Millie traveled with Millie's sister Sarah and her husband, Jerry. The two couples went everywhere together—the beach, the mountains, concerts. They were best friends. Then one year, near the end of a particularly tiring trip, a conflict developed over money. Harsh words were spoken, anger allowed to fester. Before long the two couples had stopped speaking to each other. Each couple had only harsh words for the other; each couple felt the other to be at fault. A relationship that had been a strong, positive midlife asset had turned into a liability.

We'll talk more about forgiveness later in this chapter, but for now we'll just say that it is one of the most important factors in midlife relationships. The more we resolve the bitterness, hurt, and pain in our lives, the more effectively we are freed to relate to each other and serve each other in love.

In some ways dealing with anger and hurt in relationships is like removing snow from our Midwest driveways in winter. When several inches of snow fall, we've learned that the more quickly we shovel our drive and walkway, the less chance there is of the snow becoming packed. Conversely, once we allow the snow to become packed and turn into ice, we have no end of grief trying to remove it. So it is with the hurts and bitternesses of life.

114

Looking
Both
Ways from
the Top
of the
Mountain
🜚

The extended family also includes in-laws, who can be a source of support during midlife. The classic biblical example can be seen in the relationship between Ruth and Naomi. As our friend Dee Brestin pointed out recently on our *Confident Living* radio program, "Naomi was widowed in midlife, then she lost her two sons. Ruth shows us so much about how to reach out to a friend or relative who is going through high-tide grief. She never criticized Naomi. She never told her to get over her grief and move on, or to just count her blessings. She simply came alongside, stayed with Naomi, and helped her bear her pain. I don't think Naomi was particularly kind to Ruth, and that's often true today of people who've been hurt by the circumstances of life. Ruth didn't take things personally. She just kept on loving Naomi."

Midlife Changes and Their Effects on Relationships

A variety of issues can affect our relationships at midlife. We've already mentioned the loss of a spouse, changes within the marriage relationship, and conflicts within the immediate and extended family. Some of these changes are of major significance. Other changes, however, such as the impact of hearing loss on friendships, may not seem quite as consequential. All changes, however, affect our relationships in one way or another.

By the time he had reached his late fifties, Jason had worked for almost forty years as a railroad engineer. Always relatively shy, he was married to Susy, who never met a stranger. One of the great challenges for Jason, something he found it difficult to explain to Susy or anyone else, was that he had suffered a significant hearing loss and couldn't understand what people were saying. As a result, he felt extremely uncomfortable in any social setting in which he needed to carry on a conversation. He began to withdraw socially, much to Susy's frustration. After several years of struggling with this situation, he finally decided there was nothing wrong with getting a hearing aid. Susy, in turn, adjusted to his comfort level by not always pushing him to attend every social function.

Al and Mindy found themselves increasingly isolated from friends when they were forced to move to an extended-care facility because of Mindy's Alzheimer's. Al particularly felt the frustration, since he continued to function as well as he had before. He attempted to combat his isolation, however, by reaching out to his pastor and church family. He expressed the need for assistance with transportation so he and Mindy could attend their own church even though they now lived across town. Several church members responded, providing rotating transportation and significant encouragement.

Ralph and Martha, both in their late fifties, moved to a different part of the country after Ralph's job was eliminated. Rather than settling for a lower paying job in the town in which he and his wife had lived for thirty years, Ralph chose to take a position at a company in the Northwest. They quickly experienced isolation from their friends and family and initially found it difficult to connect with people in their new location. But as Martha put it, "We just decided we had to do something about making friends. Before we moved we'd heard our pastor talk about the principle from Proverbs 18:24 that those who want to have friends must show themselves friendly. It took a while, but now we have friends at church and in our neighborhood. I'm involved in a ladies' small group Bible study, my husband meets with a group of men for prayer before work on Thursday mornings, and we've had several couples over for dinner. We don't know their spiritual condition, but we hope we can build some relationships and maybe point them to the Lord."

Cultivating Friendships

Unlike Ralph and Martha, who took the initiative to make friends, far too many of us, while recognizing that friendships are a vital component of life, do little more than complain about a lack of friendships.

There are several reasons why people lack friends. For one thing, life near the end of the twentieth century is incredibly busy. We all have far too many "important" things to do to take the time necessary to cultivate relationships or reach out to others. Furthermore, many of us are far more interested in ourselves than we are in others. Many of us have been deeply hurt, either recently or perhaps years ago, and as a result, we are reluctant to share our inner thoughts and feelings. The breakdown of basic societal restraints, the growing number of divorces, and modern patterns of moving and relocation all tend to hinder relationships. Fear of rejection is another factor, as is materialism. And the list could go on and on.

116

LOOKING
BOTH
WAYS FROM
THE TOP
OF THE
MOUNTAIN
☙

However, despite the contemporary factors that work against the cultivation of friendships, Scripture makes it clear that we are to love one another. Establishing close, healthy relationships is a vital component of successfully navigating through life. One of the best places to learn about cultivating relationships is in the Book of Proverbs.

While Solomon didn't always succeed in his own relationships, under the inspiration of the Spirit of God he provided a number of significant principles that can help us develop healthy relationships today. First, consistent, ongoing, unconditional love is the foundation for friendship. Proverbs 17:17 reads, "A friend loves at all times." In good times and bad, friends practice loyalty. Solomon also warned, "Do not forsake your own friend or your father's friend" (Prov. 27:10). Frequently, our relationships are fickle and shaky during hard times. What we need is the kind of loyal friendship Solomon's father, David, experienced with Jonathan. Over and over, as King Saul attempted to snuff out David's life, Jonathan maintained his loyalty, spoke up for his friend, and affirmed his commitment to God's ultimate plan for David to become king (1 Sam. 23:16–18).

Second, friends must take the initiative to cultivate relationships. Proverbs 18:24 reads, "A man who has friends must himself be friendly, but there is a friend who sticks closer than a brother." Some people are willing to maintain a friendship as long as the other person does most of the maintaining. However, Scripture underscores the value of our taking responsibility for the relationship. In the best friendships, both parties take responsibility and the friendship succeeds.

A third important ingredient for friendship is personal integrity. According to Proverbs 22:11, "He who loves purity of heart and has grace on his lips, the king will be his friend."

Open, honest communication is another important value in friendship. Proverbs 27:6 points out that "faithful are the wounds of a friend, but the kisses of an enemy are deceitful." A good friend isn't someone who always tells you what you want to hear; a good friend tells you the truth.

Furthermore, a good friend is one with whom you have an enjoyable relationship. There's a chemistry present that makes the relationship click. As Solomon explained in Proverbs 27:9, "Ointment and perfume delight the heart, and the sweetness of a man's friend does so by hearty counsel."

Good friends also contribute significantly to our personal growth and spiritual development. "As iron sharpens iron, so a man sharpens the countenance of his friend" (Prov. 27:17).

Finally, friends know when to give their friends sufficient space. Solomon put it this way: "He who blesses his friend with a loud voice, rising early in the morning, it will be counted a curse to him" (Prov. 27:14).

Five Keys to Healthy Relationships

Since any contact between two or more people leads to interpersonal relationships, we could write an entire book on this subject. We've chosen, however, to identify five key factors that can guide all of our relationships at midlife and beyond.

The Compassion Factor

The first key is the compassion factor. This is the ultimate factor, the one that can make the most difference in terms of relationships. Ironically, the term *compassion* is found only twelve times in the New Testament. Nine are located in the first two Gospels and are used exclusively of the Lord Jesus, while three are used of other individuals in parables recorded by Matthew and Luke.

The word *compassion* comes from the word *splagkna,* which referred to the inner parts of a sacrifice, such as the heart, liver, lungs, or kidney. Those parts were separated from the sacrificial animal, which was burned, and were often consumed at a sacrificial meal. Eventually the term came to be used in much the same way we speak of a person as having "heart." With the exception of the Good Samaritan in Luke 10, the father of the prodigal in Luke 15, and the forgiving master in Matthew 18, the term was always used to describe Jesus' compassionate approach to people. There's a great deal for us to learn about relationships from observing the way he genuinely cared.

118

LOOKING
BOTH
WAYS FROM
THE TOP
OF THE
MOUNTAIN
🍃

Matthew initially used the term to describe Jesus' response to a multitude of people he perceived as "weary and scattered like sheep having no shepherd" (Matt. 9:36). He responded in similar fashion shortly after the beheading of John the Baptist (Matt. 14:14) and still later near the Sea of Galilee when he pointed out to his disciples that the crowds did not have enough energy to go home without fainting along the way (Matt. 15:32). In response to their need, the Lord took seven loaves and a few fish and multiplied them to feed four thousand men plus women and children (compare Mark 8:1–9).

Luke's Gospel records how Jesus responded with compassion to a widow who had lost her only son, then restored the young man to life (Luke 7:11–15). Following his transfiguration, Jesus talked with the father of a young, demon-possessed man after the disciples had unsuccessfully attempted to cast out the demon (Mark 9:19). After describing his son's self-destructive, demonically induced actions, the father pleaded, "If you can do anything, have compassion on us and help us" (Mark 19:22). In response, Jesus immediately rebuked the evil spirit, charging him to come out and never enter the young man again.

The final incident in which the word was used of Jesus occurred on the road between Jericho and Jerusalem where two blind men cried out, "Have mercy on us, O Lord, Son of David" (Matt. 20:30–34). In this incident as in each of the others, Jesus became aware of a need and was moved to genuinely care. That in turn led to his taking action to selflessly meet the need. In each instance he was willing to be interrupted and he demonstrated more concern for the interests of those on whom he had compassion than for his own interests. In fact, despite his frustration over the faithlessness of an entire generation, as demonstrated by his disciples (Mark 9:19), he cared enough for the young demon-possessed man and his father to meet not only their physical and emotional need, but their ultimate spiritual need as well.

When you consider the Good Samaritan, the father of the prodigal, and the nobleman's son, the pattern for compassion becomes clear. First, since Christ came and died to meet our greatest need, laying down his life for us, we are to lay down our lives for others. In order to do this, we must learn how by studying the pattern Jesus established as he demonstrated compassion throughout his life. Furthermore, we must commit ourselves to follow his example. This includes allowing ourselves to be touched with feeling by the hurts and needs of others; permitting our schedules to be interrupted; refusing to allow ourselves to remain insulated from people, focused on our own agenda, or impervious to the pain of those around us. In short, we must become willing to reach out and touch others at their point of need in order to communicate to them that we truly care.

The Encouragement Factor

Growing out of this factor is a second, called encouragement. The term as used in the New Testament literally means "called alongside to help." It was often used in the first century in connection with a lawyer who was called in to stand alongside the accused and provide aid and defense.

Perhaps the classic role model of encouragement in the New Testament is the Holy Spirit, of whom Jesus said, "He will teach you all things, remind you of what I have said, testify about Me, convince the world of sin, righteousness and judgment, guide you into all truth, and tell you what is yet to come."[5] In its broadest sense the word for encouragement described anyone who reached out to help, encourage, or comfort someone else. Ironically, in describing the Holy Spirit as "another" comforter, Jesus used a word that meant another of the same kind. Thus, he underscored the continuity between his own compassionate ministry of encouragement and that of the Holy Spirit.

How does the Holy Spirit model encouragement for us today? The Lord promised he would dwell within us and abide with us forever. We can encourage by demonstrating loyalty, staying with those we encourage, and maintaining contact with them. The Holy Spirit teaches us the truths of Jesus, reminding us of principles we need to apply. We too have the opportunity to communicate God's encouraging and enlightening truths to others, urging people to apply these truths to their own experience. Furthermore, the Spirit's primary focus is his testimony regarding Christ. We encourage most effectively when we point others toward the Savior. Also, since the Spirit's ministry is to guide believers into all truth, we too have the privilege of encouraging others by applying God's truth to their lives to foster spiritual growth.

120

LOOKING
BOTH
WAYS FROM
THE TOP
OF THE
MOUNTAIN
🌿

Ironically, when we break the English word *encouragement* down into its components, removing the prefix "en" and the suffix "ment," we discover that the core is *courage*. Fear was the first negative emotion in Scripture (Gen. 3:10) and fear lies at the heart of virtually every other harmful emotion. The process of encouragement, therefore, can help counter the fear of those around us.

So how can we become effective encouragers? The first step involves following the pattern of others who have become skilled encouragers. I have often enjoyed pointing others to people I call "world-class encouragers." In Scripture, one example is Jonathan, the son of Saul. Reaching out to young David, he took the initiative in establishing a covenant and gave David his robe, sword, bow, and belt—an incredibly high honor and one that must have lifted the spirits of this exhausted young man after his battle with Goliath (1 Sam. 18:1, 4). Later he risked his own life to warn David of the danger of his father, spoke positively about his friend to his father the king, and even lovingly confronted Saul, reminding him it would be a sin to persecute David since David had never sinned against the king. Surely David must have been encouraged by such loyalty. As Saul continued to pursue David, Jonathan maintained his loyalty, reaffirmed his love for David, risked his own life when he spoke in David's defense (1 Sam. 20:32–33), then verbalized his love and loyal commitment to David during their final meeting (vv. 41–42).

Other encouragers in Scripture who should be studied and emulated include Nathan, who lovingly confronted King David when he had sinned, then continued to support the king and his family; and Ebed-Melech, the "Old Testament Good Samaritan." Hearing of Jeremiah's plight, Ebed-Melech secured permission from the king to take a band of soldiers to rescue the prophet from the pit, thereby saving his life (Jer. 38:1–13).

In the New Testament, Barnabas's name surfaces throughout the Book of Acts as a classic example of a man whose life was permeated with encouragement, and Paul reminded Timothy of the frequent refreshment, significant compassion, and diligent efforts of Onesiphorus, who perhaps encouraged the apostle more than anyone else in his life (2 Tim. 1:16–18).

The Forgiveness Factor

A third essential factor in successful relationships is forgiveness.

All of us have suffered hurts, some relatively minor such as a slight at a party. Others, such as the betrayal of an unfaithful spouse or the slander of a gossiping friend, can cause incredible, devastating pain. When it comes to these hurts, each of us faces an ongoing choice, one with grave consequences for all our relationships. We may choose to allow the poison of bitterness to influence our hearts, minds, and relationships, or we can choose to forgive.

In his excellent book *I Should Forgive, But . . .* , Dr. Charles Lynch identifies a number of typical arguments we give when resisting the biblical mandate to forgive.[6] These include: "I'm not angry"; "I can't forget what was done to me"; "Somebody has to pay"; "Nobody understands what I've been through"; "He won't even acknowledge what he did to me"; "I'm not the forgiving kind"; "They'll only do it again"; or "I can't let go." As Dr. Lynch points out, each of these excuses must be recognized as a form of self-deception, a sinful response. Bitterness can paralyze us emotionally, poison our relationships, and push us away from the Lord.

The apostle Paul had experienced a number of hurts in his life. As he neared the end of his life, locked away in a prison in Rome, he wrote to Timothy, urging the young man he had mentored to "come before winter" (2 Tim. 4:9, 21). In the process, he explained to Timothy how he had been deeply wronged by a man named Alexander, a coppersmith who "did me much harm" and "greatly resisted our words" (vv. 14–15). Warning Timothy to beware of this harmful individual, Paul nonetheless held no grudge and refused to become bitter. Instead he turned vengeance over to God, stating, "May the Lord repay him according to his works" (v. 14). It would have been easy for Paul to harbor bitterness over the harm he had suffered at the hand of Alexander or even from the defections of Demas, Crescens, and Titus (v. 10). However, not only did Paul refuse to become bitter over these, he even reached out to Mark, a man whose ministry he formerly rejected, urging Timothy to "bring him with you, for he is useful to me for ministry" (v. 11). Clearly Paul had learned the value of forgiveness.

122

LOOKING
BOTH
WAYS FROM
THE TOP
OF THE
MOUNTAIN
❦

Throughout his ministry the apostle urged believers to put aside bitterness and all other manifestations of selfish anger and become "kind to one another, tenderhearted, forgiving one another, just as God in Christ also forgave you" (Eph. 4:31–32). The implication of Paul's words is clear: Forgiveness is a spiritual issue. We may not be able to "forgive and forget," but God's mandate is for us to *choose* to forget. Furthermore, bitterness and other forms of "the wrath of man" produce all kinds of harm. Resentment, bitterness, and anger are all toxic to our spiritual and emotional well-being.

Finally, no matter how deeply I've been wronged, no matter how seemingly impossible it is to forgive, the fact that Christ has forgiven me for every sin makes it possible for me always to forgive, no matter what. Paul's standard of excellence in forgiveness is clear: "Just as God in Christ forgave you."

The Service Factor

But simply forgiving those who've wronged us is not sufficient. Jesus issued a radical challenge to his listeners to "love your enemies, bless those who curse you, do good to those who hate you, and pray for those who spitefully use you and persecute you" (Matt. 5:44). Paul echoed the challenge, writing, "Beloved, do not avenge yourselves, but rather give place to wrath. . . . Therefore if your enemy hungers, feed him; if he thirsts, give him a drink; for in so doing you will heap coals of fire on his head" (Rom. 12:19–20).

In this era of self focus, a time characterized by looking out for number one, we need to heed Paul's admonition: "Through love serve one another" (Gal. 5:13). We are to demonstrate love for our neighbors by willingly serving them. We are to follow the example of Jesus, who served his selfish followers in the upper room when he washed their feet.

It's easy for Christians to talk about serving others. But what does true service look like? The author of Hebrews, writing to people under intense persecution, used several words to describe authentic service. First, it was difficult. The author didn't use the normal word for service or work when he wrote, "For God is not unjust to forget your work and labor of love which you have shown toward His name, in that you have ministered to the saints, and do minister" (6:10). Instead, he used a word that indicated hard, difficult toil, the kind that isn't necessarily pleasant or enjoyable.

My (Don's) friend Seth provides an example of service. For years he directed a Christian camp. Sometimes his duties involved standing on the platform teaching; at other times he found himself unstopping a plugged toilet or cleaning dirty dishes in a kitchen. Whatever the case, no matter the degree of difficulty, Seth was willing to work hard.

Second, service is motivated by love. True service is a labor in which love and work are inextricably linked together. The link reminds us that love is not simply a sentiment or emotion. It involves a choice or decision that expresses itself in action.

Third, a work of service is "shown toward His name" (Heb. 6:10). In other words, it glorifies God. Lucille was a cantankerous older lady who had little use for God or people. Her husband's death and a series of other adversities had left her bitter. One day following a severe storm the youth group from her church showed up to help her. Someone nailed down the shingles damaged by the storm. Others picked up broken limbs and other debris. Lucille couldn't believe these teenagers actually cared enough about her to help in these ways. Her comment, "Maybe God's not so bad after all if this is how some of the people who follow him act," was a tribute to the God toward whom she had become bitter.

Finally, true service to the Lord and his people is ongoing. It's not a one-shot thing. As the author of Hebrews pointed out, "You have ministered to the saints, and do minister" (Heb. 6:10). A fairly young Christian once observed, "I can't wait until I get older when I don't have to serve others. Then they can start to serve me." The fact is we never reach such a point in our Christian living. We should never outgrow service to others.

The Mentoring Factor

One final factor is worthy of note. A person's life should involve mentoring relationships. As Donna Otto pointed out on one of our *Confident Living* broadcasts, the word *mentoring* is not in the Bible, but Scripture is loaded with examples of the process. Jethro mentored Moses, who in turn mentored Joshua. Elijah mentored Elisha. Jesus certainly mentored his twelve disciples, and Paul mentored Timothy, Titus, and other young men. Paul instructed the older women to mentor the younger women in matters of faith and practice (Titus 2:3–5).

The process of mentoring today works in much the same fashion as Jesus mentored the twelve. He described the process in John 17, pointing out that he set an example for them, presented the words of the gospel to them, prayed for them, encouraged them in the Father's name, taught them biblical truth, then sent them forth to mentor others.[7] A mentor provides spiritual direction, encouragement, and teaching. In fact, the essence of mentoring is life-changing learning in the context of relationship. It's older to younger, and it's incredibly valuable.

Shortly after his fiftieth birthday veteran pastor Ray Ortlund shared wise advice to several of his fellow church members who had passed the half century mark. "Don't huddle around with people your own age all the time," he suggested. "Pour your knowledge into people 20 or 30 years younger than you, and when you're gone, everything you've taught them will be walking around the earth for another 20 or 30 years teaching others. Extend your life."[8]

By becoming involved in the mentoring process, you will help ensure healthy relationships and interactions at midlife and leave a legacy that will outlast you.

124

LOOKING
BOTH
WAYS FROM
THE TOP
OF THE
MOUNTAIN
❦

Part Two

SLOWING

DOWN

without

FALLING

OFF

ChapterSeven

Preparing Your Finances for the Future

DEALING WITH THE THORNY FINANCIAL ISSUES that come with growing older can be threatening. Because few of our parents truly understand financial matters, they tend to put off dealing with them, often until it's too late. But with the competent help available today, there's no need to make that mistake.

As our parents grow older, their income may become fixed or even decline. These days many breadwinners find themselves forced into early retirement because of corporate downsizing or other workplace changes. Others find themselves forced into a quick adjustment from being a two-income family to a single-income family due to a loss of a job or the death of a spouse, or even a fixed-income family due to retirement.

Often our parents refuse to adjust their standard of living. They may insist on continuing in a lifestyle that is beyond their means. They may make unwise decisions about finances, purchasing an expensive car or house or taking that dream vacation. Add to this situation the onset of skyrocketing medical bills, stir in a generous dose of fear of destitution—many of our parents survived the Great Depression—and we are left with a serious financial dilemma.

When Diane Cevolani's dad, a retired shipfitter and widower, was diagnosed with lung cancer, his slow decline to death took him from middle-class status to welfare applicant almost overnight.[1] According to Cevolani, her sister and brother-in-law began providing care in their nearby home. Nurses' aides were hired to take up the slack. Then with costs and stress escalating, the family made the difficult decision to put their father in a nursing home. "We went through $12,000 in the blink of an eye," Cevolani explained. "Before long we had exhausted his entire $18,000 life savings. Then we applied for Medi-Cal for Dad."[2]

Countless families can tell similar stories. For some, the issues are relatively minor. Perhaps a mother needs more help cleaning or cooking. But often minor needs escalate into major issues, even incapacitation. A family may be faced with the sudden, shocking blow of a stroke, heart attack, or cancer. How do you prepare for this eventuality? How does the family or caregiver handle the financial pressures that come as loved ones grow older?

Whether you are an older adult or a caregiver, dealing with financial issues is something that needs to start now—right now. Everything we have from God is a gift, and often those who are good stewards throughout life are poor stewards at life's end. In the pages that follow, we address some of the financial issues you need to consider, whether you are growing older yourself or are a caregiver of someone who is growing older.

Preparing for Tomorrow, Today

Even if you haven't reached the point in your life at which you must answer the question "Do I stay put or move into a health-care facility?" there are still financial issues you need to address. You should discuss the following issues with your family, and maybe your pastor as well, as these issues touch eternity.

Let's think about the financial decisions that will not only prepare you for your older years but will also help you achieve the goal of being a steward of God.

Estate Planning

Everybody seems to be talking about estate planning these days, but what exactly is it? One common definition is, "The creation, conservation and utilization of estate resources, to secure the maximum benefit now, during disability, and at retirement" and "the best way to transfer the estate to family members, charitable organizations and others during life and death, with minimum shrinkage caused by taxes and probate."[3]

There is no reason to avoid estate planning. It doesn't mean you are going to die (you are, but not because you make plans). It means that when you die, and during all the years you live between now and then, you will know that the resources God has given you (Eccl. 5:18–20) will be used to maximize the quality of your life and make a difference after you're gone.

Here's how to do it. Begin by establishing the priorities of your estate planning. What do you want to accomplish? What are your immediate and long-range goals? Perhaps you want to provide enough money for your own assisted living, or maybe you want to fund the education of your grandchildren. You will certainly want to include giving to the Lord's work. You may wish to provide a down payment for your children's first house. Obviously you will want to be prepared to pay your funeral and burial expenses. Once you've done that, become as familiar as possible with all the estate planning tools at your disposal. There are many, and this likely will require the assistance of a qualified estate planner. You can learn more about planning from investment houses such as Merrill Lynch, financial services specialists such as American Express, or you can contact your insurance agent, bank trust department, or a well-established nonprofit ministry that has a stewardship and estate planning department. A helpful book on the subject is *Protect Your Estate: A Personal Guide to Intelligent Estate Planning* by Robert A. Esperti and Renno L. Peterson (New York: McGraw-Hill, 1993). Next, gather the data you will need in making your estate plan. Include all your assets (residence, personal property, cash, checking and savings accounts, investments, death benefit of life insurance, qualified retirement plans, and so on). Most nonprofit organizations have an inventory list, such as Back to the Bible's "Stewardship Solutions," that will assist you in gathering this data.

129

PREPARING
YOUR
FINANCES
FOR THE
FUTURE

Finally, seek out the counsel of a competent, godly person who can render technical assistance to you in drafting legal documents. Often estate planners are not attorneys, and while they are qualified to advise you on your plan, they will refer you to an attorney to do the legal work in formulating your plan.

What tools are available for your estate planning? Here are three of the more popular tools people use to plan their estate as well as plan for charitable giving.

The will. This is the place to start, but it may not be the place to end. Every Christian should have a will. Many believers are good stewards in life but poor stewards in death. A will provides an opportunity for you to give a final testimony of your faith in Christ. It authorizes payment of all your debts and disposes of your personal property according to your desires. In your will you can contribute the remainder of your estate to your individual and charitable beneficiaries, and you can nominate the person or persons you wish to have guardianship of minor children. You can do more than draft a will, but you should never do less.

Life estate agreement. A life estate agreement enables you to transfer real estate to another individual while retaining the right to use the property for a period of years or for life. Such agreements can be revocable (changeable) or irrevocable (not changeable). This agreement enables you to establish two separate interests: a life estate interest, which is the value of your use of the property, such as your home, for the rest of your life even though you have donated it to a ministry, and a remainder interest, which reflects the value of future contributions to the ministry to which you have given your home. The life estate gives you full use of your property during your life. This includes the right to live in the property or rent and receive the proceeds of the rental. This is an excellent way to transfer property to a family member, other individual, or charitable organization while still being able to live there during your life. While the life estate agreement does not eliminate inheritance tax per se, it does remove the home or real estate from the probate process, thereby eliminating significant expense and delays.

Charitable remainder trust. A charitable remainder trust, so named because it leaves the remainder value to charity upon the survivor's death, can be established during your lifetime or through your estate plan at death. When you make a lifetime transfer, meaning you transfer money, stocks, real estate, or other assets during your lifetime rather than through a will or at death, you receive an income tax charitable deduction. You also avoid capital gains tax on appreciated property, and the property is distributed outside the probate process. This vehicle is a wonderful way to achieve income, estate, and gift tax advantages.

The revocable living trust. Over the past ten years, revocable living trusts have been a popular tool in estate planning. If your estate is complicated, for example, if you own real estate or property in more than one state or hold certain types of assets such as a closely held business, or if the estate has reached a significantly high value, an amount that can vary from year to year but which at the time of this writing is approximately $650,000, it may be wise to investigate the benefits of a revocable living trust. The administration of a living trust is more private than that of a will but also more complicated. Nevertheless, it may enable your estate to avoid unnecessary probate expense when transferring assets to your beneficiaries. Your attorney or financial planner can help you determine if this is the right tool for you.

131

PREPARING
YOUR
FINANCES
FOR THE
FUTURE

These descriptions are brief because you really need the help of a trained professional to plan for your future. More details will be given in chapter 9. When seeking that professional, always secure the services of someone who is both competent in estate planning and will reflect your eternal values. Whatever you do, remember the worst thing you can do is nothing. Chart your own course. Be a steward of your own income and assets. Make sure your family and your favorite charities are cared for in your estate plans.

Perform a Family Financial Physical

Shortly after my (Wood's) father was diagnosed with Alzheimer's, I received a call from my mother. Since my dad had always handled the family finances but now was too confused to do so, Mother had to take over. She was certainly capable, but rusty. She wasn't certain where all their insurance policies were. My father had been dealing with more than one bank, and she didn't know which bank contained their savings, their checking account, and their certificates of deposit. My father's financial record keeping was, well, not professional. My mother needed some reassurance and some help.

My wife and I took a week of vacation and went to my parents' home. We were there for a visit, and we had a good one. We were also there to try to make some sense of their finances. It was time to perform a family financial physical. My brother and sister had already done some of the preliminary work, and they had left behind a written list of what they had discovered. It kept us from plowing the same ground.

My father had a safe that he never locked. It wouldn't have mattered if he had because he had written the combination to the safe on the wall above it. However, he was very protective of that safe. It was his domain. We got permission, however, to take a peak inside to see if we could locate an insurance policy no one seemed to be able to find. Opening the door of that safe was like opening Pandora's box.

The safe was full, but our search was fruitless. My dad has saved lots of things, but all the wrong things. He had his income tax records back to 1944. We found canceled checks in there predating that. Many things were saved that were useless, and those things we needed had not been saved.

We looked at the checkbook and determined what insurance companies he had written checks to in the last year. A call to the local agent netted us a new copy of the policy, even though having a copy of the policy on site was not necessary. A look at the bank statements from years gone by helped us to assess which banks he had been dealing with. My father always thought he was about to run out of money; he had little cash in his pocket. But we discovered a savings account of several thousand dollars that he had forgotten about and my mother never knew about.

You may be facing a similar situation. Perhaps you are a widow or widower and are staring at a confusing financial history yourself. You've never had to deal with the family finances; that's something your husband or wife always did. Or maybe you're a caregiver, just beginning to take care of your mother or father or both, and you're trying to make some sense out of their bookkeeping system. Don't despair. By asking the right questions and finding out who has the answers to those questions you can make an accurate analysis of a financial situation.

Whether you are taking the lead in performing a family financial physical or are just helping others in your family, do not be secretive. It is important that you inform your siblings regarding what you are doing. Send them copies of everything. It's too easy to become suspicious of the motives of our brothers or sisters. This will only cause hardship and hard feelings. Besides, distance often makes it difficult for family members to come together to discuss either the existing financial situation or a plan of action. Share with your siblings what you learn.

It is a good idea for each family member to have a copy of the following:

133

PREPARING
YOUR
FINANCES
FOR THE
FUTURE
❦

- life insurance policy numbers, amounts, types, maturity dates, current payment schedule, and so on
- other insurance policy information such as home, fire, flood, theft, auto, or long-term insurance
- a list of any "hidden" insurance policies such as the ones a travel agent may have on the purchaser of an airline ticket
- a list of any checking and savings accounts with numbers and bank branches (It is also helpful to have the name of a contact person at the bank if available.)
- a list of any other financial accounts or vehicles such as IRAs, CDs, stocks, and bonds, and the value of each
- a list of any valuables kept in the home or in a safe-deposit box
- a sealed copy of a living will or desired funeral arrangements

Keeping the family informed is an important element in keeping the family together when the tough decisions of life have to be made.

The Enigma of Health Insurance

Someone described life insurance as the company betting you won't die and you betting you will. Some Christians see owning a life insurance policy as evidence of not trusting the Lord. Most, however, see such insurance as good stewardship of resources. After all, "It is appointed for men to die once" (Heb. 9:27).

Unless the Lord returns and interrupts the normal course of life, we'll eventually win that bet with the insurance company.

We are not so much concerned here with the various forms of life insurance available to us as we are with those insurance vehicles that are directly pertinent to aging adults. If you want to know more about whole life, term insurance, and so on, call your agent and do a review of your own insurance needs. It's a good idea to have family members present if they are available. Often adults have acquired enough insurance throughout their lives that more is not needed as we grow older.

Medicare

Medicare is a health insurance program administered by the federal government. It is not available to everyone. To be eligible you must be sixty-five or older, or you must have been declared disabled for two or more years or have permanent kidney failure. Medicare health insurance is divided into two basic parts. One relates to hospital insurance (when you stay in the hospital), and the other relates to outpatient medical insurance (when you do not stay in the hospital).

Part A. Most people qualify for Part A of Medicare, the premium-free coverage that is paid through the social security system. The amount you and your employer pay into social security funds Part A. Those who do not automatically qualify for premium-free coverage can purchase Part A coverage, but the premium is overinflated.

Medicare Part A takes care of hospital allowable charges, psychiatric hospital inpatient care, nursing home stay (only Medicare approved skilled care), hospice, and some home health care. Part A will cover all allowable hospital charges except for a deductible (currently $652).

If you have a Medicare supplemental policy, it will most likely cover the Part A deductible. Since the deductible is based on the number of hospitalizations and intervals between hospitalizations, you may have to pay the deductible more than once during a calendar year.

Part B. Part B is the nonhospital stay part of your Medicare insurance. Part B pays 80 percent of all eligible outpatient and doctor charges and has an annual one-hundred-dollar deductible.

If you qualify for social security benefits, Part A is provided automatically. Part B, however, is optional. But there is a catch. If you choose not to receive Part B Medicare coverage, you must notify Medicare of your decision to refuse Part B. If you do not, you will pay a monthly charge for this coverage, currently $31.80 per month. "But," you say, "I have never been billed for Medicare Part B." That's true. This amount is being automatically subtracted from your social security check.

Here are some terms related to Medicare that may need some explanation.

Allowable charges are charges for hospital, medical, or medical supply devices that Medicare declares reasonable. These charges are made for medical services rendered to you. When actual charges exceed what Medicare deems allowable, the difference between the actual charges and allowable charges is considered the excess charge and must be paid apart from Medicare.

Accepting assignment is a key concept in the way Medicare works and whether you will be responsible for some charges after receiving medical treatment. A medical professional or provider who "accepts assignment" agrees to accept the allowable Medicare amount as payment for the medical service he or she rendered to you. The insured person—that's you—must pay the one-hundred-dollar annual deductible, plus 20 percent of the difference between what Medicare allowed and the actual amount charged.

If it seems to you Medicare doesn't go far enough, you are not alone. Many seniors share those sentiments. Medicare was intended to provide only a basic health insurance for those enrolled. The key word is *basic*. For this reason, many people have chosen to add some form of supplemental insurance to their basic coverage under Medicare.

Medigap Insurance

It is not necessary that you carry any insurance in addition to Medicare, but many experts feel it is a good investment. Policies known as Medigap or Medicare supplements may be purchased as private policies. If you hold such a policy, the insurer will pay the difference between what you are charged for medical care and what Medicare will pay.

135

PREPARING
YOUR
FINANCES
FOR THE
FUTURE

You can apply for any one of the approved federal plans for Medigap insurance. The insurer must accept your application for coverage regardless of your health status if you apply for the coverage within six months of acceptance under Medicare Part B. All insurers must write a Plan A and may decide which of the additional plans (B–J) they wish to offer. Each year the federal government publishes several Medicare/Medigap guides and informative booklets. Call the Medicare Hotline at 1-800-638-6833 to receive information. Or you may write to Consumer Information Center, Dept. 59, Pueblo, CO 81009 and ask to receive information about Medicare and Medigap insurance.

Long-Term Care Insurance

For many people one of the important questions to consider is whether to purchase long-term care insurance. It has become painfully obvious that one of the most significant issues facing an aging population is financing the cost of long-term health care. Recent studies estimate that 43 percent of people age sixty-five will enter a nursing home at some time. Half of those who enter a nursing facility will likely stay at least a year. Yet remarkably, according to one survey, 76 percent of the respondents said they did not expect to need long-term care in the future.[4]

Given the increasing lifespan and the growing elderly population, many families are likely to face a financial crisis of staggering proportions. Since a year's stay in a nursing home can cost between fifty thousand and sixty thousand dollars and the average length of stay is three years, many middle-income families could see their life's savings wiped out. Medicare covers only short-term rehabilitative care, and Medicaid, the last resort for those who become impoverished, appears to be in danger of collapsing under escalating demand. Some states even limit the number of Medicaid patients they will accept.

Basically, long-term care insurance policies are a trade-off: You pay the premiums so that the insurance company will pay the bills. Such an arrangement can be a good thing or a waste of money, depending on many variables. Who is eligible? Not everyone. If you have certain preexisting conditions or disabilities such as diabetes, which requires daily insulin, dementia, Alzheimer's, multiple sclerosis, Parkinson's, multiple TIAs (a transient ischemic attack, or mini-stroke), muscular dystrophy,

AIDS or related conditions, cirrhosis of the liver, or congestive heart failure, you are automatically ineligible. If you have had angioplasty or open heart surgery, use a walker or are in a wheelchair on a consistent basis, or need regular dialysis, you often are not eligible. In other words, to qualify for long-term care insurance, you have to be in reasonably good health. By the time most people get around to thinking about such policies, those who need them are no longer eligible.

Then there's the cost factor. For many, the cost of such long-term care insurance is prohibitive, especially if you do not subscribe to the policy until you are retired. For example, the premiums for a good policy of this type for a person in his mid-fifties may cost twelve hundred dollars annually. If you wait until age eighty to subscribe, the premiums for the same coverage may be twelve thousand dollars annually.

Long-term care insurance is best explained by someone who specializes in this complex product. Talk to an insurance broker you trust, and ask him to give you all the facts. When deciding whether to purchase such a policy, consider the following:

137

PREPARING
YOUR
FINANCES
FOR THE
FUTURE
❦

- benefit eligibility requirements (for example, is medical necessity a factor)
- coverage for mental or nervous disorders
- coverage for custodial care (the most common kind received by nursing home or retirement facility patients)
- home and community care (does the policy cover individuals who prefer to draw upon the wide range of home care services available rather than entering a nursing facility)
- cost and value
- deductibles
- the renewability of the policy

Your needs may be different from another person's needs; no single plan is best for everyone. Get the facts before you make a decision.

Division of Resources

Today, with the potential that the cost of long-term health care could dry up a family's life savings in a hurry, and with many older adults unaware of or unable to afford long-term care insurance, some alternative provisions had to be made. One such provision is the spousal impoverishment program, which is designed to keep one spouse from becoming destitute if the cost of health care destitutes the other.

What happens if your husband is diagnosed with Alzheimer's? Suppose you do not have long-term insurance and his condition worsens to the point at which he must be placed in a dementia care unit. Will paying for his care cause you to become financially destitute so that no money will be left to assist you should you need care? That need not be the case under the division of resources program. That's what Charlie and Mary found out.

Charlie and Mary had been married for fifty-eight years and had been relatively healthy during those years. At age eighty-one, however, Charlie was diagnosed with Alzheimer's. By age eighty-four, Charlie needed more care than Mary could handle. Her only recourse was to find a nursing home for Charlie. But how could she afford it? Here's how.

As of January 1, 1998, the law provides that Mary can divide their total family resources in half. This means half of everything they have is assigned to Charlie and half is assigned to her. Mary's assets, therefore, will be protected if Charlie's care requires the expenditure of the other half. A minimum of $16,152 and a maximum of one-half of Mary's countable assets up to $80,760 can be reserved by her. As the spouse not receiving treatment, Mary is considered "the community spouse." Income received in Mary's name (the community spouse) can be kept for use by her. If the community spouse is paying rent or making a mortgage payment, the minimum may be increased by $1,356 according to a set formula.

The Medicaid program will cover the health costs of Charlie's care only when his half of their assets is almost gone. Charlie would then be considered destitute. In order to qualify Charlie for Medicaid, Mary had to list all their assets owned jointly or separately and set a fair market value for each asset. Mary contacted her attorney to assist her in making this list. Often attorneys already have forms prepared to help you with this process.

Mary had to list *all* their assets, even though only some of them would be countable for the total. If your countable assets are below $20,152, your spouse is automatically eligible for Medicaid. If your countable assets are in excess of the maximum allowed to you as a couple, there are many options for reducing the total. You can purchase needed items, establish burial trusts, pay off your home mortgage, purchase a new car, or repair the family home. Again, your attorney or trusted financial professional can assist you in properly reducing your assets.

Under certain circumstances, there may be a waiting period before your spouse becomes eligible for Medicaid. For example, if you transfer some of your assets for less than the fair market value, or if you give away some of your assets to family or others, you may have to wait for your spouse to become eligible for Medicaid. Most transfers or gifts made during the thirty-six months prior to admitting your spouse to a care facility could make him or her ineligible for Medicaid. The ineligibility period is determined based on the date of the gift, the value of the asset, and the monthly cost of care in the facility at the private pay rate. The reason for transferring or giving away assets of the person receiving Medicaid benefits is also considered when determining whether the action was in violation of the Medicaid rules.

139

PREPARING
YOUR
FINANCES
FOR THE
FUTURE

When the cost of Charlie's care at the nursing home had depleted his half of their assets to four thousand dollars, Mary helped Charlie apply for Medicaid. At that point Mary's name was removed from any assets owned by Charlie. Her name could remain on Charlie's assets as attorney-in-fact, guardian, or conservator, but not as owner. Charlie's assets could also be made payable to Mary at Charlie's death to avoid probate. Only those assets in Charlie's name can legally be used for the payment of his medical expenses and to determine eligibility for Medicaid.

As mentioned earlier, not all assets Charlie and Mary listed were considered "countable assets" when determining Charlie's eligibility for Medicaid. Some were considered exempt assets. One such asset was their irrevocable burial trust. Both Charlie and Mary had each deposited three thousand dollars into an irrevocable burial trust, established to provide a burial plot, stone, casket, and vault for each of them. The trust and the interest accrued by it were not used in determining Medicaid eligibility.

Another of their assets not counted was their automobile. The law provides that one car, regardless of its value, will be exempted from determining eligibility. Some older couples purchase an expensive car as a way of legally reducing their assets, but there are downsides to this as well. You should consult your attorney when considering this option.

Life insurance with a fifteen-hundred-dollar face value for each Charlie and Mary was exempt, as were personal possessions and furniture. Charlie had been a carpenter, and Mary discovered that six thousand dollars worth of tools that had been used for his self-support were also exempt. Medicaid also exempted Charlie's stamp collection as a personal possession, as well as some oil paintings and other similar assets.

Finally, Charlie and Mary's home was exempt—a big relief to Mary. She could remain in their small but comfortable home; it would not need to be sold to pay for Charlie's ongoing health-care expenses. Mary's attorney advised her to transfer the house from joint ownership to sole ownership when Charlie entered the nursing home. By doing so, Mary could sell the house if she wanted and invest the funds in another house. If she did not transfer the house to sole ownership, the proceeds from its sale would have to be divided between Charlie and Mary. His half would then go toward paying for his care.

The title of a home can be transferred to the community spouse at any time as long as the community spouse is living in the home. This is one instance in which the thirty-six-month rule does not apply and a transfer can be made without penalty. A transfer of a home to other people (with some exceptions) is subject to the thirty-six-month rule.

Take the Right Steps

There are ways to face the dramatic life changes that come with growing older and make astute financial choices in the process. But to do that, a Christian couple has to be as "wise as serpents and as harmless as doves." You need not fear making these financial decisions, but you do need the counsel of someone you trust. Remember Solomon's warning that in the multitude of counselors is both wisdom and safety.

Contact your family attorney. Call a planned giving professional whom you trust to steer you in the right direction. Some churches and most national and international Christian ministries have a planned giving department with skilled professionals who can answer your questions or direct you to the appropriate sources to get the answers you need. There are many steps you can take right now that will ease the pressure of making those tough decisions in the future.

And remember, "The steps of a good man [or woman] are ordered by the LORD" (Ps. 37:23). As you are taking financial steps, don't forget to take steps that will make a difference in eternity.

141

PREPARING
YOUR
FINANCES
FOR THE
FUTURE

CHAPTER EIGHT

CHOOSING A LIVING ENVIRONMENT

TODAY THERE ARE THIRTY MILLION AMERICANS who are eighty-five or older. Remember Caleb in the Bible? He was faithful to God from his espionage days until the very end. And when his inheritance was finally awarded him, Caleb was eighty-five years old (Josh. 14:10). Imagine. Thirty million Caleb's in America; thirty million extraordinary people.

About 30 percent of this group have already been diagnosed with Alzheimer's. Twenty-four percent already live in nursing homes. Most of the rest are still facing the toughest decision for an elderly person and the family of that person: What living environment is right for me?

In this chapter we will explore the environmental options available for us as we grow older. No one option is right for everyone, and during the course of our lives the best option often changes. We will think out loud about the types of questions that should be asked when choosing a living environment. And we will ask some friends about the factors that brought them to their decision for their loved one.

Three Environmental Options

When faced with the decision of selecting your living environment, get lots of help. Contact the Office of Aging in your community. These people have ready answers, are willing to take sufficient time on the telephone to address the issues you raise, and have helpful literature on the subject. Your State Department of Health and Human Services also has information and can refer you to appropriate agencies. Other helpful agencies to contact include the Alzheimer's Association and Elder Care. Look in the "Human Services" directory in the back of your telephone book.

But don't stop with just a phone call. Talk with friends. Be candid. Discuss your fears and anxieties. If you are a caregiver and are helping to make the decision about a living environment for a parent or other loved one, ask your friends if they know others who have gone through this painful planning process. You may be surprised to discover how many of your friends have already had to make a similar decision. The advice of friends is not always the solution, but at least you will gain a perception you did not have before as well as some helpful information and moral support.

And always speak with your pastor. This is not just a physical decision but a spiritual one as well. You need to deal with issues of grief and regret, guilt and a sense of helplessness. Your pastor can help. If he has not already experienced the pain of making this decision, he may not be able to provide the kind of help the agencies listed in your phone book can provide, but that's not what you're looking for from him. You need spiritual counsel; you need reassurance; you need someone to pray with you.

After you have gathered all the opinions, all the advice, and all the information you can, think carefully about your options. Basically you will be faced with three choices for a living environment. You can remain in your own home, either by yourself or with your spouse. You can move in with other family members, most likely your children. Or you can choose one of the many options available through specialized care facilities.

Staying in Your Own Home

All things being equal, the best option is always to maintain your independence and freedom by living in your own home.

That's where you are most comfortable. Everything is familiar to you. It may be true that home is where the heart is, but usually our heart is in our own home.

What are some of the benefits of living in your own home? There are many.

Freedom. Remaining at home enables you to call the shots in your own life as long as possible. It gives you the freedom to be you. You can get up when you want, eat when you want, take a nap when you want, go to bed when you want. You're your own boss. You can wear what you want around the house; there's nobody to impress. You can go to the grocery store, stop by the mall for some shopping, get a haircut, do all the things you normally do (except maybe not as rapidly). You can have friends over for Sunday dinner. You are entirely free to live your life as you choose and as pleases God. Freedom. It's a wonderful feeling. Actually, if you are capable of doing all these things on your own, you probably wouldn't consider living someplace else.

Mental awareness. Remaining at home can also be good for your mind. It forces you to think through your situations. Nobody is making the decisions for you; you must make them for yourself, even if you are getting help from a family member. You must pay your own bills, balance your own checkbook, remember which day to put out the trash. That's good. It keeps you mentally alert. You must sort through the mail each day and determine what goes in the trash and what is important. You have to think about the maintenance of your own home: Whom do you call when you need the roof fixed or the furnace goes on the fritz? You need to think through the costs and benefits of repairing or replacing your VCR or television or toaster. And while it is a good idea to seek the counsel of your family or friends on any decision that involves more than a small amount of money, ultimately the decision is yours. That keeps your mind alert and ready to face the challenges of life ahead.

Familiarity. Remaining in your own home is also beneficial because it has the appeal of the familiar. Your memories are there. You know exactly when you added on that spare bedroom. You know how long it took for that tree outside your window to grow tall enough to produce shade. Everything about your environment is stable. It is permanent. It is you. Perhaps you raised your children there. If you're like my (Wood's) mother, you have chronicled the growth of your grandchildren with pencil marks on a wall. You can remember where you were in your home when the most memorable events of life took place—the assassination of John F. Kennedy, the day Neil Armstrong walked on the moon. Home is a familiar environment and a familial environment. It's a good friend. Who would want to leave a good friend?

But often life does not permit us to choose our first choice, so we have to be ready with other options. That's why alternative environments are important. And usually that's where family comes in.

Moving in with Family

Is it a good idea to move in with your family? Sometimes it is; sometimes it isn't. The answer lies in your attitudes and your family's acceptance.

Three years ago my wife and I (Wood) bought a new house. We didn't need to move; we really didn't want to move. But the home we owned, while not large, did have five sets of stairs ranging from six to nine steps each. That's fine for a midlife couple, but if my parents were ever to move in with us, they would not be able to negotiate the stairs. So we bought a home on two levels. This house has a private area for my parents with a bedroom, a sitting or TV room, and a private bath. We had talked with my mother, and she was willing to sell their house and make the move. My father, who is struggling with Alzheimer's, was less willing. To date, our spare rooms are empty.

How do you know when to make the move? How do you know if you can continue to live on your own or if moving into a house with your family is the right thing to do? These are tough questions, and the answers will vary from family to family. They will also vary based on who is making the decision. Are you the one moving, or are you a member of the family inviting a parent or other to move in with you? Are you the one receiving care, or are you the caregiver? Unfortunately, there is not a caregiver's Bible you can consult to get definitive answers to the tough questions. So how should you proceed?

Define Your Role

First, it's important that each person in the decision-making process clearly understands his or her role. That's especially true of the caregiver. As the caregiver, are you making the decision *for* your parents or are you *advising* them on how to make their own decision? This distinction is critical. Let's define our terms.

Advocate. An advocate represents a person's best interest and value system and does not take control of that person's life. An advocate, usually a son or daughter or a combination of family members, has the ability to look at the world through the older person's eyes, to view things through their value system, and to judge accurately what that older person would do. An advocate is sensitive to how their parent or other loved one lived, is living, and would like to live, and acts accordingly.

As an advocate, the decisions made by an older person may not seem reasonable to you. In fact, their decisions may even conflict with your own values. But you are not the decision maker here; you are the advocate, a helper who assists others in making a decision with which they will feel comfortable. You need to ask yourself: "How does this person live his life? What has been the most important thing in life to him? How can I help him maintain those important things?" You are there to advise, not decide. You must let your parent or other older loved one make his or her own decision.

Decision maker. There may come a time in your relationship with an older adult, however, when you must move from advocate to decision maker. Perhaps your loved one has become mentally impaired. Her judgments are unsound, not simply personal. She makes poor financial or medical decisions. She has begun to do things that are harmful to herself or her spouse. There may come a day when you will have to take charge, not just simply give advice.

That will be one of the toughest days of your life, and of your loved one's life as well. She may not be fully capable of understanding why you're making the decisions. She may resent you for making a decision for her. She may even become angry. But when an older person endangers herself or others, the advocate may have to become the decision maker. This reversal of roles is often difficult and charged with emotion, but it is usually necessary.

One of the first decisions you may have to make for your older loved one is the living environment decision. He has been at home where things are familiar and living is comfortable, but he is now a danger to himself. He forgets to turn the gas off on the stove. He loses things, including social security checks. He trips and falls often. He is beginning to see imaginary people looking in the window. The quality of his life is declining rapidly. It's time to move.

Getting Ready for the Move

There are numerous legal issues that need to be handled when a person can no longer make decisions for himself or herself. They will be discussed in chapter 9. Our concerns here are the social decisions, the emotional decisions that tear out the heart of the one making a move, and the adjustments that can cause stress in the host family.

If you are the one moving, begin considering the move early. Give yourself ample time to adapt to the idea of moving. There will never be enough time, but give yourself as much as possible. If possible, visit the home where you will be staying so you can visualize what your living environment will be like. Next, dream and plan. Think through the advantages of your move, such as the fact that you'll be closer to your family, or that you'll have loving care under the same roof, or that you'll be making new friends and seeing new places. Revel in the often missed fact that when your family invites you to live with them, they are showing that they love you very much. Enjoy the prospect of that love.

However, you must overcome two major obstacles when making such a move. The first is your spouse. If your spouse is living and has Alzheimer's or some other form of dementia, he or she may not be as willing to move as you are. In fact, your spouse may be opposed to making a move, even to move in with family. But if you are the caregiver for that spouse and their care needs are becoming much more demanding than you can handle, you must make the move. Be kind but remain firm.

The second major obstacle to overcome when moving is the disbursement of your assets. Selling your home and much of your furnishings is not the difficult task; a realtor can help you do that. The difficulty comes in parting with things you have held dear for years. That's why it's good, if you can, to begin this process long before you have to move in with your family.

Begin with those things you have absolutely no use for, things such as clothes you haven't worn in twenty years, tools you no longer have the skill to use, excess purses and shoes, a spare car or pickup. How do you know what to sell? Ask some simple questions. Have I used this item in the last twelve months? Is what I'm hanging onto stored in the attic? If I did need this item, would it take me more than ten minutes to locate it? If the answer is yes to questions such as these, chances are the item should go.

Take with you photos, a family memory for each important person in your life, a small amount of personal furniture if there is room, the clothes you wear on a regular basis, and a few other things, but not much more. One day we'll leave it all behind anyway.

Making Your Home Senior Friendly

If your parent or parents are coming to live with you, it will be as big of an adjustment for you as it will be for them. In addition to the emotional and psychological adjustments you will go through, you may also need to adjust to a physical adaptation in your home to accommodate older adults.

Patricia, seventy-six, and Paul, seventy-four, came to the conclusion, in consultation with their children, that it was time for them to live with their family. Their son and daughter-in-law, Paul Jr. and Miriam, were eager to have them move in with them. They loved their parents and had their best care at heart. Besides, Paul Jr. and Miriam had a home that would accommodate their mother and dad nicely. Even so, some physical changes had to be made to accommodate the needs of older adults. If you have a loved one coming to live with you, many of these same changes may apply to your home as well.

Accessibility. Movement for senior adults is not as easy as when they were young, so Paul Jr. and Miriam removed thresholds in doorways to prevent tripping. They widened the door on the bathroom that would be used by their parents and installed handrails in the bathtub and near the toilet. They added an additional handrail for the steps leading into the house as well as for the stairway to the family room on the lower level. These few minor changes made their house more accessible to their parents.

Lighting. After Patricia and Paul arrived, the family noticed that Patricia wasn't reading as much as she once did. She loved to read and had brought her favorite books with her. She had even stopped reading her Bible as she once did. Then Miriam noticed that when Patricia did read, she strained and squinted at every word. The problem? The lighting in Paul Jr. and Miriam's house wasn't adequate for Patricia to see in comfort. They added a bright lamp near Patricia's favorite chair and boosted the wattage in fixtures in hallways and on stairs. Also important was the outside lighting. Paul Jr. installed floodlights on the back deck and Malibu lights along the walk leading to the front door. This enabled Patricia and Paul to feel more comfortable in their new living environment.

Security. Often they won't admit it, but security is a significant worry for many older adults. They feel helpless against an intruder. Since Paul Jr. and Miriam needed to maintain a social life that did not include their parents, they decided that a security system in the house would make Paul and Patricia feel more at ease when they were home alone. It was a simple home security device, but it gave the added assurance that older adults need.

There are dozens of things people middle aged and younger never think about that loom as potential problems for older adults. To cover all the bases, Paul Jr. and Miriam asked their parents what other measures they could take to make their home more senior friendly. Here is what they found. Patricia had arthritis and found it difficult to turn the tight knobs on the living room lamps. So Miriam bought the lamps that light up with just a touch. Also, since there were no children in the house, they got rid of all childproof bottles. Patricia just couldn't open them. They also replaced door knobs with door levers, which make opening doors easier for individuals with arthritis, and began to store some things in the upper kitchen cabinets that used to be stored in the lower ones. This prevented Patricia from having to bend over to get a bowl of cereal for Paul. And speaking of Paul, he wasn't as surefooted as he used to be, so Miriam removed all the throw rugs in the house so her father-in-law wouldn't trip and fall.

When it comes to making your home senior friendly, little things mean a lot. Keep your eyes open and watch for areas in which older adults struggle. Often you can alleviate a problem with little or no expense.

If you invite your older loved ones to move in with you, make it their home too. Include them in family activities. Have them take part in your family devotions each night. Make the home as safe and comfortable for them as you can.

Alternative Living Environments

Sometimes moving in with family isn't enough. Sometimes it isn't desirable. Sometimes it isn't even wise. What do you do then? If you can't continue to live in your own home and you don't feel it is wise to move in with family, your options are still varied and attractive. Let's think about the types of alternative living environments that are available to you. After you know your options, you can make an informed decision about your future home.

Retirement Villages

Many older adults living in the North become snowbirds for three to six months out of the year. Some have decided they like the warm winters of the South and have moved into retirement villages. These are planned communities that enable older adults to live with great independence. Retirement villages may be set up as rental units or as condominiums. In a senior citizen's apartment complex the resident pays rent. In a condominium the resident pays a mortgage, plus a monthly condominium fee for services such as the maintenance of buildings and grounds, recreation facilities, security systems, transportation to shopping areas, and so on. While this type of living environment is wonderful for those who are still on the go, they generally do not offer special help for those who need medical attention or special care.

Assisted Living Centers

The assisted living or sheltered housing apartment or room is halfway between living in your own home and living in a skilled nursing facility. It is for those senior adults who do not need constant supervision yet cannot live independently. Many sheltered housing units contain safety features such as handrails, wheelchair ramps, and call bells. Some have a nurse on staff or a medical clinic in the facility. To live in these settings, people with dementing illnesses usually must be able to provide their own personal care and not be disruptive to others. They must also not be prone to wander. Since assisted living does not provide supervision, it is not suitable for most people with dementia. In fact, some programs will not accept people who suffer from dementia or Alzheimer's. Check this out before you check in.

Life-Care Facilities

A life-care facility does what the name implies. It provides varying levels of care for life. In return for an initial down payment or an entrance fee, plus a monthly living fee, the life-care facility provides a living environment similar to that of a retirement village or senior citizens' apartment or condominium. The difference is that a life-care facility will move a resident to a sheltered or skilled nursing setting when the person's health declines. Once an individual or couple is accepted in a life-care facility, the facility *may* provide care for life, even if a resident runs out of money. Be sure to ask about such policies and read the fine print before you move in. This is one of the better options for those who can afford the entrance fee and have sufficient income to pay the monthly living fee.

Adult Foster Homes

This type of facility specializes in the person with Alzheimer's or who is otherwise suffering from dementia or confusion. For a fee, the adult foster home provides a room and may provide care. Ideally, foster homes care for their guests as members of the family. They provide meals, a room, transportation to the doctor, and supervision. The quality of care in adult homes varies significantly because there is little regulation of foster care in most states. If you use such a facility for a loved one, generally you assume full responsibility for monitoring the quality of care given. Quality can decline rapidly if funds are low or if new management takes over. Be thorough in your investigation of services provided and the quality of care.

Boarding or Domiciliary Homes

Also called homes for the aged or personal care homes, boarding or domiciliary homes provide less care than adult foster homes or nursing homes. They usually provide a room, meals, supervision, and some assistance. Some specialize in dementia and offer good care. Others, however, take advantage of the vulnerable person with dementia and of lax regulations. There are no federal quality-assurance standards for these facilities, and state oversights can occur.

Making the Right Choice

Making the right choice of an alternative living environment can be difficult, both for the older adult who needs care and for the family or the caregiver. The best way to insure that you make an informed choice is to ask questions. Call all the facilities in your area and ask for literature. If you think one may be right for you, ask for an appointment and go by and check it out. Take someone along who can help you make a valued, objective assessment. Talk to the people at the facility. See if you like their demeanor, their attitudes, their responses. Talk to some of the residents. Ask the tough questions. Don't stop with one resident; that person may be an anomaly or a born complainer. Then call the Office of Aging or the Health and Human Services Agency in your area and ask them for straight answers about a particular facility.

Ultimately, however, the decision is yours. You must be satisfied you have chosen the appropriate place for you or your loved one. The questions you ask are the most important. But what should you ask? The following list of questions covers all the types of living environments you may need to consider:

- Will the entrance fee or part of it be returned to the resident's estate if it is not spent on his care?
- Does the initial investment build equity for the resident?
- What happens to the resident's investment if the facility goes bankrupt?
- Are there additional entrance fees or monthly fees charged if a resident has or develops a dementia?
- Can people with dementia be asked to leave?
- If a resident is later found to have had a preexisting dementia, which was unknown at the time of entrance, can he be asked to leave?
- Under what other conditions or circumstances might a person or couple be asked to leave the facility?
- What services and activities are included in the monthly fee?
- Is participation in community meals or activities required?
- If the resident doesn't like the food, what alternative provisions may be made?
- Does the facility have a nursing unit?
- Is there an extra charge for this unit?
- Does the nursing unit accept people with dementia?
- Is the staff trained to care for people with dementia?
- If the facility has a special care unit for people with dementia, how does that unit care differ from ordinary care?
- Does the unit accept Medicaid?
- Why types of security systems are in place in the unit?
- Are there medical specialists (dentists, podiatrists, ophthalmologists, audiologists, etc.) available to serve residents in this unit?
- Are residents allowed personal items to furnish their rooms?
- What is the policy on home visits outside the unit?
- What is the policy on family visits within the unit?
- How many staff are scheduled on each shift?
- How are staff selected, screened, and trained?
- Does the facility have a pharmacy?
- Is smoking allowed and, if so, how is it monitored?

- Are there provisions for prayer, worship, and Bible study?
- Are there any restrictions on religious practices?
- Are there any restrictions on pastoral visits to the facility?

The list could continue, but the best questions are the ones you want answered. The questions above are only to spark your thinking about what to ask about a care facility before you make up your mind. If you don't get an answer or you get an inadequate answer, ask again, and again. This is an important decision for the future.

The Next Step

If you are a caregiver, your head is probably swimming right now. There are so many things to think of. But God has entrusted to you a great treasure, your parent or other loved one. You know this is a stewardship. You want to be faithful because that is God's requirement for stewards (1 Cor. 4:2). So what do you do now? What's the next step?

The Alzheimer's Association suggests the following course of action before you make a final decision on a nursing facility for your loved one.

1. Make an appointment for a formal tour of the facility with the special dementia care unit director.
2. Return to the facility at a different time of day and make an informal tour.
3. Consider the location of the facility in relationship to that of your family.
4. Talk to families with residents currently in the unit.
5. Check to see if your private physician will make calls to the facility you select.
6. Check to see if all pharmacy costs are billed directly to the family or are included in the monthly facility charges.
7. Call everyone you think may be able to help you, including the Office on Aging, the Alzheimer's Association, and the Department of Social Services.[1]

Knowing When to Take the Step: Three Stories

Perhaps knowing the struggles others have endured in taking the next step will encourage you in your own decision. These three stories are from friends, all staff members at Back to the Bible.

Life is filled with tough choices. For Marvin and Donna Carr, the decision to place Donna's mother in a nursing home was far more difficult than the decision to invite both parents to live in their home. As Marvin explained, "My wife and her brother are the only children. They talked this over and felt it was best for their parents to be someplace where they could be cared for rather than our simply going to their home with a meal every day." But after Donna's parents moved to the Carr's home, her mom's condition deteriorated. Increased medical problems, including arthritis and serious memory lapses, led to the decision to place her in a nursing home.

"It was a tough decision," Marvin explained. "Everyone in the family had to exercise patience and understanding. It took a lot of prayer too." Yet they were all convinced that placing her in a nursing home where she could have the advanced care she needed was the right thing to do. Donna's ninety-three-year-old father continued living with them.

Several incidents brought Cherry Thompson and her siblings to the conclusion that advanced care was necessary for their mother. According to Cherry, "She moved to Lincoln in 1972 after my dad died. She did well for a long time. It's one of those tough things when you watch your parents age—especially when their physical health isn't really that bad but the mind starts to go."

Cherry's mother underwent extensive testing for Alzheimer's at a Lincoln-area hospital. "They concluded that there was a lot of depression, so we couldn't be sure, but the general assumption was that she had Alzheimer's."

Several incidents led to the decision to place Cherry's mom in a nursing home. "For a long time she was living in an apartment. She never actually lived with us. But I would go over two or three times a week. One Saturday I went over to do her hair, and she looked at me in a funny way and said, 'Did you see Mother and Dad?'

"I thought, 'What's going on?' and I said, 'No, should I have?' She said, 'Why not? They were just here. They were coming to take me to go somewhere.' At that point I knew we were in trouble," Cherry said.

"Later my brother came down from Omaha and stopped in to see her, and Mom wasn't in her apartment. She had gone across the street to a park, and when he asked her why, she said, 'They told me I had to move out.' Fortunately, it was summer. If it had been winter . . . At that point we decided something definitely had to be done."

Cherry called a family meeting. Her sister had already been through this decision with her father-in-law and advised that, given the care her mother would need, none of the kids should have her move in with them. Four of the five children were present when they told their mother that she was being placed in a nursing home. It was a family decision with total family support, but it wasn't easy.

For Judy Hansen and her brothers and sisters, distance was a factor as was their parents' inability to maintain safely their preferred life on the farm. Judy related, "My dad was one of five brothers. My grandfather homesteaded the land, and each of the brothers had received a portion of it. My dad would be the first one to have to give up his land. That was really difficult since he had spent his entire life working that land and hoped it would stay in the family."

Neither of Judy's parents was able to drive. Her mother couldn't see well enough to take care of things around the house. "We wanted them to have their independence," Judy said, "but on the other hand, we could only visit them a couple times a year." Last fall Judy's mom was driving and lapsed into a diabetic coma, destroying the family car. Judy's dad was in the hospital at the same time with complications from a kidney transplant. The doctor chose not to release either of them unless someone could stay with them.

"It was a difficult decision," Judy remembers, "but we chose to place them in an apartment in town. There was simply no other way for them to get transportation to shopping or anything, and Mother has had to go to the hospital several times this past year because of diabetic reactions. The doctor felt it would be better for her to be in town rather than living on the farm ten miles away."

Judy continued, "We made it a point not to push them to make any decisions about closing up the house or selling the farm. They certainly weren't in favor of moving to town, but the day after a big snowfall, Dad told me on the phone, 'I looked out the window this morning and saw all that snow and realized I didn't have to go out and shovel the sidewalk.' That was the first positive word from him about moving to town."

Do the Right Thing

The decision is never an easy one, but there will come a day when a decision has to be made, and usually it's the family caregivers who have to make that decision. With those loved ones who have Alzheimer's, usually the decision is made when one of two things happens. First, when those receiving care become a danger to themselves or those around them, especially their caregiver, action must be taken. Second, a decision to seek an alternative living environment is often made when the primary caregiver can no longer give adequate care. Often those suffering from Alzheimer's or other forms of dementia become so demanding, angry, and unreasonable that they cause the breakdown of their caregiver's health. When the caregiving spouse suffers a stroke or heart attack, partially induced by the stress of caregiving, that's when a reluctant spouse may finally give in and allow the family to make alternative living arrangements. Too often it's "the second victim" that brings action for the first victim.

Almost all of us who have aging parents will face the dilemma that the Carrs, Thompsons, and Hansens have faced. We will have to make a decision. Whatever that decision is, seek the Lord first. Be open and honest with your attitudes and goals, and ask him for clear direction. Do the right thing and pray that God will help the ones you love to accept the right decision.

Chapter Nine

Wills and Other Legal Issues

SAM AND JULIE SEEMED A BIT UNCOMFORTABLE as they sat in the small yet tastefully furnished waiting room for their appointment with attorney David Gibbs. "I know we need to do this," Sam whispered to Julie, rubbing his hand through his thinning, sandy hair, "but I don't believe in rushing this business of making a will or a trust. After all, I'm only fifty-two. Both my parents lived well into their eighties."

"Neither of them was twenty pounds overweight or as sedentary as you are," Julie whispered back. "We need to get this taken care of."

A fifty-two-year-old aircraft maintenance worker at Tampa International Airport, Sam and his forty-seven-year-old wife had engaged in a somewhat heated discussion after listening to attorney David Gibbs discuss midlife legal issues on a radio program. A high school teacher and mother of two grown children, Julie had insisted to Sam that they schedule an appointment with their attorney to discuss their own lack of a will. "We've never had a will," Julie said. "What if something happened to you or me? Or even both of us?"

"I don't think it's that big of a deal now," Sam had countered, pacing the tile floor in their kitchen. "After all, Sammy Jr. and Susie are both grown. We made it through their childhood without a will."

"We need to take care of this now, Sam. We've almost paid off the home, and we have enough assets that we'd probably have to pay a ton in legal fees. I was talking to my friend Valerie last week—she's in the insurance business—and she suggested that what we needed was a living trust. She says they cost more than a will, but they protect your estate from the courts. I think that's what we need to consider."

"That's not what the attorney said," Sam responded. "According to him, you're just spending a lot of extra money for nothing."

After a two-hour discussion, which had covered several topics, Julie and Sam finally agreed they needed additional counsel.

Wills

Dying without a Will

Although no statistics are available, authorities estimate that a surprising number of people at midlife have never gotten around to making a will. According to attorney David Gibbs III of the Christian Law Association, it's a critical omission. "If your children are still living at home, a will can impact where they go after you die, and that's of utmost importance for Christians who prefer not to have the state determine who will finish raising their children. After all, they consider factors other than Christian convictions. While a Christian parent may have a very specific viewpoint of what's best, the judge in a custody case in which the will hasn't defined where the children should go will generally look for relatives who have the most money and live the closest to the children. You as a Christian parent, on the other hand, may be most concerned that your children will be brought up in the nurture and admonition of the Lord. Courts as a general rule are far less concerned about spiritual matters."

According to David Gibbs and Steve Nickel, attorney and vice president for development of Back to the Bible, there is another vital reason why every Christian should have a will long before midlife. In a word, that reason is stewardship. "Since our resources belong to the Lord," Nickel explained, "we need to see to it they're disposed of with minimum tax impact or consequences and in a way that glorifies the Lord. We are certainly to render to Caesar that which is Caesar's as Jesus explained in Matthew 22, but we're also to render to God the things that are God's. Far too many Christians allow Caesar, in the form of the government, to collect taxes on funds that could go to care for other family members such as a surviving spouse, or to further the Lord's work."

Both attorneys agree that death presents an opportunity to do things for the Lord. As Gibbs put it in a *Confident Living* broadcast, "People oftentimes don't realize that through their will they can leave money to their local church or to a ministry. They can invest in the Lord's work at the point of death and allow their financial legacy to continue helping ministries, and thereby, produce ongoing spiritual fruit. Even though they've gone on to heaven, they would be leaving a spiritual investment here."

Some people, however, postpone making a will. According to Nickel, "Some people have the mistaken notion that a will is just for people who have a lot of money, who've collected a significant amount of assets, or who own their own businesses. Appropriate estate planning can certainly assist those individuals, but everyone needs to recognize the benefits of setting up an estate plan that meets the needs of their family, even families with limited assets."

Others just don't want to face their own mortality. As a friend put it recently, "I'd rather go to the dentist than make a will. I know both are important, and to be candid about it, I don't enjoy either one. But making a will reminds me too much that I'm more than half way through my life. I know it's foolish to think that making a will could hasten death—in fact I know it can't—but it makes me uncomfortable." There's something about making a will that puts many of us in more of a "prepared to die" mode than we'd like to be. While most of us recognize the fallacy in that kind of thinking, we still tend to postpone what we know to be important.

Scripture makes it clear that each of us has an appointment with death. Furthermore, according to the apostle Paul, we are to "let all things be done decently and in order" (1 Cor. 14:40).

This includes caring for the legal issues we face at midlife, including those necessary to set our households in order and prepare for death.

What Is a Will?

As attorney David Gibbs explained to Julie and Sam after they had been seated around the conference table in a room adjacent to his office, a will is a legal document in which an individual states his or her intentions regarding what people or organizations are to receive that person's property, who will see to it that his or her wishes or directives are carried out, and if necessary, who will care for minor children.

"A will is a simple legal document," David explained, holding up a copy of a draft of a will. "Generally it just has some basic provisions in it. The first part revokes all prior wills, so if you have a previous will and decide to do a new one, it eliminates the past provisions. Next it generally orders that all your debts and taxes be paid and explains what will be done with any money left over. For example, if you were to pass away and have an outstanding credit card bill or car payment, all those issues would be resolved and your credit would remain good."

David continued. "As I explained last week on the radio, you can put almost any kind of specific or general provision in your will saying, 'I want to give this to these people.' Some states allow you to have a separate document that you can attach to your will, or you can use what's called a residue provision. That's sort of the catchall for whatever isn't listed specifically. It explains how things are to be divided. Generally the residue provision indicates on a percentage basis what you want to leave to your heirs or to a church or charity. Then if you have minor children there'll be the provisions that pertain to guardianship and where your children will go. Those are the basic elements of the will."

"I have a couple of questions," Sam commented, fixing his eyes on the shirt-sleeve clad attorney seated across from him. "For one thing, is there a minimum amount that you have to earn or have before you need a will? It seems like I heard you say something about having six hundred thousand dollars or more before you had to even think about estate taxes."

"Let me explain," David responded. "Each year Congress takes a look at this issue and designates a level of income at which you can pass on your estate with no estate taxes. For this year, the threshold is $625,000. So when you look at the value of your house, your bank accounts, and any other assets you own, and you are pretty sure that the total amount is less than $625,000, a simple will can take care of things. In fact in many states the amount of your life insurance settlement is not even counted against your estate."

"That's a good thing," Sam responded, "since most of what I have is life insurance. If I drop dead tomorrow, Julie automatically becomes a wealthy widow since the union negotiated that great contract with a ton of life insurance."

"Come on, Sam," Julie frowned. But both men looked at each other and smiled.

The Executor of a Will

"I like your sense of humor, Sam," David responded. "Now what about your second question?"

"What's the story on this executor?" Sam asked. "It sounds like somebody who puts you in a position where you need a will."

Chuckling, David replied, "Not really, Sam. An executor is someone who executes or carries out the wishes of the person who writes the will. A couple of steps are involved. First, when you make a will, you have to sign it and have a specific number of witnesses watch you sign it, then they sign their names to the document as well. You may be aware that that's not only a legal requirement, but it fits Scripture."

"In the mouth of two or three witnesses," Julie responded.

"Exactly," David replied.

"So I couldn't just go home and say, 'I'm going to write my own will,' have Julie sign it, and stick it in a dresser drawer somewhere?"

"Not really, Sam," David replied. "There are specific rules of law to make sure the will is valid.

"In any case, let me get back to this issue of the executor. Sometimes an executor is referred to as a personal representative. Some people choose a family member, occasionally a close friend, often a lawyer, or even a pastor or someone in their church. The key thing is, there's a lot of flexibility in choosing an executor."

"What about someone who lives out of state?" Julie asked.

Before attorney Gibbs could answer, Sam interjected, "Not your sister—not in this lifetime."

"Actually there's no law against having someone out of state, Julie," David replied. "Nor is there a requirement that you be related to the executor. The key issue is to pick someone you really trust. Frequently, the personal representative or the executor, if he or she lives out of state, will hire a lawyer in your area who works with him or her to make sure everything is filed properly with the courts where you lived."

"I don't see why there have to be laws about things like this." Sam stretched his arms and pushed back his chair as he spoke.

"I think the concern is over potential fraud, Sam," David replied. "The courts want to be sure that when the assets of the individual who has died are distributed and the person is no longer available to ask what should be done, the legal document—the will they are working from—is an accurate reflection of what the deceased wanted. That's why special rules govern what you can do and how the will needs to be executed and signed."

Far too many people today, including Christians, are in the same situation faced by Sam and Julie. They simply haven't made a will. Does that include you? If so, take the initiative to get your will written.

Doing Your Own Will

In a day when the do-it-yourself approach has been utilized for everything from auto repair to "medicine by textbook," a growing number of people are utilizing legal software furnished by a variety of companies to do their own will. Programs such as "It's Legal"[1] provide information on wills, living wills, plus estate planning worksheets. A variety of others can be found in almost any computer software store.

According to David Gibbs, "If you look at what you own in terms of your house and your bank accounts and other assets, and if you feel fairly comfortable that you own less than $625,000 worth of assets, you can work with a computer program or some form documents that can be purchased from office supply stores or secured from bar associations and execute your own will. However, I highly recommend that individuals with more significant assets invest the time and money in talking with an attorney. The attorney may be able to help them more than offset the cost of his services by providing counsel that could save significant amounts of money at the time of their death." Most attorneys have a flat fee. If you call a reputable attorney, he or she will usually tell you exactly what it will cost to draft an entire will for you and your spouse, so there's no hidden expense.

Hiring an Attorney to Do Your Will

So what if you're at midlife, you don't have a will, and you'd like to talk with an attorney?

It's important not to be intimidated when contacting an attorney over a legal question, even as simple a matter as making a will. Remember, you are the customer. The lawyer is responsible to you. That's true whether you're considering his services or whether you've already retained them. Always explain what services you're looking for and ask in advance what the cost will be. And if you're dealing with an attorney over a will or another issue and you have difficulty hearing from him—which does happen—begin with phone calls. If you have trouble getting him to return phone calls, send a fax, then mail a letter, and explain, "I've been calling your office, and you haven't returned my calls." According to attorneys Gibbs and Nickel, when lawyers receive notice in print, they understand that you're documenting what might be their own poor performance, and they usually begin to respond more efficiently. Also remember that you have the right to fire your attorney and hire one who will handle matters more effectively. Usually, however, those kinds of issues can be worked out by straightforward communication, either by telephone, in person, or in writing.

Another thing to consider is that attorneys work across a spectrum of specialties. As Gibbs explained on the *Confident Living* radio program, "There are attorneys who do nothing but estate planning, and there are attorneys who almost never do estate planning. Generally for a person who doesn't have a lot of assets, almost any attorney will be able to help. Sometimes people say, 'There is an attorney in my family,' or 'My grandson went to law school.' This is a fairly basic area of the law in which most attorneys can provide appropriate and satisfactory assistance. However, if you're going to retain an attorney you're unfamiliar with, be sure to ask some specific questions. For example, how long has he been practicing law? What percentage of his practice deals with estate planning? Don't hesitate to ask how much the service will cost. As a consumer, you have a right to know ahead of time exactly what the bill will be. Also, many attorneys will provide an initial telephone or even an in-person consultation at no charge."

Specific Bequests in a Will

"What about specific items in the will?" Julie asked attorney Gibbs. "How are those handled? I've collected several pieces of art, some fairly valuable quilts, some carved statuary, and certain other things my daughter wants. I'm sure Sammy Jr. will want his dad's gun collection. Are those things handled automatically?"

"No," David replied, "typically these are handled under what are called specific bequests. A bequest is simply the gift of a specific item or asset to a person or organization. For example, Julie, let's say you have a piece of antique furniture or a wedding ring you wish to leave to your daughter. Sam, you may have an old car you've restored that you want to leave to a grandson. Or you may want to give five thousand dollars to each of your three grandchildren for their education. Specific bequests are typically made at the beginning of the will, followed by the distribution of the other assets. Specific bequests can include any personal item, real estate, or even a certain number of shares of stock."

Living Trusts

"What about a living trust, David?" Julie asked. "A couple of weeks ago I had lunch with a friend. She told me we'd be better off to protect our assets from probate proceedings and taxes by using a trust. What's your legal opinion about those? Maybe we should consider that instead of just a simple will."

"First, let me explain what a living trust is, then I'll give you my opinion," David replied. "A living trust is basically a trust that you create for use during your lifetime. Some other technical terms are used such as *revocable trust* or *inter vivos trust.* Typically it includes provisions that allow you to serve as trustee, managing the assets of the trust until you become either disabled or until you prefer to have someone else manage your affairs. That someone else may be an individual or even the trust department of a bank. When that occurs the provisions of the trust allow for a successor trustee to take over the management of the assets. During your lifetime, distributions are typically made to the trust in fixed, periodic amounts. If the grantor—you—should die, the trust provisions designate certain beneficiaries to receive property much like a simple will.

"Many people see certain benefits in a living trust. One is privacy, since living trusts do not go through probate. A lot of people think there are tax advantages to this as well. Here's what I've experienced. Generally to get a professional will done, even by an attorney, you will spend a hundred dollars or less. A trust can cost as much as a thousand dollars or more. I've known of instances in which individuals paid two, three, or even four thousand dollars to set up a trust. What they were told at the time is, 'This will save you from estate taxes and from probate.' The person who sold them the trust actually used the fear of those costs as a sales tool. What I've found is that most of the people who get these trusts don't need them. A simple will can easily handle your needs if your estate is valued at under $625,000, even when you include your house and all your retirement funds. Generally a simple will will handle your estate, and under federal laws you'll pay no estate taxes."

"But what about life insurance policies?" Sam asked. "We have a quarter of a million right there."

"As I mentioned before, life insurance is not considered part of your estate value. A life insurance policy is a contract, and its benefits pass directly by contract to the beneficiaries listed without going through your probate. So when you consider a $625,000 minimum, don't include your life insurance policies. Some states even exempt your home. When people get scared of probate or estate taxes and buy a trust, in my opinion they've actually spent money up front that won't save them any money down the road. I'm not saying there aren't situations in which a living trust can benefit an individual. But even when you have a living trust, it doesn't always eliminate the need for a will. Sometimes you have assets you'd rather not transfer into a living trust, for example, personal property such as a vehicle or household effects or your personal checking account. Then you have to have what's known as a pour-over will to assign those assets to the trustee of the living trust for final distribution."

"Wouldn't you save on taxes by setting up a trust and taking some of the assets like real estate out of your name?" Sam asked.

"Generally no," David replied. "Usually the income earned by the assets transferred into a living trust is still taxable on your personal income tax return, just as if those assets were still held by you personally. It's extremely important for anyone considering a living trust or for a couple considering a joint living trust to explore all the implications carefully with an attorney."

Orderly Record Keeping

Earlier we mentioned the biblical mandate to do things "decently and in order" (1 Cor. 14:40). This includes appropriate record keeping. Sometimes individuals keep their will at their attorney's office or in a safe-deposit box at the bank. Occasionally they will give a photocopy of their will to their executor or someone else they trust. Some individuals give one to their pastor or someone who would be notified in the event of their death. Occasionally, if for some reason the original cannot be found, the courts may recognize these copies of the will as legitimate. However, it's always best to make sure several people know the location of your original will and other appropriate records.

In addition to a will, it's useful to have a list of all real estate. This includes property you own both in and outside the state of your residence. Also, a list of your insurance policies would be helpful. Some individuals have life insurance policies that not even their spouse is aware of. Even though you've paid premiums for many years, the life insurance company is not under obligation to track you down when you die. Someone has to notify them that the insured has passed away before the benefits of the policy can be paid. In addition, anyone who owns a small business or has a family farm needs to keep family business records in a location where they can be accessed.

Your personal legal records should also include information regarding individual retirement accounts, mutual funds, multiple bank accounts, or any other information that would affect your personal or financial matters.

Finally, an inventory of personal property would be beneficial. It's often a good idea to place car titles, boat titles, or any other ownership documents such as shares of stock in a safe-deposit box or other safe place. Some individuals choose to keep these at home in a fireproof box or a personal safe.

A few people are hesitant to use a safe-deposit box because of the possibility of the box being sealed upon an individual's death. When asked this question on *Confident Living*, attorney David Gibbs replied, "Once you've passed away, your survivors could petition the bank for the opening of the box. Banks are set up to handle such contingencies, and they have officials with high fiduciary responsibilities who can step in, sort through the documents, and decide into whose hands they should be placed."

Living Wills

As Julie and Sam continued their conversation with attorney David Gibbs, Sam asked, "You were talking about a living trust, but I heard you answer a question on the radio about a living will. Are those the same thing?"

"Actually, they're quite different," David explained. Pushing his chair back and walking to a wall behind the conference table, he opened two paneled doors to reveal a marker board. Taking a blue colored marker, he wrote "living will." Underneath he wrote "power of attorney."

Turning back to Sam and Julie, he said, "I've already explained about a living trust. A living will is a different animal altogether. A living trust is an entity you set up while you're alive as a trust document to hold assets for the benefit of your beneficiaries.

"A living will is also a document that you execute. It gives your opinion on withholding or withdrawing life-sustaining treatment. Let me explain. In the event you're in an incurable medical situation or a bad accident and your medical condition is irreversible, the medical professionals may say, 'We can be sure that death is going to come to this individual in a relatively short period of time.' A living will would say to your family, 'I do or do not want to have a certain kind of treatment or be put on machines that will keep my body alive once medical professionals have determined that death is inevitable.' That's the position some people would take in a living will. Others would be very uncomfortable in executing such a document. They would rather have all possible treatments used, no matter what."

"You obviously couldn't make that decision on the spot," Sam nodded thoughtfully.

"No, Sam, a living will has to be executed while you're healthy and mentally competent. And, of course, it involves a very personal decision. Some individuals say, 'Well, if I'm in a bad accident, and the doctors have said my death is inevitable, for a lot of reasons—expense, emotional drain on the family—I would prefer not to have heroic measures carried out.'"

"That sounds a lot like physician-assisted suicide," Julie said. "I'm sure we wouldn't believe in that."

"I don't either. I think it's an unbiblical concept." Attorney Gibbs shook his head vigorously. "Please understand I'm not talking about something that would authorize that very dangerous trend. Physician-assisted suicide occurs when an individual who could continue to live goes to a medical professional and chooses to have his or her life ended prematurely. What I'm talking about with a living will is a situation in which a person who is inevitably going to die soon says, 'I choose not to be kept alive by machinery.'"

Physician-Assisted Suicide

According to Dr. David Stevens, physician-assisted suicide is one of the vital issues today facing individuals at midlife and beyond. According to Dr. Stevens, a family practice physician and executive director of the Christian Medical and Dental Society, there are several important terms involved. *Euthanasia*—a broad term that actually comes from two Greek words meaning "good death"—can be of either a passive or an active nature. Passive euthanasia involves the withdrawal of life support, nutrition and fluids, or a respirator when life could actually continue. Active euthanasia, the kind practiced by Dr. Jack

Kevorkian and a few others, involves injecting a substance or doing something else that actually takes a patient's life. There can even be active involuntary euthanasia in which a doctor takes a patient's life without the patient's consent.

Remarkably, the foundation of modern medical practice, the Hippocratic oath, which is over two thousand years old, came into being because doctors were taking patients' lives as well as providing health care. Patients in ancient Greece didn't know whether they could trust their physicians, so a group of doctors banded together, headed by Hippocrates, and decided, "There must be a relationship of trust between patient and physician." By taking the Hippocratic oath, physicians promise not to give deadly drugs to anyone if asked for them, nor make any suggestion to that effect.

Clearly this is an issue that, although increasingly popular today, runs counter to Scripture, which teaches that human life is sacred. Genesis 1:26 makes it clear that God is sovereign over life and death. In Deuteronomy 32:39 the Lord says, "There is no God besides Me; I kill and I make alive." The Ten Commandments prohibit murder, and 1 Corinthians 6:19 and other passages make it clear that our bodies belong to God.

A concordance study shows the word *life* appearing 496 times in over 450 verses of Scripture. The first two references, Genesis 1:30 and Genesis 2:7, underscore the fact that God is the ultimate origin of human life.

So why is this such a hot issue today? According to Dr. Stevens, "People are being sold a bill of goods under the guise of compassion. But it really isn't compassion. Compassion means coming alongside and suffering with someone. But if as a physician I assist someone in taking his life, I'm not being compassionate. I don't have to worry about coming alongside him anymore. It actually relieves me of my burden of having to show compassion.

"The other thing is people are afraid of becoming a burden to their families. Because of this fear, some of them look at physician-assisted suicide as a kind of insurance policy. They think, *Perhaps I'd never use it, but it's there in case I need it.* Pain, which is often discussed in regard to this issue, is not really the paramount question in most people's minds. In fact, today we have the best pain control we've ever had in the history of medicine."

Other phrases frequently used in discussing this issue are "right to die" and "duty to die." According to Dr. Stevens, the phrase "right to die" is almost humorous. "It kind of presupposes that doctors somewhere are locking patients up and preventing them from dying. It's really ridiculous. Everyone has the right to die. What we're talking about is not the right to die but the right for doctors to kill. That's been prohibited in our society and in our profession for over two thousand years. When physician-assisted suicide is legalized, a doctor becomes judge, juror, and executioner."

Yet according to Dr. Stevens, this is an issue that's being vigorously debated in our society, often under the dangerous guise of what is referred to as "quality of life." "That's a dangerous concept because once you say there is a life not worth living, then somebody has to define what that is. It becomes a very slippery slope because what happens is that often it's not the individual who makes that decision but those around her. It may be family members who don't want to bear the expense of her care, the doctor in the hospital, other people within the health-care administrative system, or even the government. In Holland and other places this has already happened." Numerous individuals have noted that quality of life is a wolf posing in sheep's clothing. Experience in Holland has shown that 25 percent of patients who've tried to take their lives with physician-assisted suicide were unsuccessful, and doctors have had to step in and give a lethal injection to finish the job.

The other dangerous trend according to Dr. Stevens is so-called "duty to die." "At a meeting I attended, one young man stood up and listed specific reasons that require you to take your life: You've lived a long time; you've taken up a lot of resources; you're going to be a burden on your family. In other words, you're supposed to weigh whether you live or die based on how big of a burden you are to other people. What a terrible message to send to loved ones."

Such a message is the very antithesis of love. Of course, Hebrews 9:27 makes it clear that "it is appointed for men to die once." The key question is, who sets the appointment? The timing of death rests in the sovereign hand of God. As Moses pointed out in Deuteronomy 32:39, it is the Lord who grants physical life and who withdraws it in his own time.

The Hospice Alternative

According to Dr. Stevens and his colleague Dr. Eugene Rudd, in a recent dialogue on a college campus in West Virginia, 25 percent of the students said at the beginning of the session they were in favor of physician-assisted suicide. A third said they were undecided and the rest said they were opposed to it. After a lecture and two hours of discussion, another poll was taken. "Everybody opposed it," Dr. Rudd explained. "The problem was they had bought the bill of goods and really had not thought through the issues. Trying to educate people to realize where this is all headed and the damage it will bring to the disabled, the elderly, and those who do not have power in their lives or money for health care is vital."

The Christian Medical and Dental Society and other organizations have in recent days been calling on Christians to stand up and speak out for an alternate choice. The choice that appears to be the best alternative is hospice, which provides death with dignity.

Nearly three thousand hospice programs have been introduced in the United States since 1974, with the express purpose of providing service to patients and their families. According to Derek Kerr, attending physician at Laguna Honda Hospice in Southern California, hospices "are there to help patients live as fully as they can until they die."[2] According to John Finn, vice president and cooperate medical director of Hospice of Michigan, the purpose of hospice is to serve patients and families, enabling terminally ill individuals to be cared for either at home or in a homelike setting. "Hospice does more than deal with the medical dimension—there's a concerted effort to provide emotional support, practical assistance, and what I feel is most important from a Christian perspective, spiritual insight and direction." According to Finn, the growth of the hospice movement can be seen in the response to a 1996 Gallup survey in which nine out of ten people indicated they would prefer to die at home, and a majority expressed interest in hospice care. Despite this fact, almost three Americans in four die in a hospital or nursing home under conventional medical care.

The purpose of hospice care is to provide a life-affirming climate in which dying individuals can maintain control over their circumstances, prepare for death, and live out their lives in comfort and with a sense of personal worth. Hospices typically extend care to families of terminal patients through the provision of emotional support, encouragement to participate in patient care, and support for grief. Although many people would like to use hospice care, it is not always available, frequently because most hospice policies stipulate that individuals must have fewer than six months to live.[3]

Advanced Directives

On the *Confident Living* radio program, attorney David Gibbs responded to a caller named Charlotte from Missouri who explained, "I'm a widow with one surviving daughter who works in a doctor's office. She tells me I should get a power of attorney, then give her a copy of the power of attorney. I already have an executor for my estate. Does my daughter need a separate power of attorney for health care in case I should have to go on life support or anything like that?"

David Gibbs responded, "What I would suggest, Charlotte, is that you have what's called a health-care surrogate. If anything were to happen that made you unable to make a medical decision for yourself, your daughter could be the designated person to make such decisions. If you have a physician you work with regularly, make sure that person has a copy so that he can notify the hospital and reach your daughter if a tragedy occurred or a serious medical situation arose."

Both a durable power of attorney (POA) for health care and a living will are types of advanced directives. Typically an advanced directive only comes into effect when you are terminally ill, meaning you have been given less than six months to live. A durable power of attorney for health care can also come into play whenever you are unconscious or unable to make medical decisions.[4] Your durable power of attorney, usually a family member or friend, then becomes your medical decision maker. According to the American Association of Family Physicians, a POA is generally more useful than a living will, but a POA may not be a good choice if you don't have a person you can trust to make those decisions for you.

A "do not resuscitate" order is a request not to be given cardiopulmonary resuscitation if your heart stops or if you've stopped breathing. Generally, unless given other instructions, hospital staff will try to assist all patients whose heart has stopped or who have stopped breathing. Many patients who are not likely to benefit from CPR, such as individuals who have cancer that has spread, kidneys that have stopped working, or who may otherwise be near the point of death, may have a DNR order placed in their medical chart by their physician.

Other advanced directives with specific instructions are typically written for older or seriously ill patients. For example, Julie's mother, who had terminal cancer, had given instructions that she did not want to be placed on an artificial respirator if she stopped breathing. She felt leaving these instructions would reduce her suffering, increase her peace of mind, and give her control over the circumstances of her death. Individuals who want to consider writing an advanced directive need to do so while in good health, and we recommend prayerful consideration and consultation with a pastor as well as a health-care professional. Such advanced directives can be written in several ways, either by using a form provided by your physician, securing a form from an attorney, contacting a state senator or state representative, using a computer software package for legal documents, or even simply writing down your wishes and giving them to someone else or placing them in a secure place.

Frauds

Margaret, age sixty-three, dabbed tears from her eyes as she began to tell her story to Bettye Banks, vice president of Consumer Credit Counseling Service of greater Dallas. "Bettye, I don't know what to say," she began, then paused and dabbed at her eyes again with a fresh Kleenex from her purse.

She continued, "Forty three thousand dollars. That's how much they took me for. And the worst thing is, I knew better. There's no way I'd ever get involved in the lottery here in the

States. I never even send in those letters that say, 'You may have won ten million dollars.'

"But when they called to tell me about this foreign lottery, it sounded so plausible—like money there for the taking. I used up all my savings, maxed out three credit cards—forty-three thousand dollars and that's not counting my other obligations."

According to Bettye Banks, Margaret's situation is not as rare as we might think, since there are people at every turn waiting to violate the eighth commandment. Stealing is exactly what frauds, scams, and rip-offs are—and they are proliferating at an alarming rate. All too frequently those in midlife and beyond are the targets.

"That's where the money is, and that's where rip-off artists go," Bettye recently told a national radio audience. "Younger people are typically scammed at a lower level. They still get ripped off, but the biggest scams are perpetrated against those who have the money, and that's those who've worked for twenty or thirty years and generated significant savings. They usually have money invested and have something to steal."

According to authorities, the most common fraud against the elderly utilizes the motivation of fear: fear of isolation, of loneliness, of feeling stupid, even that no one calls. After telling us about Margaret's situation, Bettye explained another incident. A man started calling an older woman virtually every day. He positioned himself as the grandson she never saw, the son who wasn't there. He actually started calling her 'Gran' and 'Granny.' She just lapped up the attention.

"In addition he'd say, 'I know you have this credit, Granny. I know your name is next on the list to win this ten million dollars. As soon as you've won, you and I will go to New York together. Then we'll visit Washington, D.C., and California.' All the things he was promising her, he had learned from previous conversations. He knew these were things she wanted to do in her life, and she'd never been able to do them. Meanwhile, he kept accessing her credit card, charging a significant amount every day, supposedly entering her in this lottery. He kept telling her he would go with her on the vacations she'd never been able to take, and she actually believed they would do it together because he left her with the feeling that she was his grandmother."

Shaking her head in exasperation and disbelief, Bettye continued. "It was all possible because her own children and grandchildren didn't let her know they were there for her. They ignored her, neglected her, seldom if ever visited her. We simply have to let our parents know that we're there for them, that we love them, and that they can count on us. Sadly, this lady didn't tell her children even when she began to realize what was going on. She didn't want to appear stupid."

Hearing Bettye's story and learning of the frequency and scope of similar frauds and rip-offs that are due in part to the isolation of older people, we were reminded of the words of Solomon many centuries ago.

> Two are better than one, because they have a good reward for their labor. For if they fall, one will lift up his companion. But woe to him who is alone when he falls, for he has no one to help him up. Again, if two lie down together, they will keep warm; but how can one be warm alone? Though one may be overpowered by another, two can withstand him. And a threefold cord is not quickly broken.
>
> ECCLESIASTES 4:9–12

When it comes to the deceptive days in which we are living, the support of family and trustworthy friends is vital. Any individual, especially one who is lonely, is vulnerable. Yet even those who may be susceptible to frauds and scams can find protection when others, especially children and grandchildren, remain involved in their lives, demonstrating love and showing interest.

According to Bettye Banks, it is quite common for crooks to pose as the absent child. "Those repeated calls almost always begin with some expression of 'I love you' or some variable of that. Often the scam artist will claim to have lost his own mother or grandmother, then say, 'You remind me so much of her. Please let me talk to you. I care. You are exactly what I need in my life right now.' Suddenly that elderly person again feels loved, needed, and important. They are getting a phone call daily—

at least weekly—from an individual who seems to need them but who is actually setting them up for a fall."

Another common ploy, according to authorities, takes advantage of the fact that older people watch the news and are aware of news reports of criminal activity. Typically a call may come from someone who sounds official and professional, frequently posing as a bank officer. "Do you have an account in this bank? Here's what we need for you to do to help us catch a crook. Go to your bank, withdraw X thousands of dollars, and bring it to me in a paper bag." Sometimes the request is not as blatant. Often it is. Another variation on this scam technique is to use a familiar name—a police chief, an officer, or someone the victim knows.

While those kinds of scams are frequently used against individuals who are beyond midlife, even those who are at midlife are susceptible to the preapproved credit application scam. Bettye stated, "Individuals will actually sift through your trash and your debris, find those preapproved credit applications you may have tossed without tearing up, and use them to open accounts in your name. Then they charge those accounts up to their limits—and you're at risk because you haven't been prudent in managing your debris.

"In addition, individuals will actually copy down the license plate number of someone whom they've seen using credit for a major purchase in a store, then report a near-miss accident, perhaps contacting the Department of Motor Vehicles, giving them a license number and saying, 'This person ran me off the road. I'd like to find them.' They get your name, your address, your social security number. Before long, they have all they need to establish access to your credit."

Bettye Banks warns against the frauds that capitalize on the desire to get rich quick, including fake lotteries and free vacation offers. As she urges, "Never pay for anything that's supposed to be free."

According to financial adviser Tom Teckmeyer, president of Teckmeyer Financial Services, there are a variety of fraudulent investment schemes. On one of our *Confident Living* programs, Tom noted, "A lot of different financial scams continue to surface from time to time. Some of the major ones we see are people selling limited partnerships in oil wells. Another typical one is partnerships in equipment-leasing programs (computers, railroad cars, or those kinds of things). Scam artists also prey on people by telling them there's a foreign bank account, in Nigeria or the Cayman Islands or someplace, that's idle, and they can have access to great sums of money if they'll just send five or ten thousand dollars to run the paperwork.

"People need to be aware that these things continue to crop up. Con people are looking to prey on innocent victims at every corner. To protect ourselves and our loved ones, we need to look at the people who are talking to us about this investment. Do you know them? How long have you known them? How well do you know them? Have they been at this a long time? What are their credentials? Do they have any expertise or experience in this area? Any educational background?

"In addition, consider how quickly they are asking you to take advantage of this once-in-a-lifetime opportunity. If you have to do it immediately, or within the next day or two, it's probably not a good thing.

"Furthermore, how much money are they asking for? If it seems unrealistic, it probably is. Don't get caught giving money to people you don't know very well or who want it in a hurry. Also, remember the truism, 'If it sounds too good to be true, it probably is.' Let your conscience guide you. If you have an uneasy feeling, there's probably a reason you feel that way. Listen to the Holy Spirit's leading. He will help you avoid those types of things.

"It's also wise to limit your investments to products you know and trust. I've learned over the fifteen years I've been in the investment business that if I stray very far from high quality individual stocks, bonds, and mutual funds, I get into uncharted waters where the sharks are swimming. If you're being offered the latest game in town, you should be wary."

These frauds, scams, and rip-offs bring to mind the warning of Proverbs 13:11: "Wealth gained by dishonesty will be diminished, but he who gathers by labor [little by little] will increase." Many times we or our parents may succumb to get-rich-quick schemes that are quite dishonest. If it sounds too good to be true, it usually is.

As they wrapped up their meeting with attorney David Gibbs, Julie and Sam learned about another potential hazard: funeral planning. Julie had suggested that at their age she and Sam needed to consider purchasing a plan they had seen advertised on television. She decided to ask David for his opinion.

"Funerals are incredibly expensive," David replied. "If you look into what a burial service, casket, and memorial markers cost, you'll find the amount can be quite substantial. Some people are saying, 'I'd like to bear some of that cost now as opposed to putting that on my family or my estate at the time of my passing.'

"Certainly there are legitimate plans by which you can pay the costs ahead of time. However, let me warn you that there are some illegitimate plans that are essentially cons, in which people sell you something that doesn't even exist or will be of absolutely no benefit at the time of your homegoing. Be sure that if you're considering such an option it's with a reputable funeral home or a service in your area. Read the contract carefully—in fact, I recommend having your attorney look over the contract. Make sure you know exactly what you're paying for."

Legal Terminology

The following list of definitions is not meant to be a replacement for consulting with a qualified lawyer. However, it may make the communication between you and your legal adviser more profitable.

Guardianship. This is the most restrictive of the alternative decision-making options and requires a court order. The guardian is responsible to the court system and must report annually. The "ward," or person who is the object of the guardianship, loses all legal rights and is not deemed competent to make any decisions. The person desiring such guardianship must prove conclusively that his or her ward is not able to make competent decisions on their own.

Conservatorship. This extends only to making financial decisions. The person who is appointed as conservator has complete control over the ward's finances.

Representative payee. A representative payee is appointed by the Social Security Administration to care for all issues dealing with social security affairs. To qualify, a person must file an application with the social security office and medically certify that the ward is not capable of handling their own social security issues.

Durable power of attorney (POA). This is a legal document in which an individual appoints someone to serve as his or her representative or agent. By signing a POA, a person does not give up any of his or her legal rights, and this agreement can be changed or even revoked at any time prior to disability or incapacity. This document has the benefit of allowing a person to make his or her own decision to the fullest extent possible and to choose who will serve as their alternate decision maker. It is important, however, to appoint a new agent in the event the first agent passes away before the ward does. A durable power of attorney must be completed while a person is still considered competent, and it must be notarized. Two witnesses are also recommended.

Springing durable power of attorney. This agreement is the same as a durable power of attorney except that it becomes effective only upon disability or incapacity. A definition of disability or incapacity must be included in the document.

Medical durable power of attorney. This is the same as a durable power of attorney except specifically designed for medical decision making.

Living will. A living will is a document in which a person expresses his or her desires in the event of a terminal illness or irreversible coma. Living wills do not have a legal status in some states. It is likely, however, that a court would find a living will valid if challenged. It should be notarized and witnessed and can be part of a durable power of attorney.

Trust. A trust is a legal entity that is able to own property and is managed by a trustee for the benefit of the beneficiary. It has both benefits and drawbacks. On the positive side, a trust can be managed by the person who establishes it and can be a good estate planning tool. At the same time, though, it can be more expensive than a will or probate, depending on the size of the estate.

After they had given attorney Gibbs the information to be used in drafting their will, he promised to send them a copy in the mail, then schedule an appointment to meet with them to review the details and have the will executed.

"So will this be the last will we'll ever need?"

David replied, "Probably not. I recommend that wills be updated whenever there's a question as to whether it's still accurate. Generally when people move, change addresses, experience the death of a spouse or a child, a divorce, or any other kind of change in the family, their will should be revised to accurately reflect their wishes." According to attorney Gibbs, it is preferable to redraft a will rather than modify it with a codicil, which is an amendment, as they can be quite confusing.

"I'm glad we've taken care of our will," Sam said to Julie as he started their sport utility vehicle in the parking lot outside David Gibbs's law office. The sun was just beginning to sink into a bank of clouds to the west.

"But there are so many legal issues to know about at midlife: wills, trusts, living wills, living trusts, power of attorney. You almost need to be an attorney to understand it all."

"Or at least know a good one," Julie replied, smiling.

SLOWING
DOWN
WITHOUT
FALLING OFF

PART THREE

CARING
for YOUR
AGING
PARENTS

CHAPTER TEN

WHAT ABOUT MY PARENTS?

As THE YEARS PASS, our relationship with our parents undergoes dramatic changes. We've navigated the transitions from childhood to adolescence to adulthood, modifying our relationship with Mom and Dad in the process. We've enjoyed, perhaps for decades, an adult-adult relationship with them. There comes a time, however, when we have to face a new transition in our relationship with our parents.

What's the worst thing about growing older? Today two factors seem to be dominating the landscape of aging and demanding greater care for aging parents. One is Alzheimer's. The other involves physical or visual inability. These ailments make it difficult or impossible for parents to care for themselves.

Frank Kroll

Frank Kroll was a hardworking pastor who successfully shepherded the same church for thirty-three years. His heart was as big as I've ever seen. He was the kind of man for whom almost nothing was an obstacle. If something needed to be done, he'd find a way to do it.

Once our youth group needed transportation to a national convention, but the church had no money. So my father bought a bus and took the teens to the convention. On another occasion when the church needed more space for Sunday school rooms, the deacons of the church decided to raise the church, dig a basement, and return the building to its foundation. But, again, there was no money. My father bought a bulldozer and did the work himself. As a young boy, I thought my father could do anything.

At the time of this writing, my father is eighty-three years old. His years of ministry are over. He served long and he served well. I'd like to say that at least he still has his memories, but he doesn't even have all of them. My dad has Alzheimer's disease, and much of his past seems to have been erased.

A Bewildered Family

Alzheimer's is cruel. It robs its victims of life before life is over. It is a slow death, with its victims dying thousands of days before their final day. It's not only a personal difficulty, it's a family disaster. It affects the spouse and children as much, and many times more, than it does the person with the disease. As a family we were bewildered at what we saw happening right before our eyes. It couldn't be true; it couldn't be happening; it couldn't be happening to us! But it was.

On November 16, 1990, a convocation was held in Lincoln, Nebraska, at which I was installed as the third general director and Bible teacher of Back to the Bible. An impressive assortment of radio and ministry bigwigs were there, but the person whose presence was the most meaningful to me was my father. He gave the dedication prayer as the others gathered around with their hands on me.

It was on that occasion that I began to suspect something might be wrong. My father decided to say a few words before he prayed, "because he's my son and he can't stop me." At the time I thought the confusion in his remarks was due to nervousness. Now it seems more likely that this was the first evidence of Alzheimer's. It would be several years before we knew for sure.

In May 1993, my youngest daughter, Tiffany, graduated from high school. Her grandma and grandpa flew to Nebraska to join in the festivities. My father was a skilled craftsman with wood and had always been able to do just about anything with his hands. During the visit, my wife, Linda, asked him to install a shelf above her range for a microwave. It was a simple task, yet my father measured the space for the shelf, then measured it again and again. In fact, he measured it for more than an hour, but he couldn't interpret what the measurements meant. And when it came time to attach the shelf, he simply stared at his hammer, his screwdriver, his rule and drill. He couldn't remember which tool he needed to screw the shelf to the wall. Linda and I looked at each other with teary eyes. Something was happening to our father.

Suspicions Confirmed

There is usually a defining event that confirms all suspicions of Alzheimer's. For my father, that defining event involved a surgery that took place on April 4, 1995.

My mother needed a second knee replacement and my father had been having difficulty with his hip. My brothers and I live hundreds of miles from their town in western Pennsylvania. My older brother and his wife—Jerry and Linda—live in Virginia. My younger brother and his wife—Ron and Kathy—reside in Florida. Linda and I live in Nebraska. We knew neither of our parents could take care of the other after a surgery, so we arranged for their surgeries to occur together. That way we could take turns caring for them at the same time.

After their surgeries, my mother did wonderfully well. My father did not. Physically he was fine; mentally he was a different man. He told everyone who visited him that he was in the hospital because he had been mugged in the parking lot. Sadly, he believed that was true. His demeanor in the hospital was also not that of my pastor-father. He would not stay in bed; he refused to listen to the nurses; he kept pulling out tubes and disconnecting monitors. Finally he had to be restrained. His anger level rose dramatically. He complained about almost everything— and that certainly wasn't my father. Do you know that stereotypical elderly man who cries out and complains about everything? Strangely, that was my father. His personality had become dramatically different.

We spoke with his family physician and related some earlier instances of what appeared to be aberrant behavior. The doctor invited a neurologist and a psychiatrist to evaluate him. After a CAT scan and a series of other tests, the doctors came to a conclusion: My father was suffering from Alzheimer's disease.

"Who's That outside My Window?"

A few days after my father was released from the hospital, his doctor started him on 10 mg of Cognex. He also began treating him for depression with Paxil. Adjusting to these medicines wasn't easy. As the dosage of Cognex increased, so did my father's nausea. Often he complained of being too sick to eat or even get out of bed. To what degree the sickness was real we do not know, but it was real to him.

Everything seemed to trouble my father at this point. He had continual difficulty with his hearing. He had worn hearing aids for many years, but now there was the added frustration of not understanding how to work them. He wouldn't talk to us on the phone because "all the buzzing" irritated him. His hearing aids contain a switch to control the volume, as well as to turn them on and off. Although he was suffering from 70 percent hearing loss, most of the time he couldn't hear because he had turned his hearing aids off instead of on. He just didn't understand, and what's worse, he couldn't be made to understand.

Paranoia began to torment him. He insisted that my mother keep all the windows locked. Their house was not air-conditioned, but he would not let her open any windows, regardless of how oppressive the heat became in the summer. My father constantly saw a face looking in. He was certain there was someone there. The drapes had to be drawn throughout the house every night. Fortunately, that period of paranoia passed. Even though the windows still have to remain shut and locked, he no longer sees people outside.

My father's understanding and memory continued to fail. His inability to follow the story line on a television program, combined with his incapacity to hear well, meant that passing the evenings by watching television was not an option for him. There were two exceptions, however. My father has never been interested in politics, but increasingly he began watching

C-Span for hours. When he became bored with that, he'd watch the Weather Channel. We knew it wasn't an interest in government or changing weather patterns that intrigued him. These programs provided nonthreatening companionship. They demanded nothing of him. They simply left him alone.

"I'm Sure I Paid That Bill"

At this point, things began to fall apart rapidly for my dad. He had always handled the family finances, wrote all the checks, paid all the bills. But suddenly things were so confusing. Bills were not being paid. He began to accuse the banks of hiding his money or not giving it to him when he wanted. When we questioned him, he didn't know how much money he had in his checking and savings accounts. He had never trusted my mother with financial matters, so everything was new to her.

Shortly after Christmas 1995, Linda's father became ill. His illness was diagnosed as a fast-growing cancer. We flew to Pennsylvania in January 1996 to be with him, and shortly thereafter, February 11, he died. We returned to Pennsylvania for the funeral and spent a week with our family there.

Since we don't often get home, we decided to take a part of that week to help my parents assess their finances. In my dad's safe we found canceled checks dating back to the 1940s. There were other documents that were horribly out of date. My parents had life and other forms of insurance, but neither of them knew where their policies were or how much insurance was in force. We called the companies and had duplicates of the policies mailed to us.

We knew my parents had some retirement money invested in certificates of deposit, but they didn't know how much or which banks held them. We investigated and had them consolidated to one bank so that every other month one of the CDs matured. That way, if they needed the money, they could reclaim it without penalty. We also discovered Dad had a savings account at another bank containing several thousand dollars that my mother didn't even know about. We transferred those funds to an account with a higher yield.

My father was willing to accept our help. He agreed with all that we suggested, but he was unwilling to throw anything away. We placed hundreds of useless papers and canceled checks in brown grocery bags. He took them to the basement to discard them, but after we were gone, he returned most of them to the safe.

It was evident that taking care of the family finances was now beyond his ability. My mother had to take over. That was difficult for my dad, but he agreed—agreed, but still refused to help. If he wasn't going to do it, he wasn't going to help her do it either. We showed her what she needed to know, and with occasional telephone calls to my brothers and me for clarification or advice, she has done well.

"I Might as Well Be Dead!"

With Dad's diminished ability came greater despondency. He couldn't use his tools, which he had mastered over the years and loved so much. His depression grew, often to the point of serious concern. A number of times he would say, "I can't get my words out. I can't remember anything. Everybody thinks I'm a dummy. Life isn't worth living anymore. I might as well be dead!"

Of the many things I have seen Alzheimer's do to my dad, perhaps the worst is the way it has robbed him of himself. He is not the same man I knew all my life. He is angry, often childish, sometimes even a threat. He still can pray, he still attends church, he continues to read the Word, he still retains the hope of life eternal, but life here and now is very different for him. He does not enjoy life the way he did. My father would never have said, "I might as well be dead." But Alzheimer's has robbed him of the man he was.

We took these veiled references to suicide seriously. My father had some guns and a few rifles from World War II. We got rid of them. We hid a couple of his prized World War II relics in the attic just in case we had to produce them someday to show him. He was getting more despondent all the time. But things would get much worse.

"Who's That Guy Who Keeps Going Upstairs?"

It was no longer safe for my mother and father to be alone in their home, but they had built their house in 1939, and shaking heaven and earth would not get him to move out. He saw no need for any form of in-home care, and he certainly saw no value in moving to a smaller house, apartment, or retirement facility. Meanwhile, he couldn't or wouldn't help my mother with the housework because in his opinion men just didn't do that sort of thing. The burden of his care was increasing, and he didn't know it. Everything had fallen on my mother. Something had to be done.

Near the end of 1996 the church my father had pastored for so many years began searching for a part-time youth director. The congregation was looking for a young couple with no children who could give impetus and direction to their youth outreach. After the search process, Park Gate Baptist Church called Matt and Tina Work. That in itself was a truly amazing answer to prayer. You see, Matt is my son-in-law and Tina is my daughter. Someone from the family would now live close enough to check on my parents.

But God's answer to prayer was even greater than we assumed possible. God always does "exceedingly abundantly above all that we ask or think" (Eph. 3:20). My parents' house is quite large, and my mother was having difficulty cleaning it all. It is a lovely country home with lots of room. In fact, three huge bedrooms and a bath upstairs hadn't been used in years. Matt and Tina had only been married two years and needed an economical place to live, especially since they wouldn't be making much money at the church. Problem solved. Matt and Tina moved in upstairs. We felt relieved knowing that someone was there in the evening hours and through the night to watch over my parents on a day-to-day basis.

But even this remarkable answer to prayer was not without its problems. Alzheimer's not only robs the mind of memory but often produces childlike behavior. Matt had been a part of our family for only two years, and even though my dad knew him, he often would say to my mother, "Who's that guy who keeps coming into our house and going upstairs?" At other times, he acted as if he had known Matt forever.

Strangely enough, Matt presented another challenge. Suddenly there was another man in the house. "Why was he there? What did he want? Was he trying to take over? Is he moving in on my wife?" As odd as it may seem, all these questions surfaced in my father's mind. I'm grateful to Matt for showing the maturity of character to deal with these questions without complaint or response.

"I Can Drive Better Than All of Them"

A few paragraphs back I said things would get worse for my father, and they did. Everyone in our family knew his driving wasn't as safe as it should have been, so we decided to talk to the doctor about it. It seemed as if everything had been taken away from my dad. The things he enjoyed most in life he could no longer comprehend, let alone do. He had been stripped of his personality, his pride, and his ability. There was only one thing left that gave him a sense of control: driving his car or pickup. The doctor was cool to the idea of denying my father the privilege of driving.

But Dad's driving had become a threat to himself and those around him. In April of 1997 he drove the wrong way down a one-way street and was stopped by a police officer. The officer was extremely kind and gentle, but he told my father he would probably have to take a driver's test. My dad was devastated. "They all think I can't drive anymore. They think I'm a dummy. I can drive better than all of them."

In August 1997, the state of Pennsylvania sent Dad a notice informing him that he needed to surrender his driver's license due to medical reasons. The letter said that if his medical condition improved and the doctor notified them, the state would review his case and he could have his license back. My brother Jerry had the unenviable task of dealing this final blow to my father's manhood. Initially my father seemed surprisingly accepting, but he has exhibited frequent flare-ups of anger and has said he intends to drive regardless of what anyone says. He hasn't because my mother and Tina have been able to talk him out of it.

Where Are We Now?

As of this writing, where is my family in caring for my father? My parents are still living at home, although we have continually encouraged them to move in with one of their sons. We have also tried to keep other options open for them. We have taken them to visit retirement centers and life-care facilities. Once after touring a facility here in Lincoln for an hour, my father, who had been bent over walking with his cane, asked Linda what this place was. When she responded that it was a place for people to live who need a little help, he straightened right up and literally ran down the hall, just to prove to us he didn't need to be in a place like that!

Matt and Tina are still living above my parents in their home. My father's medicine has been changed to 10 mg of Aricept, a new treatment that seems to work better for him. He experiences fewer delusions since he no longer takes Paxil for depression and less nausea since the change from Cognex. He continues to have good days and bad days. Some days every little thing angers him. Other days he is tender and kind, the father we all remember.

In many respects, Alzheimer's returns a person to childhood. Their behavior as well as their attitudes and emotions often become childish. Jealousy, anger, impatience, paranoia, selfishness, and stubbornness are all common among victims of this disease. My father has experienced all of them, most of which were totally foreign to him. When his anger rises or anything threatening happens, he retreats to the safety of his bed. It's not uncommon to see my dad in a fetal position in bed until the middle of the afternoon. When he awakens, it's for an exciting hour of C-Span or a nap in his favorite chair.

The most alive I have seen him in the last few years was during a visit to Nebraska some months ago. Linda wanted me to build some wooden storage shelves in our garage. My dad went to the lumber yard with me to get the materials. On the way home, with the back of the van open and the windows down, I looked over at him. He was riding with his head out the window. The wind was blowing his hair and he had a huge smile on his face. He was in seventh heaven. His mind was wandering through a meadow of fond memories. He was excited and happy. He was useful. He was working with wood again.

Once during the construction project I slid a hammer over to him and nonchalantly said, "Drive a few nails in that end to hold it down." I looked away immediately to express full confidence in his ability. The man who used to drive an eightpenny nail with three hits took fifteen to put this one away, but I have not seen him happier in a half dozen years.

Continuing Concerns

As a family, our concerns for my father are actually exceeded by our concerns for my mother. Much of the verbal or emotional stress at home is borne by her. She is strong and loving and understands that much of what my father says does not come from his heart, but it is still difficult for her. Convincing my father that he is demanding more of her than she is able to give has not been easy. But if she were not at his side, he would need twenty-four-hour care. She gives him his medicine. She convinces him to get up and shower. My mother prepares all the meals for him, except when Tina comes home early enough. She gives round the clock care, and this is taking its toll on her.

The day will come, perhaps soon, when we will have to override Dad's will in order to preserve the quality of her life. It has not been easy watching what Alzheimer's has done because it has taken a toll on both of them. My brothers and I have experienced amazing unity as a family, but we continue to take our cues from our parents—what they want, what they think they can handle.

For years I have taught the wonderful truths found in 2 Corinthians 5:17: "Therefore, if anyone is in Christ, he is a new creation; old things have passed away; behold, all things have become new." I have seen that happen spiritually to hundreds of people. I never thought I would see an emotional and mental change in the reverse direction. But with my father's Alzheimer's, I have seen the closest thing to an emotional reversal I may ever experience, and I don't like what I've seen.

For him, in the last five or six years, everything has changed. His lifestyle, his daily habits, his interests, his demeanor—all these things have changed, but not for the better. The most comforting thing is the absolute assurance that what is eternal cannot change. My father's eternal salvation will not change. His eternal destiny will not change. One day his body will change, but for the better. Now things are not changing the way we want, but our family is confident of better things ahead.

For years we all needed him. My dad was our strength. He was the can-do pastor. He was the hardworking father. He was all his sons ever wanted to be. Now he needs us. We need to be strong for him and for my mother, and by God's grace we will be. We pray to that end every day.

Jim and Juanita Hawkins

The hills appeared ablaze with various shades of red and orange as my plane banked into its final approach to the Birmingham airport. I was en route to a speaking engagement, and something of even greater personal importance—a meeting with my two brothers and two sisters to discuss present and future care options for my parents, both of whom are approaching fourscore years of age.

Mother and Dad met through Dad's sister Margie. Mother and Aunt Margie worked together as legal secretaries in a law office in Birmingham. Mother had the incredible ability to type nearly one hundred words per minute on an old Royal manual typewriter.

Dad worked for forty-two years with the Southern Railway, shoveling coal as a fireman. One of my earliest memories involves seeing him perched beside a steam engine, a big smile on a face streaked with soot from the coal, the huge steam engine puffing and belching like some prehistoric monster.

During World War II, Dad served in the U.S. Marines. He spent several years in the Pacific theater, primarily involved in aviation repair and maintenance, part of the famous "Black Sheep Squadron" of Colonel John "Pappy" Boyington.

Mother and Dad have been blessed with health and strength. Both came to know the Lord as Savior in 1952, just before I made that decision as a child of seven. Dad and I were baptized the same evening at Westwood Baptist Church. Although Dad worked long hours with the railroad, making freight and occasional passenger runs from Birmingham to nearby states, he and mother made our spiritual growth a priority. Dad had become a firm believer in what he called the "family altar," and whether he was home or not, evenings were marked by reading Scripture and praying. Faithful church attendance was also an important part of our family regimen. In addition, I was encouraged to attend Christian camps. Each summer, camp played a key role in my own spiritual development.

Mother's Stroke

In recent years we have become much more aware of a growing need to provide care for our parents. That awareness intensified in February of 1991. Kathy and I were living in Dallas, and Mother flew out for a weeklong visit. We enjoyed a delightful time visiting friends, children, and grandchildren, shopping at the huge Galleria Mall, sightseeing around the Dallas/Fort Worth Metroplex, and spending many hours reminiscing with Mother.

The day she returned home, Mother told my sister Suzi she didn't feel well. The following Monday as her condition worsened, Suzi took her to the doctor. Mother's physician, Dr. Olson, immediately admitted her to Brookwood Hospital. "You're having a stroke, Mrs. Hawkins," was her terse diagnosis.

As a result of the stroke, Mother was left with no left-side vision from either eye. She also began experiencing significant short-term memory loss. Her days of actively driving around the Birmingham area were over. Before long she would be forced to give up her decades-long role teaching Sunday school at Westwood Baptist.

The previous year Mother had begun experiencing hearing and balance problems. The diagnosis: Ménière's disease. During the early nineties she was also given a battery of skin tests and was found to be allergic to at least fifteen common environmental substances including newsprint, glue, and even photographs (because of the formaldehyde used in the developing process).

Mother's health seemed at low ebb as she and Dad approached their fiftieth anniversary in January of 1995. Her dermatologist diagnosed her with pityriasis, a condition that left her hypersensitive to ultraviolet rays and unable to spend more than a few minutes in the sunshine. A fall in May of 1996 led to hip replacement surgery, and even after extensive physical therapy, she was able to walk only with the use of a walker. Often she needed a wheelchair.

Dad's Vision Loss

While mother's health deteriorated, Dad continued to do well. Since she was unable to drive, he became the primary chauffeur for their frequent trips to the doctor and the grocery store, among other errands, including regular trips across town to the Homewood YMCA for physical exercise and hydrotherapy.

Although he had lost most of the vision in his right eye in the spring of 1986, Dad had excellent sight in his left eye; in fact for most of his forty-two years as an engineer on the Southern Railway—now the Norfolk Southern—he had never needed glasses.

Then one morning in May of 1995, Dad awakened and felt, as he put it, "like I had sand in my eye." A hastily arranged appointment with Dr. Lanning Cline, one of the top ophthalmologists in the area, led to an initial diagnosis of macula degeneration. Dad told the doctor, "It is as though I'm looking at a clock and everything between the three and the six is blank." After a series of tests, Dr. Cline concluded that the smaller nerves around the eye had been damaged because of a lack of circulation. For a time surgery was considered, but as Dr. Cline explained to Dad, "Within just the past month, we've concluded that those who have the surgery actually wind up worse off in most instances than those who don't. If we had operated you might have lost all your sight and been totally blind."

As it was, my sister Becky explained, "Dad's legally blind. He's lost 80 percent of his ability to see."

Daily Difficulties

As my plane landed, I looked over the series of questions I had written down, questions to help determine what needed to be done for Mother and Dad.

1. How are they doing now?
2. What do they need?
3. What are they willing to do?

The following morning I met my two brothers, Paul and John, and my two sisters, Suzi and Becky, for breakfast in the coffee shop in the hotel where I was staying. Since I wasn't scheduled to speak until noon, we had a significant window of time to discuss Mother and Dad's condition.

First we reviewed the significant facts. They still live in the same home on Arcadia Road where I grew up. When it was first built almost fifty years ago, it was a small, two-bedroom home without indoor plumbing, located on a dirt road in the country. Today, after extensive remodeling, it's become a moderately sized, three-bedroom, two-bath home on a suburban corner. Needless to say, it's where Mother and Dad prefer to continue living. Whenever the subject of assisted living or a move to a retirement facility comes up, one or the other of them—usually both—express their strong preference to remain there.

However, we also recognized and considered the difficulties, even dangers, inherent in their continuing to live at home. Since neither can see very well, it's quite difficult for them to keep up with chores around the house. Dad takes care of most of the household responsibilities such as cleaning, since he is better able to move about. He washes dishes, takes out the garbage, even takes care of the laundry and the household mopping and vacuuming. Since he can't see very well, he often misses a lot. We're also concerned about the danger that they may forget to turn off one of the burners on the stove.

A few months ago, Mother, who has difficulty getting into the tub, tried to bathe while Dad was lying down resting. She fell into the tub—fortunately the bottom was cushioned with some dirty clothes she had placed there—but she found herself stranded for nearly three hours! She called out, but Dad, who is hard of hearing because of his years operating diesel locomotives, was unable to hear her cries and had fallen asleep. Eventually he awakened, went to check on her, and found her in the tub, unable to get out. He was forced to call 911 and have a rescue team remove her. She was shaken but otherwise unharmed by the experience. However, one of the concerns we expressed in our meeting was that something like this not happen again.

We discussed the fact that both parents, although generally in good spirits, had experienced some depression because of their losses. In addition, Mother's physician indicated the possibility of beginning stages of Alzheimer's, as evidenced by her increasing short-term memory difficulties.

Mother's physician had arranged for an RN to make an in-house visit once a week to check on her condition—a great help since Mother takes approximately sixteen medications per day. In addition, a nurse's aide, a delightful woman named Eartha, came in three times a week to assist Mother with her bath. During the time I spent with them over the weekend, I discovered that Becky had set up a notebook from which Mother and Dad, working together, could keep track as Mother takes her various medications, including an antidepressant. Becky's husband, Tommy, had given Dad a watch last Christmas with a feature uniquely suited to him—press a button and it gives the time audibly. Four times a day, he and Mother carefully work through her list of medicines, documenting the exact time she takes each tablet. One medication even has to be ground up and taken in three teaspoons of applesauce.

Care Options

Part of our discussion as siblings covered the variety of living options available to our parents, including assisted living and extended care. Yet we all realized that, if possible, the most desirable choice was to keep Mother and Dad in the familiar surroundings in which they had lived for so long. But how could we ensure their safety and well-being?

We decided to investigate the possibility of a security alarm. Paul would check out several companies to determine whether one might have an option of a remote, which Mother could carry like a pager, to be used in case she fell or couldn't rouse Dad. Our preference was that she have a device that could sound an alarm and also dial 911.

The second decision we made was to seek someone Mother and Dad would be comfortable with, perhaps someone they already knew, who could come in once a week to clean. Our preference was to find a Christian woman who could make sure things were clean around the house as well as provide a bit of encouragement and cheer for Mother and Dad.

I brought up what I considered to be one of the best potential sources of help—Westwood Baptist Church. The little church where the three of us had been baptized in 1952 had grown to a membership of approximately two thousand. The senior pastor, Cecil Sewell, and his wife, Sharon, had become very close to Mother and Dad, visiting them in their home on several occasions as well as calling on Mother in the hospital. Although Mother and Dad were unable to attend church as regularly as before, Dad still attended about half the time. A member of his senior men's Sunday school class, Charles McCreary, called at least once a week to check on them and ask if Dad or both of them needed a ride to church. On occasion Mother felt able to attend; most often, however, she stayed home. Since the services are televised, they've been able to continue feeling a part of the church, and Mother has had telephone contact with a number of her friends.

Although my plan had been to contact Pastor Sewell that Saturday, he was out of town. With his help I had hoped to find a prospective part-time housekeeper since I had volunteered to take the initiative on this.

That Sunday I was scheduled to speak at McCalla Bible Church. Mother and Dad felt well that morning, so I picked them up and we drove out to McCalla together. We saw many old friends there, and we met Clarence and Kathy Bahlmann. Clarence is a student at Southeastern Bible College, and Kathy and Mother just seemed to hit it off perfectly—in fact they must have talked for ten or fifteen minutes after the service.

Just before we were to leave to go to lunch with our longtime friends Tom and Ilona Dyson, it occurred to me that since Mother and Kathy had gotten along so well, perhaps I should approach her about our need for someone to provide cleaning and encouragement. Kathy expressed interest and a willingness to pray about the possibility, and we agreed to make contact again soon. Since Mother brought up Kathy's name several times afterward, I couldn't help thinking that perhaps it was best that I hadn't been able to contact Pastor Sewell. After all, we had prayed that the Lord would lead us to just the right person to provide this additional care. Although Kathy was unable to become Mother's regular caregiver due to her own family commitment, all of us were encouraged by the reminder that God has the right person to fill every need and is capable of bringing those people into our lives in his time.

For the short term, the bases seemed covered. Paul volunteered to check on the alarm system, and I offered to pursue the cleaning service. John would take care of handyman items, along with Paul, and both Becky and Suzi would provide transportation and check on the folks regularly. The only thing left for us to discuss was our long-term strategy.

After discussing issues ranging from our parents' feelings to what might happen if their health continued to deteriorate, we determined our first step would be to consider a live-in caregiver as an interim step before considering a move to an assisted living facility. Our goal: to respect their dignity, wishes, and freedom while doing everything we could to protect them, physically and otherwise.

Thanksgiving in Lincoln

Two weeks later, my parents flew to Nebraska for their first visit since we moved here from Texas four years ago. Mother had been extremely anxious about flying, and we had arranged for wheelchairs for her and Dad, which proved extremely helpful at Chicago's busy O'Hare International Airport.

Mother's first words to me were, "Thank you for praying. I didn't feel any anxiety whatsoever." Since she takes anxiety medication for an obsessive-compulsive disorder, we were all delighted at how well her trip had gone.

Both of my parents are avid *Back to the Bible* listeners and supporters. Their visit gave us an opportunity to take them to a special pre-Thanksgiving chapel at Back to the Bible, where they were able to meet Wood for the first time. We spent Thanksgiving with four generations, as two of our three children and three grandchildren were able to enjoy the occasion with us. We took advantage of the occasion to add to the memoirs we had begun recording in previous visits—a process we hope to continue during future visits.

When I helped them into their seats for their flight home, Mother's comment was, "I can't believe how well this has gone. This has been a wonderful time."

Since none of us knows how long we will have our parents, I couldn't have agreed more.

CHAPTER ELEVEN

FAMILY TIES

AN OLD DUTCH PROVERB SAYS, "We get too soon old and too late smart." Without question we all need wisdom to know what to do in providing care for our parents as they grow older.

While Scripture speaks clearly and specifically to some of the issues related to caring for our parents, on others it is silent. We are clearly told to honor our parents (Eph. 6:2) and to plan in advance to provide for their needs (1 Tim. 5:8). Yet nowhere does Scripture tell us that we should or shouldn't move them into our own home or place them in a retirement facility or a nursing home.

As you read in the last chapter, both of us have been confronted with the need for additional care for our parents as they grow older. Yet as we noted after a recent prayer time at Back to the Bible, we are not alone in facing this issue.

Dave Hansen, our vice president of international ministries, and his wife, Judy, have devoted a great deal of time and energy to caring for Judy's parents, who have spent much of their lives on a farm near a small community in eastern Montana. Marvin Carr, our director of general services, and his wife, Donna, moved her parents in with them nearly four years ago. When health issues forced Donna's mother to be placed in a nursing home,

Marvin and Donna continued to care for her father, now nearly ninety-four, in their home while visiting Donna's mom nearly every day until her death. Cherry Thompson, who served for many years in our accounting department, also faced the agonizing decision of placing her mother in a nursing home. We've detailed their stories in chapter 8.

Janet Miller, executive secretary to several of our vice presidents, became aware of her mother's problem with Alzheimer's less than a year ago. But as Janet noted, "She's progressed to the stage now where we are talking about putting her in a nursing home sooner rather than later." Complicating the decision for Janet and her brothers and sisters is the need to provide additional care for their eighty-five-year-old father.

The Biblical Mandate for the Family

Scripture makes it clear that God expects us to care for members of our family. In 1 Timothy 5 the apostle Paul provides instructions to a pastor, Timothy, on how the church is to deal with those who are growing older. Paul's opening exhortation urges believers to treat those who are aging with respect: "Do not rebuke an older man, but exhort him as a father . . . the older women as mothers" (vv. 1–2).

Unfortunately, growing numbers of older Americans are being neglected, battered, and financially exploited by their children or other caretakers. According to federally funded research by the National Center on Elder Abuse, reports of domestic abuse against elderly Americans increased from 117,000 in 1986 to 241,000 in 1994. According to the Center, less than 10 percent of the nearly two million annual cases of elder abuse are reported.[1] Another study that focused on nursing home personnel revealed that 10 percent have physically abused patients by shoving, pinching, grabbing, or slapping them.[2] According to Fernando Torres-Gil, assistant to the U.S. Health and Human Services' Secretary for Aging, seniors are "embarrassed to admit that a relative, a loved one, or their own child is abusing them either physically or financially, or neglecting or exploiting them."[3] Clearly such behavior runs counter to the commands of Scripture.

As Paul pointed out in 1 Timothy 5:4, "If any widow has children or grandchildren, let them first learn to show piety at home and to repay their parents; for this is good and acceptable before God." According to these clear-cut instructions, the first line of provision for aging parents, including widows, is the immediate family—children and grandchildren.

Verse eight is even more explicit: "But if anyone does not provide for his own, and especially for those of his household, he has denied the faith and is worse than an unbeliever."

From this verse we can draw three clear requirements. First, caring for aging parents is a requirement for every believer. While government programs and outside aid can help, this is a responsibility that ultimately doesn't rest on social security or Medicare. Nor is this mandate just for the wealthy. The word *anyone* indicates each of us has a responsibility to care for family members as they grow older.

Second, the word *provide* actually indicates advanced planning. The implication of this compound term in the Greek is that caring for aging parents demands careful forethought and planning. In recent days, financial counselors have drilled into us the importance of planning our finances so we can put our children through college, purchase a home, or retire. This passage indicates another important item that should be included on our list of financial planning matters: caring for parents as they age.

Recently, we asked financial consultant Tom Teckmeyer, president of Teckmeyer Financial Services, whether any of his clients had specifically included care for aging parents in their financial planning. Tom, whose clientele includes many Christians, responded that such advanced financial planning was almost nonexistent, based on his experience.

However, Tom and his wife, Lori, decided almost a decade ago to set up a parental care fund and begin saving for the day when they might have to care for their parents. As Tom explained, "My folks took care of us. One day I know we'll need to take care of them. I wish more people would see the value of this. I have only one client who's taken this step."

Finally, when it comes to caring for our parents, nothing less than our Christian testimony is at stake. Paul's words are as pointed as the proverbial ice pick. We are guilty of worse behavior than the pagans when we fail to care for our parents. As the apostle John writes, "Whoever does not practice righteousness is not of God, nor is he who does not love his brother" (1 John 3:10). When we fail to demonstrate love and care for those who raised us, how can we claim to be demonstrating love for God?

Clear Principle, Complex Issues

Despite the clear-cut nature of Paul's instruction in 1 Timothy and the command to "honor thy father and mother" found in Ephesians 6:2, the application of these principles to our various circumstances raises complex dilemmas. The following is a list of several important issues to be considered.

First, independence is an important value to us all. Everyone—including our parents—would like to enjoy the freedom to make our own choices so we can experience a fulfilling life.

"Mother and Dad can't continue living at home," Cynthia asserted. "That's the third time in three months I've come over and found a stove burner on. They'll set the house on fire. I'm going to have to insist that they sell their home and move into an assisted living facility."

"I'm taking Dad's keys," Bob declared emphatically. "Last week he almost ran over the child next door! Plus he's had two fender benders in the last six months. Just because he's too stubborn to admit he can't see well enough to drive doesn't mean I should let him kill somebody."

These may seem like cut-and-dried situations. Yet the reality is our parents have lived independently for many years. Now impairments threaten to encroach on their freedoms, compounding their stress and ours. They may need more help around the home with cleaning, cooking, taking out the trash, paying bills, or shopping. Trips to the doctor may increase, and they are likely to require transportation assistance on a regular basis.

A second issue involves physical and mental well-being. As our bodies age, their functions deteriorate. Sometimes the loss is gradual. On other occasions it may occur suddenly. Just walking or climbing stairs becomes more difficult. Infections may take longer to heal. Parents may experience the shame of a lack of bladder control. Elderly people are also at greater risk for falls, which could result in such serious consequences as hip and knee replacement surgeries. Arthritis and other kinds of joint pain may increase from occasional and mild to chronic and severe. Cancer becomes a greater risk, and even routine checkups may uncover life-threatening physical problems.

Mental stability also becomes a factor. While some individuals retain a sharp, clear mind, others often begin experiencing memory loss and confusion over simple things. Forgetfulness is not just a symptom of Alzheimer's; it can have other causes as well.

Third, many caregivers face an increasing burden coupled with an unwillingness on the part of other siblings to help. A recent letter to advice columnist Ann Landers read,

> This is for all the sisters and brothers of caregivers who are too busy with their own lives to lend a hand.
>
> Four years ago my life changed when my mother became ill with a progressive disease. I put all my plans on hold and little by little gave up visiting my friends and doing volunteer work, socializing, attending night school and spending time with my husband. I must now use all my free time to take my parents to their doctors' appointments and tend to their needs. I'm not complaining—my parents are wonderful people, and I consider it a privilege to care for them. But I am upset because my siblings do nothing to help me.
>
> In the beginning my brother and sister bombarded me with questions about "the folks" but now after almost five years, they never ask how Mom and Dad are getting along nor do they offer to give me any relief. I don't think I should need to hire a stranger to take care of my parents, but it looks like I may have to. . . . My life is so stressful right now that my health is suffering.[4]

Ann Landers observed that this is a story heard far too many times. She explained to "No Name" that although "there is no way you can force your siblings to step up to the plate and give you a hand," they need to be told of the needs. If they refuse to help, either other family members need to be enlisted or outside assistance must be secured and the financial implications addressed.

A final dilemma for the family involves the mobile society in which we live. Some elderly people have large, caring families who live nearby. Several children may have ample resources, or some may have money while others have time. Responsibilities may be shared, leaving no one overburdened.

On the other hand, since two out of five families move each year, many parents live far from their children. Both of us are examples of this, since we live thousands of miles from our parents, who reside in Pennsylvania (Wood's) and Alabama (Don's). Though we make it a point to keep in touch with frequent telephone calls and visits, there is still a keen sense of physical separation.

In other families the distance may be more emotional than geographic. Or it may be both. One of us has been friends for many years with a couple who raised an only son. They are all Christians and have been active for years in a local church. When the son married, he and his wife at first lived in the same city, just a few miles from his parents. They felt they would never lack for their son's love and attention.

A few years later a career opportunity prompted the son and his wife to move to another city. The parents were concerned about the distance, yet they felt their son's ongoing love and concern would overcome that obstacle. Within a few years, however, he began to express indifference toward them, then anger, claiming he was unhappy with the way they had raised him. Sadly, this couple has missed much of their grandchildren's lives, plus the encouragement and help of their only son and daughter-in-law, because of this geographic and emotional distance. While their local church pitches in to help meet their needs, emotionally and even physically at times, theirs has been a tragic situation.

Sometimes when our parents live far away or become incapacitated, we may face the question of moving closer to them or having them move in with us. Should we uproot them from familiar surroundings, their dwindling number of friends, and the home in which they have lived for so long? Or should we uproot ourselves and perhaps our own children, changing careers or ministries in order to position ourselves closer to our parents in order to help them?

When we face such difficult decisions, we definitely need direction. Fortunately, we're not left to our own resources. As God promised through David, his Word is designed to function as "a lamp to my feet and a light to my path" (Ps. 119:105).

James promises, "If any one of you lacks wisdom, let him ask of God . . . and it will be given to him" (James 1:5).

In view of these facts, and the scriptural exhortation to honor and care for our parents, what practical steps should we take?

Practical Steps

First, we need to pay close attention to changes in our parents' lives. Since both of us live some distance from our parents and generally see them two or three times a year, we're usually able to spot changes pretty quickly. For adult children who live nearby, changes in their parents may be more gradual and more difficult to notice. Look for signs such as failing memory, a weakened ability to get around, tendencies to leave stove burners on or water running, and difficulty keeping up with housecleaning or personal hygiene.

Second, it's important that we recognize the variety of issues our parents face. For many, especially those who have lost a spouse, loneliness is a major factor. For others, health becomes a primary concern. Medical problems can range from Alzheimer's to cancer, from dementia to depression. For still others the major pressures may be financial.

Third, it is essential that we choose to forgive our parents for any wrongs they may have done us. This means following biblical instructions not to hold grudges. Perhaps our parents neglected us in the past, favored our siblings, or even abused us. The only option that pleases God and helps maintain our own spiritual and emotional well-being is to choose to forgive them. This also includes choosing not to become bitter over any impositions their circumstances may place on us in the present. It's tempting to resent the demands and pressures of parent care, but it will help if we remember all the Lord has done for us, and even the things our parents have done for us in the past.

Frequently, both parents and children need to process long-held bitterness. Recently "Beth" called our radio program to express her concerns over a bitter, angry mother-in-law who is not a Christian. "She's sixty-two and facing heart surgery," Beth said. "How do I handle her bitterness?" We encouraged Beth to extend and model the forgiveness we have in Christ based on Ephesians 4:32. We suggested she gently encourage her mother-in-law to discuss the issues of bitterness and forgiveness, to continue maintaining contact with her, and to keep showing love in tangible ways. Most important of all we used Luke 18:1 as a basis for urging her to continue praying for her mother-in-law.

Fourth, when facing the tough decisions demanded by the needs of aging parents, it is important to seek wise counsel.

Another radio listener, Joan, phoned to talk about her seventy-five-year-old mother who was in relatively good health but who seemed paranoid over the prospect that she might be placed in a nursing home. Joan and her husband had been discussing whether or not to move in with her mother. We encouraged her to talk with her pastor about the issue and to survey resources to see what was available in her community. Often people can be hired to do household chores, provide lawn care, and help with transportation to the doctor or the grocery store.

A fifth step involves recognizing the value God places on the wisdom of age. All of us who are involved in ministry, including local churches and media ministries, must avoid the temptation to limit our efforts to the young and the hearty. As the senior segment of our population continues to grow and their problems increase, we must provide compassionate, biblical help on a wide range of issues. As a Christian community, we cannot allow the secular world to set the pace in serving those who are in the homestretch of their lifespans.

Sixth, when you are forced to make a difficult decision, pray about it, seek counsel, then make the decision without regrets. It's always important to count the cost of any option. John Gillies points this out as he explains how he and his wife cared for two aging parents. "Home care is a glorious proposition, but it is costly—in dollars and cents and in energy and life-style."[5] Sometimes the best option is to move parents into your home. Other times it may be more important to provide additional care, even if it requires remodeling or renovating the home in which they have lived for years in order to allow them to remain there. Whatever decision you make, trust God to guide you as you seek his wisdom, and be sure to avoid the traps of guilt and second-guessing.

Recently, a woman from California wrote to Ann Landers:

After my father died, my brothers and I knew that my mother would be unable to cope by herself in her big house. Although they discussed modifying their own homes to accommodate Mother, I was very strong in my opposition to this. I told them there was no way Mother could live in my home without destroying my marriage. And I suspected the same was true for them. They eventually agreed and [we moved] Mother into a facility where she could get more and more attention as her physical and mental abilities deteriorated.

Guilt, you bet. Every time I visited her I felt guilty. Did she rub it in? Of course. "How can you make me live in a place like this?" she would ask. But after I left I knew that this was the best solution for a bad situation. Mother had better care in that facility than my family or I would ever have been able to provide.

I realize this may not be the best answer for everyone, but it was the best one for us. It was a tough decision but I've never regretted it.[6]

Clearly this California woman's decision is not the right one for everyone, but apparently it was right for her. Whatever decision you make, make it with prayer, wise counsel, and a mind saturated with the principles of God's Word.

Finally, whether your parents live in your home, their own home, or a retirement or extended care facility, it's vital for the children and grandchildren to visit as often as possible and to let them know they have not been forgotten. Spend time with your parents. Take a tape recorder or a video camera along and record their reminiscences. After they're gone, you may be absolutely thrilled that you made those tapes.

Most important of all, the love and honor you will be extending to your parents through your regular personal contact will help you fulfill your God-given responsibility to provide Christlike parent care.

CHAPTER **TWELVE**

ALZHEIMER'S 1: THE SCOURGE OF AGING

DRIVE FAR ENOUGH DOWN A ROAD in Minnesota, and you'll probably pass a lake. If you've ever traveled across Minnesota, or if you know the state's motto, you'll understand why. The state is known as the "land of ten thousand lakes," and if you fly across the state on a clear day, you may think the number is even higher.

Travel far enough in Minnesota, and you'll encounter a lake. Live long enough, and you'll probably encounter Alzheimer's. Today more of us than ever are encountering Alzheimer's disease as we cross the span of life. It's something many of us used to joke about when we'd forgotten an appointment or misplaced our car keys. But for those who have begun to experience the devastating effects of Alzheimer's, either as a patient or a relative, the disease is no laughing matter.

Some people have wrongly concluded that the term comes from a slurred pronunciation of "old timer's disease," since it primarily affects individuals later in life. Actually the disease was named for a German neurologist, Alois Alzheimer, who in 1906 observed a patient in her fifties who demonstrated symptoms that are characteristic of a syndrome known as "dementia."[1] Because the woman demonstrated symptoms of brain function loss that normally occurred in people much older, Dr. Alzheimer labeled her condition presenile dementia. When Dr. Alzheimer's patient died, an autopsy revealed significant changes in her brain, which were believed to have caused memory impairment, disorganized thinking, and her overall mental and emotional decline.

A Growing Problem

At one point Alzheimer's was considered rare and was believed to occur only in people under age sixty. Today it's been estimated that anywhere from 5 to 15 percent of those over sixty-five have Alzheimer's, and as many as 20 percent of those over age eighty have the disease.[2] It's been estimated that up to four million people had Alzheimer's in 1998, and the number is expected to grow unless a cure is found. In fact, one researcher, Paul Bell, claims that most people will have Alzheimer's or a similar brain disorder if they live long enough. According to his view, it's part of the aging process.[3]

Alzheimer's has been labeled "the disease of the century" by Steven Post, associate professor for the Center for Bio-Medical Ethics at Case Western Reserve University in Cleveland, Ohio. According to Dr. Post, the number of Alzheimer's patients could soar to fifteen million by the year 2040.[4] Of course, by the year 2030, it's been estimated that 22 percent of the U.S. population will be sixty-five or older.[5] Alzheimer's is currently the fourth leading cause of death in the United States among those age seventy-five to eighty-four, taking more than one hundred thousand lives each year.[6] Studies have indicated that almost 60 percent of the nursing home population in the United States is afflicted with this disease.

More Than Forgetfulness

Alzheimer's disease is far more serious than the occasional forgetfulness many of us experience at midlife. However, in its early stages it may be difficult to distinguish from other illnesses.

A recently identified brain disease called Diffuse Lewy Body (DLB) has symptoms that are similar to Alzheimer's (as well as Parkinson's). Researchers are speculating that DLB may account for as much as 30 percent of dementia cases. One important difference between this newly discovered disease and Alzheimer's is that DLB is treatable if diagnosed correctly; Alzheimer's is not.[7] Furthermore, the effects of Alzheimer's on the brain are gradual and could be mistaken for ordinary forgetfulness. Some individuals frequently are able to compensate for early symptoms. At first the victim and those around him may not even suspect a medical problem. The effects of Alzheimer's increase slowly but inexorably. Some have actually termed the disease "the death of the mind." Eventually the patient experiences greater than normal stress, and the symptoms worsen.

Alzheimer's is one of a number of diseases generally grouped under the category of dementia, the primary clinical name given to diseases with symptoms of memory loss and impaired thinking and reasoning in adults. Other terms that have been used include Organic Brain Syndrome, Chronic Brain Disorder, senility, and even hardening of the arteries. Physicians may also use the terms senile dementia, or even multi-infarct disease, although normally multi-infarct disease results from a series of strokes rather than the gradual deterioration of Alzheimer's.

Many patients with Alzheimer's develop behavior problems such as agitation (being upset, frustrated, and confused), shouting, disturbed sleep, wandering away, and resisting efforts to care for them. They may have strange thoughts, imagine they hear or see things that are upsetting to them, or experience hallucinations.[8]

Brain Deterioration

The human brain is one of the most incredible components of God's creation. About 80 percent of its total mass, called the cerebral cortex, is divided into two nearly symmetrical hemispheres. Each hemisphere in turn is divided into four lobes. The frontal lobes govern motor function, emotional behavior, speech, personality, coordination, and social behavior. Since Alzheimer's disease primarily affects this area of the brain, patients typically undergo personality changes, lose inhibitions, become less able to organize behavior, and fail to recognize their erratic behavior.

Alzheimer's can also affect the temporal lobe, where hearing, memory, vision, and verbal comprehension are centered, and the wiener-shaped limbic region, which contains components that affect emotion and short- and long-term memory.[9]

Among the symptoms of the disease identified by Dr. Alzheimer in the early 1900s was the presence in the brain of what he called neurofibrillary tangles. As the term suggests, these are bundles of ordinary brain filaments that have become badly twisted. If you can imagine what a room in your local telephone exchange might look like after vandals have twisted all the wires together, you can understand what has happened in the brain of the Alzheimer's patient. When these tangles are viewed under an electron microscope during an autopsy, the filaments appear to have become wrapped around each other in a spiral-like fashion, as if two pieces of yarn had been twisted together, then stretched tightly. Medical professionals refer to these as paired helical filaments.[10] The filaments themselves are a normal part of the brain structure. The problem occurs when their form is changed by twisting. Pathologists also report that autopsies performed on Alzheimer's patients actually show some physical shrinkage of the brain.

Recently, during a radio program on caring for aging parents, Dr. Dale Michels, founder of the Lincoln Family Medical Group of Lincoln, Nebraska, and a family practice physician with a subspecialty in geriatrics, observed that "it's impossible to make a totally accurate diagnosis of Alzheimer's unless the patient has died and the brain can be examined." According to Dr. Michels and others, some degree of tangling can be found in specific brain areas of most normal middle-aged and older persons. Thus, it seems possible that the development of slight short-term memory loss with age can be associated with the normal development of some of these tangles. If this is the case, it is likely that the more severe memory disorders of Alzheimer's patients, as well as related problems, might be related to this kind of deterioration.

Charlotte: A Case Study

For several years Charlotte had realized that her memory was beginning to slip. When her children would bring home friends from high school or college, she had trouble remembering their names. One day she purchased several months' worth of meat at the supermarket, intending to store it in the deep freeze in the basement. A foul smell a few days later alerted Charlotte's husband, Bob, to the fact that Charlotte had taken the meat to the basement yet forgotten to store it in the freezer.

While talking with a group of friends following her Sunday school class at church the following week, Charlotte realized she had forgotten more than just someone's name—she had totally lost the thread of the conversation. After this happened on several occasions, she began to compensate by working harder to keep up with the conversation. She always tried to come up with an appropriate answer or comment, even if she felt confusion on the inside.

After several embarrassing conversations, however, Charlotte began to attend church less frequently. Then it was discovered that as treasurer of her Sunday school class she had lost track of several hundred dollars. When the pastor and one of the elders asked her about it, Charlotte insisted angrily that someone had stolen the money. However, her husband found it a few weeks later in an envelope between the pages of her previous quarter's Sunday school materials.

Before long Charlotte began to spend more time at home, a departure from her usual outgoing nature. Her neighbors and her friends at church, with whom she had visited frequently, became concerned. When the pastor came for a visit, Charlotte was uncharacteristically rude to him.

Bob began to notice that household chores, normally cared for in timely fashion, began to be neglected. When he offered to help, Charlotte refused. Frequently, she failed to put leftovers away; at times she would leave items out for two or three days, then place them back in the refrigerator. After she and Bob both experienced bouts with food poisoning, he expressed his concern that she was beginning to lose her memory.

It was not a pleasant conversation, nor did it last long. Charlotte simply denied having any memory problem. She told her husband and her daughter, who was visiting at the time, she was tired of their attempts to meddle in her life.

The following week, Bob learned that both the electricity and telephone services had been cut off. He soon discovered Charlotte had failed to pay the bills for more than three months.

A week later, Charlotte's neighbors were awakened at 3:00 A.M. by screaming outside her home. It was cold—almost freezing—and she had run outside dressed in only a thin nightgown. In a hysterical tone of voice she told the neighbors that a stranger had broken into her home and attempted to attack her. When they took her to the door and rang the doorbell, Bob answered. Charlotte pointed a finger and exclaimed hysterically, "That's him. That's the burglar." The police were called, and when they arrived on the scene, Charlotte was still frightened and confused. She kept talking about the stranger who had broken in and attempted to assault her. She insisted that her husband—to whom she had been married for over thirty years—was her assailant.

Charlotte's family and friends were confused. Perhaps she was just growing older. Maybe the stresses of life were affecting her. After hospitalization and a thorough checkup, Dr. Richard Sanders, her family physician of many years, called Bob into his office.

"I'm pretty sure we understand the problem now, Bob. Charlotte is in the first stage of Alzheimer's."

A Biblical Perspective

When Alzheimer's is diagnosed, we are frequently tempted to ask, "Why? Why me? Why this? Why my loved one, my spouse, my parent? Why now? Lord," we say. "You may have picked the wrong person for this trial."

Yet the apostle Peter wrote to remind suffering Christians, "Beloved, do not think it strange concerning the fiery trial which is to try you, as though some strange thing happened to you; but rejoice to the extent that you partake of Christ's sufferings, that when His glory is revealed, you may also be glad with exceeding joy" (1 Peter 4:12–13). Each of us would prefer to skip certain trials of life, particularly Alzheimer's. This dreaded disease is only one of a wide range of adversities encountered by God's people from all walks of life virtually every day. Yet trials still surprise us. From Peter's perspective, they shouldn't.

Trials such as Alzheimer's drive us back to the promises of God—promises such as "ask, and it will be given to you" (Matt. 7:7), or "all things work together for good" (Rom. 8:28), or "You will make me full of joy in Your presence" (Acts 2:28). These are promises we cannot only frame and hang on our walls but claim in our hearts when we experience problems.

Scripture frequently points out that all the Lord's godly children will experience adversity. Jesus reminded his disciples that "in the world you will have tribulation" (John 16:33). As Paul expressed it in Romans 8:17, we are "heirs of God and joint heirs with Christ, if indeed we suffer with Him, that we may also be glorified together." While we may prefer to bypass the adversity, weed out the pain, and skip the discomfort, God doesn't operate that way.

Furthermore, Alzheimer's is but one evidence that we live in a fallen world. When Adam and Eve decided to disobey God—and each of us individually chose to follow in our first parents' footsteps—consequences were visited on our planet, including deterioration, decay, disease, and ultimately death. While we may feel dismayed that a good and loving God would allow the kind of suffering that comes with Alzheimer's, it is important that we lay the blame for such suffering where it belongs—not with a God who is absolutely perfect and unable to be tempted with respect to wrong, but with a world separated from God by the effects of sin.

Our response when Alzheimer's comes should be to follow the example of the apostle Paul, who viewed one of the great adversities in his life as having the purpose "that we should not trust in ourselves but in God who raises the dead" (2 Cor. 1:9). Frequently, our response when problems strike is to try to retain some measure of control over life. Alzheimer's reminds us that life isn't under our control at all. Instead, we must learn to cast ourselves on the Lord in utter dependence.

David wrote Psalm 61 at what may have been the darkest moment of his life. His favorite son, Absalom, had led a coup, and many of his closest friends and aides had defected. As he expressed it in Psalm 61:2, "From the end of the earth I will cry to You, when my heart is overwhelmed." The psalmist was at the point of despair, feeling like he couldn't cope. Yet even as he admitted feeling overwhelmed, David reached out in dependence to the Lord.

> Hear my cry, O God; attend to my prayer. . . . When my heart is overwhelmed; lead me to the rock that is higher than I. For You have been a shelter for me, and a strong tower from the enemy. I will abide in Your tabernacle forever; I will trust in the shelter of Your wings.
>
> PSALM 61:1–4

When David felt life had handed him a crushing blow, his confidence rested securely in the Lord. Instead of attempting to handle his overwhelming adversity in his own strength, he sought the secure shelter in the Lord's person, character, and lovingkindness. Ultimately, when something as devastating and irreversible as Alzheimer's strikes, that's our only possible hope.

Causes

Although much has been learned about the symptoms of Alzheimer's, researchers have made little progress in identifying the causes. Some researchers theorize that the disease has a single cause; others feel that Alzheimer's results from the interaction of several contributing factors, including genetic predisposition, immune system imbalances, environment, and stress, as well as others.

Research into dementia in general has led to several important conclusions in recent years:

1. Dementia is not the natural result of aging. One of the most common misconceptions about Alzheimer's, which is a form of dementia, is that the disease's symptoms are simply a normal sign of old age. Even though symptoms such as forgetfulness may correspond with our common ideas of aging, the memory loss caused by Alzheimer's ultimately becomes far more severe and progressive than simple forgetfulness.

2. Dementia (including Alzheimer's) is caused by specific identifiable diseases and factors.

3. Diagnosis is important to identify treatable conditions.

4. A proper evaluation or diagnosis is essential in the management of diseases that at present are not curable, including Alzheimer's.[11]

One difficulty facing those who are carrying on research in this field is that the study of the brain is unlike the study of any other organ. Scientists can study the structure of other organs under a microscope and often can observe a living organ at work. However, the brain's function cannot be understood from its appearance, and the chemical and neurotransmitters that cause the brain to work dissipate almost immediately at death. Until the development of the PET scan, a medical tool that provides a picture showing which areas of the brain are working hardest during a particular kind of mental activity, scientists had been unable to grasp the complex interactions of the brain.

Genetic factors are known to play a part in other brain diseases and disorders, including Down's syndrome, which shares several features in common with Alzheimer's disease. Since there are extra copies of one chromosome in Down's syndrome victims, several studies have sought to pinpoint a possible chromosome defect in the brains of some Alzheimer's patients. However, to date, researchers have been unable to clarify the role of genetic factors or to establish that relatives of Alzheimer's have any significantly higher risk of getting the disease.

Other theories concerning the causes of Alzheimer's include the possibility of an extremely slow infectious virus, the development of autoimmune antibodies by the immune system, or even high concentrations of aluminum caused by cookware and other environmental factors. Most research suggests, however, that the high levels of aluminum found in the brains of Alzheimer's patients is probably a result rather than a cause of the disease.

Families at times attempt to blame traumatic stresses or past events. In the case of Charlotte, Bob told both his physician and his pastor that he felt a particularly stressful period in their marriage a decade earlier may have contributed to Charlotte's condition. However, Dr. Sanders and Pastor Scott Richards both assured Bob that research indicates that neither past traumatic events nor even a history of psychiatric problems such as depression or an addiction have been shown to have a causal link to Alzheimer's.

Cures

There are no known cures for Alzheimer's, but a popular Alzheimer's site on the Internet (Alzheimers.com) lists a number of treatments that have relieved some of the symptoms for certain patients. Such diverse treatments include the following:

Ginkgo

An extract of ginkgo (*Ginkgo biloba*) leaves are used to help prevent or treat some conditions associated with aging such as stroke, heart disease, impotence, deafness, blindness, and memory loss. Medical science has been interested in the herb's ability to interfere with the action of a substance the body produces called platelet activation factor (PAF). These platelets can restrict blood flow through the brain and cause memory lapses, problem-solving difficulties, and other mental deficits. Numerous European studies indicate that ginkgo extract can help restore blood flow and reverse these symptoms. Studies done recently suggest ginkgo might also help Alzheimer's patients. In 1996 German researchers recruited 156 Alzheimer's patients. One half were given a placebo, the others a twice-daily dose (120 mg) of ginkgo extract. The group taking the ginkgo showed significant improvement in cognitive abilities.

Acetyl-L-Carnitine

Alzheimer's disease is characterized by decreased levels of the neurotransmitter acetylcholine in the brain. Three studies (a 1991 Italian study, a 1992 study at the Neurological Institute in New York City, and a 1995 study at the University of Pittsburgh) revealed that taking Acetyl-L-Carnitine did not prevent brain deterioration but slowed it down significantly.[12]

Ampakines

Ampakines are a new class of drugs that improve memory. In animal studies, those taking Ampalex scored 35 percent higher on memory functions than the animals that didn't. A study in Germany and Sweden of fifty-four people ages twenty-one to seventy-three revealed that those using Ampalex scored twice as well on short-term memory tests.[13] In 1996 Cortex Pharmaceuticals in Southern California contracted with the National Institute on Aging to treat a small group of patients with Alzheimer's. The results have not been released at the time of this writing.

Calcium Channel Blockers

Alzheimer's symptoms are the result of the deterioration and eventual death of the body's nerve cells. As these nerve cells deteriorate, they lose the ability to regulate the flow of calcium across the cell membranes. Some researchers suggest that calcium channel blockers (drugs that affect this mineral flow) may prolong nerve cell life.

Other treatments have also been suggested, and new ones appear on the scene frequently as medical researchers expand their understanding of the disease and the brain. Many scientists are pinning their hope on the rapidly developing field of genetic engineering for an Alzheimer's cure. At this point, however, there is no cure, only the hope of slowing down the symptoms.[14]

Is It Really Alzheimer's?

It is important for those who exhibit Alzheimer's symptoms to receive a complete clinical assessment. While they are not infallible, physicians have a high percentage of success in identifying those who have the illness. Researchers recently performed brain autopsies (the only sure way of diagnosing Alzheimer's) on 220 people who had been diagnosed with Alzheimer's while living. Eighty-eight percent exhibited the characteristic brain abnormalities of the disease.

A clinical assessment usually begins with a thorough case history. The affected individual, family members, and friends describe the symptoms they have experienced or seen compared with how the patient functioned in the past.

Next a doctor performs a medical workup to see if something else might be causing the symptoms such as Parkinson's, a stroke, or major depression. Part of this process involves several standard laboratory tests. These include a blood count (CBC) to check for vitamin deficiencies and lead poisoning, a blood chemistry workup to rule out kidney failure or thyroid problems, tests for HIV and other sexually transmitted diseases, possibly a lumbar puncture to obtain cerebrospinal fluid to eliminate meningitis or encephalitis, an EEG to check for Creutzfeldt-Jakob disease, and a CT Scan or MRI to look for brain tumors, stroke, or other dementing brain conditions.

In addition, physicians have developed several specific sets of criteria to diagnosis Alzheimer's disease. These diagnostic factors include memory impairment—difficulty in learning new information or recalling previously learned information—and at least one of the following:

1. Loss of word comprehension ability, for example, the inability to respond to a statement such as "Your daughter is on the phone" (aphasia).

2. Loss of ability to perform complex tasks involving muscle coordination such as bathing or dressing (apraxia).

3. Loss of ability to recognize and use familiar objects such as clothing or a toothbrush (agnosia).

4. Loss of ability to plan, organize, and carry out normal activities such as shopping.[15]

These problems may begin slowly, then become more severe. For an Alzheimer's diagnosis, however, there must be a substantial decline from previous abilities and significant problems in everyday functioning.

If the various tests indicate the possibility of Alzheimer's, medical authorities suggest it is still wise to have the entire testing process repeated to avoid the possibility of misdiagnosis. Typically this is done by a neurologist who specializes in dementia-type illnesses.

Stages of Alzheimer's

Alzheimer's is a disease of progressive stages.[16] The first could be called the "denial stage" for both the patient and the family.

In the beginning, the patient is still able to take care of most of his or her personal needs and generally continues living a normal life. This was the case with Lincoln professional Hughes Hannibal Shanks, as described by his wife, Lela, during a radio interview on Nebraska Public Radio. She explained that during the first stage Hughes was for the most part able to care for himself in every area and recognized her most of the time. By the second stage he needed significant assistance, and by the third stage—his condition at the time of the interview—he required total care and had essentially forgotten how to bathe and dress himself.

Characteristics of first-stage Alzheimer's include indecision, progressive short-term memory loss, confusion and disorganization, withdrawal from family, insecurity, and spontaneous emotional outbursts—both laughter and weeping. During his meeting with Dr. Sanders, Bob nodded affirmative to each of these items as the doctor read them from his checklist. Charlotte had been withdrawing from family gatherings as well as from church. In the same fashion, Lela Knox Shanks described how her husband, Hughes, had been withdrawing from the family.

> Before [Alzheimer's disease] he had been a main player if not the center of every lively discussion taking place at our special family dinners. We often had three different debates going at one time, always controversial with loud dogmatic voices for every side. Hughes was usually the family radical, not our children. When he was no longer able to prepare the big dinners, he withdrew from the rest of the family. We would find him in the basement puttering among his wood pieces trying to remember how he once put them together to make picture frames.[17]

Although denial is common in the first stage, it is quickly replaced by concern on the part of family members as stage two arrives, frequently in regard to driving ability. The Alzheimer's patient may continue to navigate familiar routes with reasonable safety. However, he becomes increasingly vulnerable to mistakes and improper responses to sudden or unforeseen situations, either overreacting or failing to react to potentially dangerous traffic conditions.

As the Alzheimer's patient senses his own capabilities slipping away during stage two, he is likely to become increasingly self-absorbed, depressed, and insensitive to the feelings of others. Lela Knox Shanks describes second-stage Alzheimer's disease as the "aggression and hostility" stage.[18] As patients feel a greater loss of personal control, they frequently react by striking out in anger, perhaps even violence, toward those who are closest to them. At this point, agonizing decisions as to whether to keep the Alzheimer's patient at home or seek a long-term care facility must be made. Numerous factors including legal issues such as a durable power of attorney, arrangements in the event that you or other caregivers become ill, and provision for times away must be considered.

In the third stage of Alzheimer's, the patient's mental capacities have diminished to the point that "the brain appears to no longer be able to tell the body what to do."[19] By this time the patient refuses to eat and becomes emaciated. Physical movement becomes difficult. Incontinence is a given. Frequently, the patient will sit up and rock or carry out other repetitive movements. The inability to recognize family or friends increases, while anger and other strong emotions diminish. At this stage the need for tranquilizers or other medications may lessen as motor abilities deteriorate. Ultimately, stupor will occur in the final stage and lead to coma and death.

Obviously, these final days are very difficult, especially for the caregiver. To see a loved one slowly deteriorate and eventually slip away breaks one's heart. Yet, as believers, we have the assurance of God's presence through it all. David says in Psalm 23:4, "Yea, though I walk through the valley of the shadow of death, I will fear no evil; for You are with me; Your rod and Your staff, they comfort me." The phrase in this verse translated "the valley of the shadow of death" in Hebrew actually is "the valley of dark shadows." The effects of Alzheimer's, both physically and mentally, cast dark shadows, but we don't face them alone. In order for something to cast a shadow, there must be a light behind it. Standing behind all the struggle and tragedies of this illness is the light of God's Son, Jesus Christ, who is able to comfort us. Find your strength in him. Let his rod guide you and his staff support you during a time that many find overwhelming. Jesus has said, "I will never leave you nor forsake you" (Heb. 13:5). Trust him to keep that promise in your life.

In the next chapter we will provide some practical strategies for dealing with the challenges of Alzheimer's.

CHAPTER THIRTEEN

ALZHEIMER'S 2: CAREGIVING AND COPING

ALMOST FOUR MILLION PEOPLE who suffer from Alzheimer's (nearly 70 percent of those with the disease) are cared for at home by a spouse or another close relative. Such home care can be more frustrating, demanding, and exhausting than anyone can imagine. It is apparent that Alzheimer's has two victims: the one with the disease and the one responsible for the care.

The stress-induced physical and psychological illnesses resulting from the constant responsibilities involved in caring for an Alzheimer's patient should not be taken lightly. These afflictions can sometimes be serious enough to cause the caregiver to be hospitalized.

Stage-Two Alzheimer's

Catastrophic Reactions

Many would say the real stress in caring for an Alzheimer's patient begins as the individual enters stage two of the disease. Frequently, this is the point at which catastrophic reactions begin to occur. On one occasion, Bob had told Charlotte at least ten times that this was the day they were to visit Dr. Sanders. However, Bob and their daughter Nancy were literally forced to drag Charlotte screaming and resisting to the car. All the way to Dr. Sanders's office, she yelled for help and even attempted to jump out of the car. When she reached the waiting room, she tried to run away.

Later that evening she accused her husband of stealing her glasses. "You threw them away," she angrily told Bob.

"I didn't touch them," he answered calmly.

"You always say that," she responded. "How do you explain the fact that they're gone?"

Patiently, he replied, "Charlotte, you do this to me every time you lose your glasses."

"I did not lose them. You threw them away. I know you did."

Bob reflected on the fact that his wife had changed drastically. In the past she would have simply asked if he knew where her glasses were. She would never have started an argument or accused him of throwing them away.

Individuals in stage two frequently become excessively upset and experience rapidly changing moods. They can exhibit such behavioral problems as shouting, becoming agitated (frustrated and confused), and resisting care. Alzheimer's patients may become so agitated that they will simply break down in tears or try to hit or kick. They also may have strange thoughts or imagine that they hear or see things that upset them. However, such agitation can also be caused by an infection, injury, or even a medication. Consequently, if someone should become suddenly agitated, he or she should be evaluated by a physician.

When these kinds of catastrophic responses occur, it's important to remember the following five suggestions:

1. Don't become offended. Instead, try to listen carefully to what is upsetting the patient. His concerns may not seem logical, but try to view the situation from the perspective of his reality. Try to reassure him and let him know you care.

2. Don't try to argue or appeal to reason. Let her express her opinions and acknowledge her thoughts.

3. Don't offer complicated explanations. When a situation overwhelms their limited thinking capacity, people with

Alzheimer's may overreact. Even normal people sometimes do this when bombarded with more crises than they can manage at one time. Those with Alzheimer's have an even lower threshold of tolerance.

4. Try to distract the patient. Draw her attention to another activity or perhaps ask her to help with some simple chore.

5. Duplicate items in case they get lost. If he often loses a specific item, such as a wallet, buy an extra so you can have a spare on hand. This keeps the frustration level lower for both of you.

By the time she had reached stage two, Charlotte usually became upset when it was time for her bath and refused to co-operate. When her daughter Nancy would insist, Charlotte would argue and even shout. The entire family became tense and began to dread the evening routine.

Those who counsel caregivers suggest that the best way to manage these catastrophic reactions is to try to stop them before they happen. Keep in mind that these responses are not from stubbornness or nastiness but a behavior born out of confusion. These reactions are not a manipulative tactic; in fact the caregiver may have more control over the patient's reaction than the patient himself.

As the author of Proverbs pointed out, "A soft answer turns away wrath, but a harsh word stirs up anger" (Prov. 15:1). When an Alzheimer's patient responds negatively, family members and close friends must maintain control. Remember that the patient, faced with the need to think about several things at once, simply experiences mental overload when trying to sort out all the tasks involved in something as simple as taking a bath. Trying to do something one can no longer manage, feeling upset about that inability, not wanting to appear or feel inadequate, feeling rushed, not understanding what he or she has been asked to do, feeling frustrated, being treated like a child, and not being able to make himself or herself understood creates a volatile mix, a prescription for catastrophe. The antidote for the caregiver includes responding calmly, maintaining routine, simplifying things, taking things one step at a time, and giving careful step-by-step reactions.

When Charlotte reacted angrily to her bath, Nancy simply said, "Mom, I'm going to unbutton your blouse. It's all right. Now I'm going to slip off your blouse. It's fine. You're helping me. Let's slip out of your slacks. Now let's step into the tub. Here, I'll hold your arm."

It's always best to give the confused person time to respond. Scripture has a lot to say about patience and waiting. Remember the words of James 1:19: "Be swift to hear, slow to speak, slow to wrath." Simplify the approach, modify the approach when necessary, and if the patient becomes upset or resistant, remain calm. If necessary, remove him or her from the situation in a quiet, unhurried way. Frequently, the emotional storm will end as quickly as it began. In these situations the short memory of the patient may work to your advantage.

If catastrophic responses happen frequently, keeping a log may help you identify their cause. When the outburst is over, write down what happened and when, list the people present and the events that led up to the response. Look for a pattern. For the benefit of the patient as well as the caregiver, it may become necessary for a sedative to be used if the person becomes too aggressive.

Combativeness

Another common characteristic of second-stage Alzheimer's is combativeness. One day Bob took Charlotte to the beautician who had done her hair every week for the past five years. As the beautician worked on the back of her head, Charlotte kept trying to turn around. Whenever this happened, the beautician would turn Charlotte's head back. Before long, Charlotte began batting at the beautician's hands. She looked as if she were about to cry. Finally Charlotte turned around in the chair and hit the beautician. Bob felt mortified.

One of the keys to dealing with combativeness is for caregivers to be alert to the patient's signals that her stress level is rising. Perhaps if Bob had talked with the beautician and asked her to explain to Charlotte what she was doing and to pause periodically to show her in a mirror how her hair was turning out, Charlotte might have understood what was happening and would not have become upset. Whenever a patient becomes agitated, it's always best to remove the patient from whatever is upsetting him or her and allow for a period of relaxation.

Lela Knox Shank described an incident that occurred during the second stage of her husband's Alzheimer's.

> I was in the kitchen drawing a glass of water. Hughes came into the room and ordered me to put the glass down. Then he shouted, "Get out of this house, you're an impostor trying to break up my marriage." Suddenly he reached for my gold necklace and broke it off my neck. I was not hurt, but I was afraid, not knowing what he might do next. I ran out the back door and sat in the sun. I cried and moaned, praying for an answer to what to do. After about twenty or thirty minutes, I tapped lightly on the back door. Hughes opened the door and expressed great relief that I was all right. He said, "Where have you been? I looked all over for you. I was just getting ready to call the police and report you as missing."[1]

This incident underscores another common yet frequently underused resource: prayer. Since the Alzheimer's patient's ability to function has been impaired, those around him or her need extraordinary wisdom and coping ability. James 1:5 promises that God gives such wisdom to those who ask of him in faith.

Other Traits

Other common traits of second-stage Alzheimer's include hiding objects, repetitive acts, a tendency toward wandering, an inability to communicate verbally, a tendency to drink or eat anything, incontinence, and inability to recognize family members.

A few months after her diagnosis, Charlotte had to start wearing protective underwear. Her incontinence, perhaps the most dreaded of all symptoms for caregivers, began when she started having trouble recognizing the bathroom or finding her way to it. On several occasions Bob found her using the closet for a restroom. Within months she began losing control of her bladder and bowels regularly. The same thing happened to Hughes Shanks, according to his wife. "Sometimes he would be in the bathroom and still looking for it. On more than one occasion he mistook the floor heat vent, the wash basin or the bathtub for the commode. . . . He usually gives a clue to care providers, however, by standing up suddenly and moving about. At least half the time he makes some effort to help himself within his limited mental abilities."[2]

At this point in time, no medicines exist to help prevent wandering. The caretaker, however, can implement a few simple coping strategies. For example, provide a safe place for the person with Alzheimer's to wander such as a fenced-in yard. This allows you to avoid confrontations. If this is not possible, place a piece of furniture in front of the door or tie a ribbon across it to remind your loved one she isn't supposed to go out that door. Hiding the doorknob by placing a cloth over it may be helpful in some situations. You may even set up an alarm system (something as simple as a few empty cans tied to a string on the doorknob or a string of bells) to alert you that she is trying to leave a certain area. Locks are another possibility, but be aware that these can present a hazard in the event of a fire.

The person afflicted with Alzheimer's is also plagued by an inability to sleep at night. This can become quite stressful for caregivers. Putting a clock in the bedroom and keeping the curtains open may help alert the patient to the time of day. Restricting the patient's caffeine intake may help, as well as making sure she gets some exercise every day. Limit the number of naps taken by the patient during the day as well. If the Alzheimer's patient has a painful condition such as arthritis, see if it would be acceptable to give her some type of medicine for pain right before bed so the pain will not interrupt sleep.

One of the most difficult factors to cope with at this stage is the patient's inability to recognize family members. For years Bob and Charlotte had hosted the children, their spouses, and grandchildren at their home for Christmas Day dinner. The celebration always included a reading of the account of the birth of Jesus, Christmas carols, sharing with family members what had happened during the previous months, exchanging gifts, and, of course, a delicious meal—cooked mostly by Charlotte. However, the Christmas after her diagnosis, Charlotte found cooking beyond her ability. Throughout the meal she was unable to recognize Robert Jr., Richard, or Carol. At times she seemed to understand who Nancy was, and for most of the day she recognized Bob. She was pleasant toward the grandchildren but didn't seem to know who they were either.

One factor that contributed to her confusion, according to Dr. Sanders, was that the Christmas gathering, which traditionally had been held in their home, was held at Nancy's house—a less familiar setting for Charlotte.

Stage-Three Alzheimer's

By the time the third stage arrives, individuals with Alzheimer's have generally become unaware of their surroundings, the time of year, the year itself, or other indications of time and place. Memory has deteriorated to a fragmentary knowledge of home, address, or whereabouts. Getting lost becomes almost inevitable, and the patient may be unable to distinguish strangers from friends and family. Often he or she is unable to recognize even the spouse. For the Alzheimer's victim, the world has become a frightening and unmanageable place. The loss of ability to think, remember, and perceive prevents him from organizing the fragments of life into a meaningful whole.

In late second- and third-stage Alzheimer's, caregiving becomes an overwhelming task, demanding almost more than twenty-four hours a day. Writing in the graphically titled *The Thirty Six Hour Day*, Nancy Mace and Peter Rabins observe:

> Family members tell us that they experience many feelings as they care for a person with a chronic dementing illness. They feel sad, discouraged and alone. They feel angry, guilty or hopeful. They feel tired or depressed. . . . Emotional distress is appropriate and understandable. Sometimes families of people with dementing illnesses find themselves overwhelmed by their feelings.[3]

These feelings seem to parallel those of the prophet Jeremiah in Lamentations 3. After he had witnessed the overwhelming disaster of the fall of his hometown, Jerusalem, the prophet lamented, "I am the man who has seen affliction by the rod of His wrath. . . . I have forgotten prosperity. And I said, 'My strength and my hope have perished from the LORD.' Remember my affliction and roaming, the wormwood and the gall. My soul still remembers and sinks within me" (Lam. 3:1, 17–20). Surrounded by overwhelming circumstances, memories of a past far different than the chaotic and hopeless present, the prophet's words are particularly suited to provide hope, strength, and encouragement for those who struggle with caring for a loved one with Alzheimer's. "This I recall to my mind, therefore I have hope. Through the LORD's mercies we are not consumed, because His compassions fail not. They are new every morning. Great is Your faithfulness. 'The LORD is my portion,' says my soul, 'Therefore I hope in Him!' The LORD is good to those who wait for Him, to the soul who seeks Him" (Lam. 3:21–25).

Throughout the illness, caregivers have faced one challenge after another. Even though it may seem things have been hopeless and useless, the contact has been important, even though the patient may have been unable to respond.

Protect Yourself

Considering the potentially serious consequences associated with caregiving, the Alzheimer's caregiver needs to take steps to protect his or her own physical and emotional health. Such steps include the following:

1. Come to terms with reality.

Frequently, family members choose to deny there is a problem even when it is obvious. Since the symptoms of Alzheimer's often begin imperceptibly and progress slowly, you may be tempted to use the common defense mechanism of denial, even as you find yourself giving an increasing amount of time and energy to cope with your loved one's growing problem. Thus, the pressure in a caregiver's life increases imperceptibly yet inexorably. The quicker you acknowledge the existence and magnitude of the problem, the sooner you and your loved one can get the help you need.

2. Begin legal and financial planning.

Such issues as power of attorney, a will, appointing a trustee to manage assets, guardianship, and property ownership should be resolved as soon as possible. Since caretaking may involve in-home nursing care, a nursing home, or hospice, financial planning is also essential.

3. Find out as much as possible about the disease.

Alzheimer's is a progressive illness with each stage along the way requiring differing levels of caregiving skills. Knowing the symptoms of each stage will help you to offer the best possible care and maximize the quality of life for your loved one.

4. Enlist help.

If you are trying to do everything yourself, chances are you will become exhausted, and you may even become ill yourself. Accept the support of family and friends, use respite care, and find a support group. For the sake of yourself and your loved one, find out what assistance is available—and use it. Learn to let go and allow others to help you.

5. Deliberately take care of yourself.

Don't feel guilty about taking steps to ensure that you stay healthy. Remember, Jesus told his disciples to "come aside" and take time to rest from their responsibilities (Mark 6:31). In addition to taking regular breaks from the caregiving routine, watch your diet, exercise, and make sure you get enough sleep. Be sensitive to symptoms that your stress level may be rising. Such symptoms include physical symptoms such as blurred vision, digestive problems, loss of appetite, or high blood pressure; emotional responses such as depression or frustration; or behavioral reactions such as irritability and lack of concentration.

Caring for the Caregiver

Someone defined a friend as a person who walks in when the rest of the world has walked out. If there is one thing a person caring for someone with Alzheimer's needs, it's a friend. If you want to be such a friend, here are some suggestions to keep in mind.

1. Give them a break.

Probably at the top of every caregiver's need list is the chance to take a break. This may mean going to dinner or a movie, shopping, attending a support group meeting, or just getting some sleep. The change in routine is not only good for the caregiver but also for the person with Alzheimer's, who may enjoy a change of pace as well. Even a short respite can do wonders for a caregiver's spirit.

2. Consider the little things.

Look for even small ways to show your support and concern for a caregiver. When cooking a meal for your family, make a little extra and deliver it in disposable containers. As you do your own errands, find out if you can drop something off at the cleaners, return a library book, or pick up an item at the grocery store. Just the realization that people care enough to ask will help lift the caregiver's burden.

3. Keep communication channels open.

A card or short phone call can mean a great deal. Stop in for a brief visit, but realize that the caregiver will probably not be able to give you his or her full attention. Keep reaching out, even if you do not receive a response. Remember that the stress of caregiving may leave the caregiver with little or no energy to give back to others.

4. Learn to listen.

Sometimes a caregiver simply needs someone to listen—not give answers. Try not to ask questions; let the caregiver talk about whatever is important to him or her. Use nonverbal cues and good eye contact to show your interest.

5. Make specific offers.

General offers of help are often passed up because the caregiver may not be comfortable expressing his or her specific needs. Instead, ask for a list of chores that the caregiver finds difficult to get done because of caregiving responsibilities, such as dusting, washing clothes, or mowing the lawn. Consider which ones you might be able to do on a weekly or monthly basis. Then dedicate some time in your schedule to doing those chores.

The number of people with Alzheimer's continues to grow, which means that the need for individuals who are willing to give of their time is increasing as well. If you are fortunate enough not to have a loved one with Alzheimer's, consider the possibility of helping to carry the load for someone who does.

Encouragement from Scripture

The words of the prophet Jeremiah, which we considered earlier, can provide a source of significant peace and encouragement as you face Alzheimer's yourself or as you cope with the drain of caring for a close relative with the disease.

First, Jeremiah's words make it clear that hope comes from choosing to focus on the Lord rather than circumstances. While this may seem impossible for those who are caught in the web of Alzheimer's, the prophet shows the need for and the reward of this action.

Throughout Lamentations 3:1–20, Jeremiah provides an example of his need to focus on the Lord rather than his circumstances. "I am the man who has seen affliction by the rod of His wrath" (v. 1). "My strength and my hope have perished from the LORD. Remember my affliction and roaming, the wormwood and the gall. My soul still remembers and sinks within me" (vv. 18–20). The prophet desperately needed to focus on the Lord. When he made a conscious choice to recall the Lord's mercies, compassions, and faithfulness (vv. 21–23), he experienced the reward of viewing the Lord as his portion and life as good (vv. 24–27).

Furthermore, the prophet uses a number of words to indicate shades of meaning regarding the nature of hope. *Toheleth*, for example, refers to a positive expectation, which he confesses has perished along with his strength (Lam. 3:18). Despite this he continues waiting or "stretching out" (*yachal*) in hope to God by remembering the Lord's mercies, great compassions, and consistent faithfulness (vv. 21–23). The word for hope, *toheleth*, appears frequently in the Book of Job as the patriarch dealt with great personal loss and serious physical and emotional impairment.

Jeremiah further observed that "the LORD is good to those who wait for Him, to the soul who seeks Him" (v. 25). The word translated seek, *kavah*, comes from the root *mikvah*, which indicates a longing or an expectation. The lesson is obvious. When human expectation is depleted, the only solution is to focus all our expectations and longings on the Lord and to seek after him.

In the following verse, the prophet used another word for hope, *chul*. This Hebrew word describes a person writhing in pain—the term was actually used to describe the contractions of childbirth. Jeremiah used this common human experience as a metaphor of just how painful waiting and hoping can be before the goal sought is "delivered." The prophet continued, "It is good that one should hope and wait quietly for the salvation of the LORD" (v. 26). This same word was used in Micah 1:12 of the residents of Mareth who hoped—literally pined and became sick—for good. Instead, disaster came.

When you hear the diagnosis of Alzheimer's for yourself or your loved one, you may feel disaster has come. "How could this have happened?" you may ask. "Why? Why me? Why my loved one? This is disaster—nothing good can come of it." Or you may focus on dredging up failures from the past. "I must be suffering God's judgment because of some sin."

Scripture can provide significant encouragement regarding both God's sovereignty and his loving care for us. As the psalmist pointed out in Psalm 139, God knows us intimately and thoroughly, since he fully understands our path in life and is completely acquainted with all our ways (vv. 1–3). He carefully formed our genetic structure before we were born (vv. 13–15), and every day of our lives was written in his book before we lived a single one (v. 16). Thus, while Alzheimer's, and for that matter every human disease, can be traced back to sin and the effects of the fall, this truth is counterbalanced by the reality of God's personal involvement, love, and care in our lives. It is important that we allow Scripture to encourage us by helping us focus on the goodness and loving care of God rather than the typical why questions we are all prone to ask.

Twelve Spiritual Principles for Coping

Based on Jeremiah's words in Lamentations 3, we have developed twelve spiritual principles for coping with Alzheimer's, either as a patient in the early stages or as a caregiver.

1. Focus on God, his mercies and character.

Jeremiah's conscious choice to turn away from his "bitterness and woe" (v. 5) to the Lord's mercies, compassions, and faithfulness (vv. 22–23) made it possible for him to cope with an unbearable situation.

2. Be honest in assessing your situation.

Throughout the Book of Lamentations, Jeremiah never glossed over the problems or the pain. Even in 3:22 he admitted, "Through the LORD's mercies we are not consumed." Like the apostle Paul acknowledging the "sentence of death" in 2 Corinthians 1, Jeremiah recognized the desperate situation he faced. We can never improve our circumstances through denial.

3. Trust the Lord for daily strength.

As Jeremiah noted in 3:22–23, "His compassions fail not. They are new every morning." Both of us have found it essential to meet the Lord every morning, confess any sin, and stay close to him. It is only in this way that we can obtain that new mercy and strength based on his incredible compassion, loyal love, and faithfulness. Loyal love speaks of God's trustworthy character that reminds us we can rely on him no matter what the circumstance. His compassions describe the abundant emotion with which he reaches out to us in love. His faithfulness reminds us that, though life may seem unfair and unjust, we can rest in his righteous sovereignty in every situation.

4. Let God, not people or circumstances, become your ultimate resource.

Left with no one else to trust, the prophet Jeremiah reminded himself, "'The LORD is my portion,' says my soul, 'Therefore I hope in Him!'" (Lam. 3:24). One of the greatest burdens of caring for an Alzheimer's patient is getting nothing in return. Frequently, this is compounded by a sense of abandonment by others who could help. The key is to gain whatever we need from the Lord, not from the patient or others. Certainly it is appropriate to seek encouragement from others, and we need this in the body of Christ. Galatians 6:2 reminds us to "bear one another's burdens, and so fulfill the law of Christ." Yet it is best to allow the Lord, the God of all comfort, to be our ultimate burden bearer.

5. Be willing to wait on the Lord.

This is easier said than done. Yet Jeremiah reminds us that the Lord is good to those who wait for him and seek him (v. 25). The apostle Paul learned this lesson while asking the Lord three times to remove his thorn in the flesh. He learned that God's plan was for him to experience God's sufficient grace, and he was able to use this lesson in a wide range of adverse experiences. So it was with the prophet Jeremiah. Frequently, when we are forced to wait, we are tempted to question God's goodness. May we instead follow the example of Jeremiah and acknowledge the Lord to be good, even while we wait.

6. Focus on the ultimate hope.

Three times in these verses Jeremiah used the word *good*. First it is used to describe the Lord (v. 25). Then it is used of the process of hoping (v. 26) and of waiting quietly for God's salvation (v. 27). The phrase "the salvation of the Lord" is used in a number of ways in Scripture, not the least of which is to speak of the ultimate hope of heaven. It is in the presence of the Lord that the Alzheimer's patient will ultimately have all impairments and limitations removed, and where those who have patiently waited for the Lord will find themselves delivered from the incredible burdens they bore in this life. We find it helpful to spend time thinking about heaven and remembering the fact that we will one day stand before the Lord at the judgment seat of Christ, then spend eternity in his presence reaping the rewards of a life invested in serving God and others here.

7. *Remember it is biblical for the younger to serve the older.*

The third time *good* is cited by the prophet Jeremiah is in verse 27. Frequently we may resent having to invest time in parents who have Alzheimer's. Yet Jeremiah remembered, "It is good for a man to bear the yoke in his youth." When we are young and possess the energy, God is pleased when we use those energies to serve him and others, including those with Alzheimer's.

8. *Entrust your temporal hopes to the Lord.*

Frequently, we may be tempted to complain and gripe, or even cry bitterly to the Lord insisting that he heal our loved one. As Jeremiah observed, the appropriate response is to "sit alone and keep silent." Since God is sovereign, bow before him (Jeremiah puts it even more graphically: "Let him put his mouth in the dust" [v. 29]). There may yet be hope, the prophet noted, yet we must continue waiting quietly and patiently for the Lord. There are times when God chooses to reverse serious illness. God chose to restore children to Job—not the same children who died, but others. He also restored Job's fortunes. However, he never promises to reverse or restore, only to remain faithful and to give us grace for every situation.

9. *Take time to meditate.*

Just as the body relaxes through exercise, our spirit relaxes through meditation. Meditation is like a good spiritual workout with a Bible verse, a favorite hymn, or even a favorite poem. Even when circumstances around you may be chaotic, meditation will help you keep your thoughts and emotions together. If you feel ready to fall apart, think about some especially meaningful portion of Scripture. The prophet Jeremiah reflected this principle when he wrote, "Your words were found, and I ate them, and Your word was to me the joy and rejoicing of my heart" (Jer. 15:16). Meditating on Scripture, like digesting a nourishing meal, can provide both satisfaction and strength.

10. *Communicate through prayer.*

There will be times when you desperately feel the need to talk to someone, but no one will be there. That's when you need to avail yourself of prayer. We may get discouraged with prayer because God doesn't seem to be answering. But remember prayer is not reciting a shopping list; prayer is a conversation with our heavenly Father, who invites us to call on him for unanticipated answers (Jer. 33:3). Prayer gives us the opportunity to vent our feelings and share our frustrations with someone who truly cares.

11. *Confess any sin and stay close to the Lord.*

Unlike many around him, Jeremiah had maintained a godly life. Nonetheless, he included himself in the exhortation to "search out and examine our ways, and turn back to the LORD" (Lam. 3:40). Although it is wrong to assume that Alzheimer's is a judgment from God on either us or our loved ones (see the example in John 9 of the young man who was born blind), it is appropriate for us to regularly examine our hearts and lives, confess any sin, and maintain a close walk with the Lord. We may be particularly susceptible to bitterness, criticism, or improper attitudes.

12. *Maintain an attitude of praise.*

Paul reminded the Thessalonians to "in everything give thanks; for this is the will of God in Christ Jesus for you" (1 Thess. 5:18). Likewise, Jeremiah urged his people in the face of incredible devastation, "Let us lift our hearts and hands to God in heaven" (Lam. 3:41). This is a logical response when we have confessed and God has forgiven. When he cleanses our hands and purifies our hearts, we are in a position to praise him. The prophet had wept bitterly and incessantly over his circumstances (v. 49), yet the Lord had observed his plight (v. 50). The prophet felt hopeless (v. 54), yet when he called on the Lord (v. 55), God graciously answered (v. 56). Because of the Lord's comforting presence, Jeremiah's fears were alleviated (v. 57). The Lord restored meaning to his life (v. 58) despite many seeming injustices (v. 59). Ultimately, the prophet acknowledged, "You, O LORD, remain forever; Your throne from generation to generation" (Lam. 5:19).

As we praise our God, meditate on his promises, confess our failures, and trust him for grace each day, we discover that his mercies are new every morning and his faithfulness great—even when Alzheimer's is the diagnosis.

CONCLUSION

FINALLY HOME

As you drive east on Interstate 10 across the Atchafalaya River, you finally reach a point at which you've moved beyond the bridge, past the swamps, and into the rich farmland of the Mississippi Delta. If you're driving at night, you begin to see a light glowing up ahead. Before long you recognize that light as the city of Baton Rouge. If that's your destination, you know you're finally home.

As seventy million of us travel across the growing span of midlife, it's important for us to recognize that our ultimate goal isn't some milepost along the midlife span, or even to reach a golden age. For all who know Jesus Christ as savior, there's another destination far more brilliant at the end of the bridge—the celestial city. When you cross that last bridge, you're finally Home.

The ancient sheik of the desert, a rich nomad named Abraham, is an excellent example of a fellow traveler. He lived in a tent, moving from place to place. For Abraham and his wife, Sarah, as for all of us, life was a journey—much of it spent in a foreign environment among hostile people. And yet the author of the Book of Hebrews says that Abraham "waited for the city which has foundations, whose builder and maker is God" (Heb.

11:10). Abraham wandered through life, but at the end his wandering ceased. He finally reached home.

Anxious to Get There

During the summer of 1984, my family and I (Wood) set out across America in a Dodge maxivan. We drove from New York State, across the prairie expanse of the Heartland to the Great Northwest, then down the coast of California, across the Southwest and South to Alabama, then back to New York. On one occasion we had to drive from San Diego, California, to Vanderwagen, New Mexico, in one stretch. We drove north and then east to Barstow, crossed the desert at night, and arrived at the north rim of the Grand Canyon in time to watch the sunrise. Then we continued to Window Rock, Arizona, east to Gallup, New Mexico, and finally to Vanderwagen, where I was to speak that night at the Broken Arrow Bible Camp. What a day. We were barely into that long day when one of my children began a chorus of "Dad, are we there yet?" It was good to finally get there.

For the Christian, life is a journey. We set out barely able to walk, then we learn to run. After that we learn how to slow down a bit, and finally we reach the end of our earthly journey. We arrive at our heavenly home. Along the way we encounter times when we are anxious to get there. If the journey is hard, the eagerness increases.

Ed Siemens was a good friend. He had served as a pastor and a salesman, then in midlife had returned to seminary for graduate studies. Finally, Ed and his wife, June, joined our Back to the Bible staff as stewardship representatives. Ed assisted others in planning for the future, so his thoughts were often on finally getting home.

Ed was tall, gifted, and a people person. Robust and active, he traveled the southwestern United States, talking to Back to the Bible's supporters and spreading good cheer wherever he went. Less than two years ago he seemed at the peak of health. I'll never forget the day June and Ed came to the office to see me. They had just been to the doctor. I met them in our prayer chapel, a secluded place dedicated to prayer. I asked Herb, our chaplain at Back to the Bible, and Selma Epp to join us. That's when Ed gave us the news.

He had been diagnosed with prostate cancer. It was in an advanced stage and spreading rapidly. The prospects were grim. We held on to each other. We cried. We prayed. We trusted God. Within six months, Ed was finally home.

I remember visiting Ed during the last weeks of his life. He was at home under hospice care. Each time my purpose in going there was to bring cheer to Ed, but each time I would come away cheered myself. Ed wasn't afraid to die. He knew where home was, and he was ready to go there. Time after time I heard Ed say, "All I want is to glorify my Lord in life and death." Ed Siemens got his wish. I participated in his funeral service and have never been at an occasion that focused more on the Lord Jesus.

Ed had crossed the span of midlife. He could see the specter of the grave, yet he never flinched. The Lord had pulled the stinger of death for him. Beyond the grave he could see the lights of the eternal city. Ed's Lord Jesus had broken Satan's power, and the intimidation of death was gone.

In light of the fact that we are all getting older and one day will face death, three questions come to mind that bear directly on our final destination. If you haven't faced these three questions, you aren't ready to grow old. If you have faced them and like Ed Siemens can face the specter of death without flinching, you are ready for your final approach. What is your answer to these three questions?

Why Is Death So Difficult?

"And he died."

Adam must have been a remarkable man. He was the very first human creation of God. He was made in the image of God (Gen. 1:26). He was blessed by God (Gen. 1:28). Only of Adam can it be said that God breathed into his nostrils the breath of life (Gen. 2:7). God communicated directly with him and Adam enjoyed the company of his Creator God (Gen. 3:8–10). But because of Adam's sin, the most agonizing notation about the life of Adam is found in Genesis 5:5: "All the days that Adam lived were nine hundred and thirty years; *and he died*" (italics mine).

God did not create us just to watch us grow old and die. Aging, pain, and death were not in God's original blueprint for men and women. God created man for life, not death. He warned Adam not to eat of the tree of the knowledge of good and evil because that alone would interrupt God's life plan for humankind. But Eve was tempted and Adam disobeyed God (Gen. 3:1–6) and, as they say, the rest is history.

Why is death so difficult? It is difficult because it is punishment, and punishment, by its very nature, is never easy. God had placed before Adam and Eve an idyllic environment. No pollution. No taxes. No long-term nursing facilities. Just a beautiful paradise. It would be their home forever, and God would bless their life with children and grandchildren and the whole world would experience the wonderful gift of life.

But all this was lost in one day when Adam and Eve disobeyed God's plan and sinned. Adam and Eve made a tactical error: They listened to the lies of Satan rather than the truth of God. And they paid dearly. God said that Adam's punishment for his sin would be as follows: "In the sweat of your face you shall eat bread till you return to the ground, for out of it you were taken; for dust you are, and to dust you shall return" (Gen. 3:19). "Dust to dust" was not part of God's plan; it was the amendment of punishment that came as a result of Adam's sin.

Now that amendment is applied to every one of our lives. The apostle Paul explained it this way: "Therefore, just as through one man sin entered the world, and death through sin, and thus death spread to all men, because all sinned" (Rom. 5:12). Sin spread through the ranks of humankind like wildfire. And death came right along as the consequence of sin. "For the wages of sin is death" (Rom. 6:23).

In fact, we don't even have to do anything wrong to be a sinner; we are born sinners because we are born of sinful parents. King David said, "Behold, I was brought forth in iniquity, and in sin my mother conceived me" (Ps. 51:5). The wise patriarch Job sized up our situation correctly when he asked, "Who can bring a clean thing out of an unclean? No one" (Job 14:4). Sinful parents will give birth to sinful infants 100 percent of the time.

Although we'd rather not think about it, the subject of death is a dominant one in Scripture. The word occurs 143 times in

128 verses in the New Testament. Paul used the word five times in 1 Corinthians 15, explaining that death originated because of sin (v. 21). It is our bitter enemy (v. 26). And it will be ultimately destroyed by Jesus Christ (v. 54). Like a wasp, a bee, or a hornet, it has a painful sting (v. 55). And that sting is sin and its effect (v. 56). Yet the resurrection of Jesus Christ has pulled the stinger of death.

The author of Hebrews added to our understanding of this subject by explaining that even though Jesus suffered death, he has been crowned with glory and honor (Heb. 1:9). Under God's plan, he tasted death for everyone in order to provide salvation. Furthermore, through his death, he destroyed the one who holds the power of death, the devil (v. 14), and provides release for those under the bondage of the fear of death (v. 15).

Death is difficult because death is the consequence of our sin. As long as we are bearing that consequence alone, we should not expect death to be easy.

I have watched weeping funeral processions as they passed me in the lanes and country roads of many countries. In Israel I have seen a contingent of men carrying a coffin in silence as a contingent of wailing women followed behind. There was no hope, no relief from the sadness. In Poland I have seen people steeped in the church and religion stand at a grave and look as grim as possible. There was no hope beyond the grave. I saw utterly blank stares on the faces of Chinese people who had lost their loved one. No hope.

Why is death so difficult? Because it's not meant to be easy. Death is difficult because death is punishment. Our sin has brought to us the most unbearable consequence. "And he died."

How Should I View Death?

There's an old African tribal saying that goes something like this: "The man who isn't hungry says the coconut has a hard shell." Interpretation: "Attitude is everything."

Much of our fear of death arises from our attitude toward death. We view death incorrectly, therefore we approach it incorrectly.

Because death is so distasteful and dreaded, many have come to view it in a way that is very different from God's view. They view death through their own lenses, even though they can only see death from this side. They see death as painful, an enemy to be feared, something to be avoided at all costs, the final out of the game. It's little wonder growing older has become such a depressing occurrence for many.

Dr. Ira Brock, a hospice physician, was quoted in the *Washington Post* as saying, "Approaching the end of life through the lens of assisted suicide is like looking through the wrong end of binoculars; the view is narrowed and distorted."[1]

God's view of death is dramatically different. Humans see death as something to be dreaded; God views it as something to be anticipated. Humans see death as a gloomy dark night; God describes it as a glorious new day. Humans see death as the end of the journey; God sees it as a layover on the journey. Your perspective on death—humankind's or God's perspective—will dramatically affect whether or not death is bearable.

Something to Be Anticipated

In 1970 I (Wood) went to France to study at the University of Strasbourg. My wife, Linda, and our two young children were not able to go with me. We were facing months of separation. We wrote back and forth, I taped little messages on my cassette recorder for the kids, but let's face it, letters and cassettes are not like being there in person. We missed each other terribly. As the months wore on I began to look forward to the day when I would return to them and we would be together again. Finally the day came. I flew from Brussels, Belgium, to New York City and was finally home. There they were. All at the airport. All waiting to greet me. My anticipation had been rewarded with the reality of joy.

For the Christian, approaching death and knowing that you are almost home is also a time of anticipation. It's not that we don't enjoy what we presently have, it's that what we presently have cannot compare to what awaits us. It's not that we're not happy on this side of death, it's that God promises us we will be ecstatic on the other side, when we're finally home. It's not that we don't enjoy life, it's just that with our heavenly Father we will enjoy eternal life so much more!

Death is not anticipated by the Christian because we enjoy dying; death is anticipated because we enjoy God. Like Abraham, we are looking for a city whose builder and maker is God (Heb. 11:10). Like Paul, we are looking forward with anticipation to the time when our departure is at hand (2 Tim. 4:6). We have fought a good fight, finished our course, kept the faith. Now it's time to move on to our eternal reward. Death is not a time to be feared or shunned, it is a time to anticipate hearing our Master say, "Well done, good and faithful servant. . . . Enter into the joy of your Lord" (Matt. 25:21). Who would not anticipate that reception!

No, God does not view death as something to be dreaded; rather it is something to be joyfully anticipated. Only the one who has trusted Jesus Christ as savior can know that kind of anticipation.

There is an inscription in the crypt of the Allegheny Observatory at the University of Pittsburgh that reads, "We have loved the stars too fondly to be fearful of the night." When we love and enjoy God completely, we never fear the night that takes us to him.

A Glorious New Day

Many of us fear death because we always fear the unknown. When Christopher Columbus set out to sail west on the Atlantic, his crew and he did so with no little trepidation. They were facing the unknown. When Neil Armstrong first set foot on the moon, he did so with no little apprehension. And why not? He was facing the unknown. Intelligent people always fear the unknown.

So why do Christians not fear death? Because what follows death is not entirely unknown. God describes it for us in his Word. It's not a gloomy dark tunnel. It's not an out-of-body experience. It's not even a lit tunnel to nowhere. It's home. And there's no better feeling than finally arriving home.

When we get to heaven our family will be there, that great cloud of witnesses mentioned in Hebrews 12 who have passed through death before us. They are awaiting our arrival. Many of my brothers and sisters in Christ, people dear to me in this life, are already home. It will be good to see M. L. Lowe and Paul Tell again. I can't wait to hear Charles Haddon Spurgeon preach. My grandmother and grandfather whom I haven't seen in decades are awaiting me there. Members of my immediate family faced death long before most people do. I want to get their perspective on being greeted by our heavenly Father in their teen years instead of old age.

But best of all, when we Christians pass through death and are finally home, we'll see Jesus there, the one who died for us to make heaven possible. We'll join that great choir of angels around the throne and sing with voices louder and more beautiful than ever before possible, "Worthy is the Lamb who was slain to receive power and riches and wisdom, and strength and honor and glory and blessing" (Rev. 5:12). We'll be home, home with the one who loved us and gave himself for us. That will be a glorious day.

What's more, when we are finally home, we'll have to leave a lot of things behind on this side of the grave, because on the other side of the grave, after we pass through death, we have this astonishing and hopeful promise: "And God will wipe away every tear from their eyes; there shall be no more death, nor sorrow, nor crying; and there shall be no more pain, for the former things have passed away" (Rev. 21:4). After we face death, we'll have to do without sorrow, crying, and pain. I think I can do without those things!

God's view of heaven is that of a glorious new day that dawns as brightly as the city lights of Baton Rouge on a dark Louisiana night, only a thousand times brighter. The dark gloom of death itself is transformed into the glorious light of God.

A Layover on the Journey

Because I live in Lincoln, Nebraska, which isn't exactly the hub to anywhere, I have to fly somewhere to fly somewhere. That means once or twice a week I pass through the busiest airport in the world—Chicago's O'Hare International Airport. O'Hare is a nice airport, easy to maneuver around in (even if you do have to go through that New Age tunnel from concourse B to concourse C), and there are hundreds of flights from there each day.

Many people today view death as the end. They see death as the terminus of their journey. You are born, you live, then you die. That's it. The only sure things are death and taxes. We all know the feeling. For this reason, many physicians today see the loss of a patient as the ultimate failure. They will take extreme measures to keep a person alive. Their call is not to provide meaningful and loving care for a person while he or she is alive; their call is to extend life indefinitely. People fear death to such an extreme that they will encourage physicians to take any heroic measures available to them to extend a person's life one more day. Why? Because people believe death is the end. Our humanistic, evolutionary thinking has driven much of society to believe that there is nothing more tragic than death.

God's view of death is very different. It is not the end. Death is a door to a bright new future. It is a passageway. It brings closure to one phase of life but opens up to an eternal phase of life that is much more desired than the temporal phase.

I view death a bit like flying to Chicago's O'Hare Airport. When I land in Chicago, the windy city is usually not my final destination. In fact, when I check my luggage in Lincoln, I never check it to Chicago. I always check it to my final destination. Chicago is just a layover on the journey. Usually in Chicago I board a plane that is bigger, more powerful, faster, more luxurious than the one I got off. Why? Because Chicago is not the end of my journey; it's just the place I change planes.

Death is like that. God doesn't view death as the terminus of our journey; it's just the place we change bodies from the earthly variety to the heavenly variety. "So also is the resurrection of the dead. The body is sown in corruption, it is raised in incorruption. It is sown in dishonor, it is raised in glory. It is sown in weakness, it is raised in power. It is sown a natural body, it is raised a spiritual body. There is a natural body, and there is a spiritual body" (1 Cor. 15:42–44).

If we view death as the end, then how do we view heaven? If we view death as the end, how do we view the resurrection from the dead? If we view death as the end, how do we view the resurrection body? God views death as I view changing planes. I'm just there to catch a better flight to my real destination.

Get a proper view of death and death itself will become more bearable. In fact, if we share God's view of death, it will be far more than bearable; it will be a triumph. "O Death, where is your sting? O Hades, where is your victory? The sting of death is sin, and the strength of sin is the law. But thanks be to God, who gives us the victory through our Lord Jesus Christ" (1 Cor. 15:55–57). Through faith in Jesus Christ as our savior, we can know that death is not our destination, it's just our connecting city. Heaven is our ultimate home.

But that may not be true for you. Heaven is not automatically your ultimate home. It's only the home of those who are prepared to go there. That brings me to the final question we all must confront as we grow older and get ready to face death. Am I prepared to die? Am I ready to go? If I died tonight, would I wake up in heaven tomorrow?

Am I Prepared to Die?

No one is foolish enough to suggest that death will become easy. But death can become bearable. It wasn't easy for June Siemens to stand with her family at Ed's graveside and say good-bye. Death is a time of sorrow and sadness, even for Christians. When Jesus heard that his friend Lazarus had died, Jesus wept (John 11:35). Should we do any less? But while death can never be easy, it can be bearable. The Bible tells us how.

When my family and I set out across the United States in 1984 for our family adventure, we didn't just get up one morning, go out to the van, load it up, and take off. There were months of preparation beforehand. We gathered information as a family. I asked everyone where they wanted to go and what they wanted to see along the way. We checked our calendar for the time we had available. I plotted our course. We spread out maps, and the kids memorized our route. We built a place to hang clothes in the back of the maxivan so that we would not have to take suitcases into the motels or homes where we were staying each night. We just took in the clothes we would change into. A six-week adventure like this took a lot of planning and preparation.

Should we entrust our eternal future to anything less than full preparation? Do you want to grow older and face not having done anything to prepare for what you know is certain? Probably not. Yet that's exactly what millions of people do. They face an uncertain future with uncertain plans. It's little wonder death is so difficult.

The Bible is clear about how to prepare for your eternal future. In fact, it's as simple as ABC.

A. *Admit* that you are not ready to go to heaven when you die because you are a sinner. That's what the Bible says about all of us. "There is none righteous, no, not one" (Rom. 3:10). "For all have sinned and fall short of the glory of God" (Rom. 3:23). I was born a sinner, I became a sinner the first time I personally disobeyed God, and I will die a sinner. I had to freely admit that in order to be able to face the specter of death. If death is going to become bearable, you must admit it as well.

B. *Believe* that although you are a sinner, Jesus Christ died to pay the penalty for your sin and save you from its punishment. When the jail keeper at Philippi asked the apostle Paul what he needed to do to be saved, Paul responded, "Believe on the Lord Jesus Christ, and you will be saved" (Acts. 16:31). Salvation isn't a matter of turning over a new leaf or trying to live so your good works outweigh your bad works. It's not living a moral life and doing good. Salvation is the loving act of God whereby he sent his Son, Jesus, to die on Calvary's cross specifically to pay the penalty for your sin, which is death. "For God so loved the world that He gave His only begotten Son, that whoever believes in Him should not perish but have everlasting life" (John 3:16). That's God's Word, and if you believe that only Jesus' death can forgive the penalty of your sin, you can face death with hope. Death becomes bearable.

C. *Confess* to God that you believe what his Word says, that you are a sinner, and that you believe Jesus died to save you from your sin and its penalty. Admit you are lost without Jesus, without hope. Believe that Jesus can give you the hope you need because he died for your sin. And confess to God that you believe and want him to save you. To the Romans the apostle Paul said, "If you confess with your mouth the Lord Jesus and believe in your heart that God raised Him from the dead, you will be saved. For with the heart one believes to righteousness, and with the mouth confession is made to salvation" (Rom. 10:9–10).

That's really all there is to it. When you trust Jesus Christ to be your personal savior from sin and death, the penalty for sin, you can face death with new confidence and new hope. You can say with Ed Siemens, "I'm not afraid to die. All I want to do is glorify my Lord Jesus." When you trust Jesus, you are prepared for death.

How Will It All End?

Look at life around you. You or someone close to you may be facing reduced physical abilities, depleted energy, failing health, limited finances, the unknowns of aging. You're scared. Maybe you're all alone. You wonder how it's all going to turn out. Will your days as you approach death be filled with fear or with faith? Will you face death as most do, or as Ed Siemens did? The way we approach life is the way we approach death. Either we trust God's love and his many promises of care, or we face the specter of death as a cold, tragic end. Which will it be for you?

In *The Caregiver Journal*, Edward P. Wimberly puts it all in perspective. He says,

> The Bible has an eschatological plot rather than a tragic plot. Tragedy has a negative ending because evil and suffering overwhelm the person. The eschatological plot takes tragedy seriously, but eventually tragedy is overcome and there is a positive ending.
>
> The positive ending of the eschatological plot has everything to do with healing and wholeness of persons. Despite suffering and evil, the eschatological plot believes that God will transform pain and suffering into some meaningful possibility. In the eschatological plot, pain and suffering have a word, but not the last word. Pain and suffering's triumph is temporary rather than permanent. Suffering and pain will not always last in the eschatological plot.[2]

For the Christian, the physical pain and suffering may not be alleviated, but we know it is only temporary. God has a glorious future for us because we have trusted Jesus Christ as our savior, our healer, our coming king. For the Christian, death is not the end. It is a doorway to our final destination—eternal life with God in heaven. Only then is the Christian finally home.

NOTES

Introduction: Navigating Life's Span

1. *Guerrilla Marketing Newsletter*, 28 April 1997, Guerrilla Marketing International, Mill Valley, California.

2. Thomas R. Cole and Mary C. Winkle, *The Oxford Book of Aging* (New York: Oxford University Press, 1994), 3.

3. Robert Rosenblatt, "Over Eighty Five Population in US to Double by 2020," *Los Angeles Times*, 21 May 1996, A16.

4. "Elderly Disability Rates Dropping; Increase in Home Care Expected," *The Maturing Marketplace* 2, no. 8 (22 April 1997), 63.

Chapter 1: Help, I'm Growing Older!

1. Bob Buford, *Game Plan* (Grand Rapids: Zondervan, 1997), 12.

2. Ibid., 20.

3. This is true of the New King James Version but may not be true of all versions.

4. Keil and Delitzsch, *Old Testament Commentaries*, vol. 4 (Grand Rapids: Eerdmans, n.d.), 92.

5. Edyth Draper, *Draper's Book of Quotations for the Christian World* (Wheaton: Tyndale, 1992), 8128.

6. George Wells Arms, "Glory in the Autumn Years," *Good News Broadcaster*, Back to the Bible, December 1980, 16.

Chapter 2: Health Issues at Midlife

1. "Pharmaceutical Firms Developing Drugs to Combat Aging Diseases," *The Maturing Marketplace* 2, no. 13 (September 1997), 112–13.

2. Rick Boling, "Listen Up," *Modern Maturity*, July–August 1997, 64–65.

3. W. David Hager, M.D., and Linda Carruth Hager, *Stress and the Woman's Body* (Grand Rapids: Revell, 1996), 76.

4. Tom Hickey, *Health and Aging* (Monterey, Calif.: Brooks/Cole Publishing, 1980), 6.

5. Mark Clements and Dianne Ahls, "How Healthy Are We?" *Parade*, 7 September 1997, 4–7.

6. Don Hawkins, Daniel L. Koppersmith, M.D., and Ginger Koppersmith, *When Cancer Comes* (Chicago: Moody Press, 1993), 77.

7. Cathy Perlmutter with Laura Goldstein, "The Heart of the Matter," *Prevention*, February 1998, 100–107, 170–74.

8. Ibid.

9. Ibid., 105.

10. Malin Dollinger, M.D., Ernest Rosenbaum, M.D., and Greg Cable, *Everyone's Guide to Cancer Therapy* (New York: Andrews and McNeel, 1991), 11.

11. Dr. Sharon Sneed and Dr. David Sneed, *Prime Time* (Dallas: Word, 1989), 72.

12. Ibid., 88.

Chapter 3: Career Changes at Midlife

1. Dick Ennis, "ACTS International," *Encounter Magazine*, January 1991, 5.

2. Described in "Transition through Change," *Leadership Network* 3, no. 3 (July 1993), 1.

3. Ruby MacDonald, *Ruby MacDonald's Forty Plus and Feeling Fabulous Book* (Old Tappan, N.J.: Revell, 1982).

4. Gary R. Collins, *Christian Counseling: A Comprehensive Guide* (Dallas: Word, 1988), 198.

5. Victor Frankl, *Man's Search for Meaning* (Boston: Beacon Press, 1993), 124.

6. Annetta Miller, "Stress on the Job," *Newsweek*, 25 April 1988, 40.

7. Lee Ellis and Larry Burkett, *Your Career in Changing Times* (Chicago: Moody Press, 1993), 165.

8. For a more complete discussion, see ibid., 168–74.

9. Gary Smalley and John Trent, *The Two Sides of Love* (Colorado Springs: Focus on the Family, 1992), 34–36.

Chapter 4: The Emotions of Midlife

1. Dr. Dan Allender and Dr. Tremper Longman, *The Cry of the Soul* (Colorado Springs: NavPress, 1994), 31.

2. Ibid., 30.

3. C. S. Lewis, *Letters to an American Lady*, (Grand Rapids: Eerdmans, 1967), 93.

4. C. M. Parkes, *Bereavement: Studies of Grief in Adult Life* (New York: International University's Press, 1972), 124.

5. C. S. Lewis, *A Grief Observed* (New York: Seabury, 1961), 1.

6. Allender and Longman, *Cry of the Soul*, 58.

7. James I. Packer, *Knowing God* (Downers Grove, Ill.: InterVarsity Press, 1973), 136.

8. Les Carter, *Mind over Emotions* (Grand Rapids: Baker, 1985), 17–18.

9. Charles Swindoll, *Growing Strong in the Seasons of Life* (Portland, Ore.: Multnomah Press, 1983), 45.

10. This translation of *paraklētos* is used by many Bible teachers, including the authors. See the discussion in W. E. Vine, *An Expository Dictionary of New Testament Words* (Nashville: Nelson, 1984), 200.

Chapter 5: Spiritual Changes at Midlife

1. D. W. Moore, "Most Americans Say Religion Is Important to Them," *The Gallup Poll Monthly* 353 (February 1995): 20.

2. Stephanie Rohlfs-Young, "Research on the Physical Affects of Spirituality," *Alzheimer's Association*, March 1998, 1.

3. Harold G. Koenig, L. B. Bearon, and R. Dayringer, "Physician Perspective on the Role of Religion in the Physician–Older Patient Relationship," *The Journal of Family Practice* 28, no. 4 (1989): 441–48.

4. *Health*, 9605/15/nfm/holy.smokes/index.html.

5. Harold G. Koenig, *Aging and God: Spiritual Pathways to Mental Health in Midlife and Later Years* (Binghamton, N.Y.: Haworth Pastoral Press, 1994).

6. David O. Moberg, "Book Reviews of *Religion in Gerontology: From Benign Neglect to Belated Respect*," *The Gerontologist* 36, no. 2 (1996): 264.

Chapter 6: Relationships at Midlife

1. Guy Greenfield, *We Need Each Other* (Grand Rapids: Baker, 1984), 17.

2. *Theological Dictionary of the New Testament,* ed. Gerhard Kittel and Gerhard Friedrich, trans. Geoffrey Bromiley (Grand Rapids: Eerdmans, 1964), 1:22, s.v. "Agnos Agnizo."

3. Don Hawkins, *Friends in Deed* (Chicago: Moody Press, 1995), 74.

4. Donald and Rita Cushenberry, *Coping with Life after Your Mate Dies* (Grand Rapids: Baker, 1991), 15–23.

5. For an enlightening discussion on the connection between encouragement and the Holy Spirit, see Gene Getz, *Encouraging One Another* (Wheaton: Victor Books, 1974), 23–25.

6. Dr. Charles Lynch, *I Should Forgive, But* . . . (Nashville: Word, 1998).

7. For a more complete discussion of the six-step process of discipleship used by Jesus, plus a discussion of the relationship between mentoring and discipling, see Don Hawkins, *Master Discipleship* (Grand Rapids: Kregel, 1996).

8. Ray and Anne Ortlund, *The Best Half of Life* (Waco: World Books, 1988), 116.

Chapter 7: Preparing Your Finances for the Future

1. Annie Nakao, "Middle-Class to Welfare in the Blink of an Eye," *Electric Examiner,* 4 April 1995.

2. Ibid.

3. "Will and Trust Planning Guide," Back to the Bible *SOLUTIONS*, Lincoln, Nebraska 68501.

4. Harry Crosby, "Should I Buy Long-Term Insurance?" 1997.

Chapter 8: Choosing a Living Environment

1. Nancy L. Mace, M.A., and Lisa P. Gwyther, A.C.S.W., "Selecting a Nursing Home with a Dedicated Dementia Care Unit," Alzheimer's Association.

Chapter 9: Wills and Other Legal Issues

1. Produced by Parsons Technology, Inc., the 5.0 version of It's Legal, © 1994.

2. Leah Glasheen and Susan Crowley, A *Family Affair*, AARP Bulletin, 39, no. 5, May 1998, 2.

3. Elinor B. Waters and Jane Goodman, *Empowering Older Adults* (San Francisco: Jossey-Bass Publishers, 1990), 155.

4. www.aafp.org, "Advanced Directives and Do Not Resuscitate Orders."

Chapter 11: Family Ties

1. Andrew Weaver and Harold Koenig, "Uncovering Elder Abuse," *Christian Ministry*, July–August 1997, 18–19.

2. "How Pastors Can Aid the Abused Elderly," *Current Thoughts and Trends* 13, no. 11 (November 1997), 15.

3. "Abuse of Elderly Thought Rising," *Lincoln Journal Star*, 2 May 1995, 3.

4. Ann Landers, "Siblings Not Helping with Aging Parents," *Lincoln Journal Star*, 25 November 1997, 8B.

5. John Gillies, *A Guide to Caring for and Coping with Aging Parents* (Nashville: Thomas Nelson, 1981), 89.

6. Ann Landers, "Haven't Regretted Putting Mom in Home," *Lincoln Journal Star*, 2 September 1997, 8B.

Chapter 12: Alzheimer's 1: The Scourge of Aging

1. Nancy Mace and Peter V. Rabins, M.D., *A Family Guide to Caring for Persons with Alzheimer's Disease, Related Dementing Illnesses, and Memory Loss in Later Life*, rev. ed. (Baltimore: Johns Hopkins University Press, 1981), 1991.

2. Howard Gruetzner, *Alzheimer's: A Caregiver's Guide and Source Book* (New York: John Wiley and Sons, 1992), 7.

3. "New Found Brain Disease Mimics Alzheimer's," *Young at Heart* (Lincoln: SCG Publishing), November–December 1997, 11.

4. David Schwartzlander, "Symposium Puts Human Face on Alzheimer's Toll," *Lincoln Journal Star*, 28 February 1998, B1.

5. Lela Knox Shanks, *Your Name Is Hughes Hannibal Shanks: A Caregiver's Guide to Alzheimer's* (Lincoln: University of Nebraska Press, 1996), 31.

6. America's Pharmaceutical Companies, *Alzheimer's Disease* (n.p., n.d.), 3.

7. *Young at Heart*, 11.

8. "Caring for a Family Member with Dementia," *American Academy of Family Physicians* (1996): 1 (www.aafp.org.).

9. Gruetzner, *Alzheimer's*, 207–10.

10. Ibid., 210.

11. Mace and Rabins, *Family Guide*, 291.

12. "One-Year Multicenter Placebo Controlled Study of Acetyl-L-Carnitine in Patients with Alzheimer's Dementia," *Neurology* 47, no. 3 (September 1996): 705–11; "Acetyl-L-Carnitine in Alzheimer's Disease: A Short-Term Study of CSF Neurotransmitters and Neuropeptides," *Alzheimer's Disease Association Discord* 9, no. 3 (fall 1995): 128–31; "The Effect of Acetyl-L-Carnitine in Alzheimer's," *Neurobiology-Aging* 16, no. 1 (January–February 1995): 1–4.

13. "Comparison of the Effects of an Ampakine with Those of Methamphetamine on Aggregate Neuronal Activity in the Cortex versus the Striatum," *Brain Research. Molecular Brain Research* 46, no. 1–2 (1997): 127–35.

14. "Other Treatments," www.Alzheimers.com, http://www.alzheimers.com/site/L3TABLES/L3T10413.HTM.

15. Adapted from the *Diagnostic and Statistical Manual of Mental Disorders*, 4th ed., (DSM-IV), (Washington, D.C.: American Psychiatric Association, 1994).

16. For more comprehensive explanation of these stages, see Shanks, *Hughes Hannibal Shanks*, 16–30.

17. Ibid., 19.

18. Ibid.

19. Barry Reisberg et al., "The Global Deterioration Scale for Assessment of Primary Degenerative Dementia," *American Journal of Psychiatry* 139 (September 1982): 1138.

Chapter 13: Alzheimer's 2: Caregiving and Coping

1. Shanks, *Hughes Hannibal Shanks*, 20.

2. Ibid., 25.

3. Mace and Rabins, *The Thirty Six Hour Day*, 200.

Conclusion: Finally Home

1. Dr. Ira Brock, "Why Do We Make Dying So Miserable?" *Washington Post*, 2 January 1997, A-23.

2. Edward P. Wimberly, *The Caregiver Journal* (1996).

Woodrow Kroll is president of Back to the Bible in Lincoln, Nebraska, and Bible teacher on the *Back to the Bible* broadcast heard daily around the world.

Before assuming his responsibilities at Back to the Bible in 1990, Kroll spent more than twenty years training men and women for ministry at colleges and universities. He served ten years as president of Practical Bible College in Binghamton, New York. The author of dozens of books, he is a popular speaker at Bible conferences throughout the world.

Kroll received the M.Div. degree from Gordon-Conwell Theological Seminary, the Th.M. and Th.D. from Geneva-St. Alban's Theological College.

Woodrow and his wife, Linda, live in Lincoln, Nebraska.

Don Hawkins is cohost and producer of the *Back to the Bible* radio program, which is heard on over six hundred stations worldwide. He also hosts the live nationwide call-in program *Live Perspectives*.

The former executive director of the Minirth Meier Clinic, Don has authored or co-authored many best-selling books, including *Never Give Up, How to Beat Burnout, Worry-Free Living, Before Burnout, The Stress Factor, When Cancer Comes, Happy Holidays, Prodigal People, Friends in Deed, Master Discipleship, Overworked, The Roots of Inner Peace,* and *Parent Care.*

A graduate of Southeastern Bible College (B.A.) and Dallas Theological Seminary (Th.M.), Don received the D.Min. from Calvary Theological Seminary in 1998. He is a veteran conference and seminar speaker and has nineteen years of pastoral experience.

He and his wife, Kathy, are the parents of three grown children and live in Lincoln, Nebraska.